EU Criminal Law and Justice

ELGAR EUROPEAN LAW

Series editor: John Usher, *Professor of European Law and Head, School of Law, University of Exeter, UK*

European integration is the driving force behind constant evolution and change in the laws of the member states and the institutions of the European Union. This important series will offer short, state-of-the-art overviews of many specific areas of EU law, from competition law to consumer law and from environmental law to labour law. Whilst most books will take a thematic, vertical approach, others will offer a more horizontal approach and consider the overarching themes of EU law.

Distilled from rigorous substantive analysis, and written by some of the best names in the field, as well as the new generation of scholars, these books are designed both to guide the reader through the changing legislation itself, and to provide a firm theoretical foundation for advanced study. They will be an invaluable source of reference for scholars and postgraduate students in the fields of EU law and European integration, as well as lawyers from the respective individual fields and policymakers within the EU.

Titles in the series include:

EU Consumer Law and Policy
Stephen Weatherill

EU Private International Law
Harmonization of Laws
Peter Stone

EU Public Procurement Law
Christopher H. Bovis

EU Criminal Law and Justice
Maria Fletcher and Robin Lööf with Bill Gilmore

EU Criminal Law and Justice

Maria Fletcher

School of Law, University of Glasgow, UK

and

Robin Lööf

European University Institute, Florence, Italy

with

Bill Gilmore

School of Law, University of Edinburgh, UK

ELGAR EUROPEAN LAW

Edward Elgar

Cheltenham, UK • Northampton, MA, USA

Published by
Edward Elgar Publishing Limited
The Lypiatts
15 Lansdown Road
Cheltenham
Glos GL50 2JA
UK

Edward Elgar Publishing, Inc.
William Pratt House
9 Dewey Court
Northampton
Massachusetts 01060
USA

A catalogue record for this book
is available from the British Library

Library of Congress Control Number: 2008930896

ISBN 978 1 84542 697 2 (cased)

Printed and bound in Great Britain by MPG Books Ltd, Bodmin, Cornwall

Contents

Foreword

The automatic corollary of agreeing to write the introduction to a book is that one then has to sit down to read it. In the case of the present work, this has been a pleasant duty. With the odd exception, my practice at the Bar did not lead me to do much criminal work. I was a dyed-in-the-wool Euro-lawyer. After two years at the Court of Justice of the EC, I found myself awaiting (with a certain degree of trepidation, it must be said) the entry into force on 1 March 2008 of the new 'urgent preliminary ruling' procedure that has been put in place to deal with references under Part IV of the EC Treaty (immigration, asylum and certain civil law matters) and Title VI of the TEU (police and judicial cooperation). I decided that, before the first references under the new procedure hit the Court like unfamiliar express trains, it would be eminently sensible to improve my level of background knowledge. A pre-proof copy of this book therefore found its way both immediately and painlessly onto my reading list.

Because of its sensitivity (it is, after all, traditionally closely associated with the exercise of sovereignty), criminal law was packaged at Maastricht, together with immigration and asylum issues, within 'justice and home affairs' ('JHA'), safely away from 'mainstream' EC law. Subsequently, it has been maintained in lonely splendour within Title VI of the 'third pillar'. If the Lisbon Treaty is ratified, it will move into the 'area of freedom, security and justice'[1] ('AFSJ') – an umbrella Title IV within the Treaty on the Functioning of the European Union ('TFEU') – albeit with important reservations for the United Kingdom and Ireland. Possibly because EC criminal law has tended to move around in company with other big, sensitive topics, there have been relatively few attempts to treat it coherently, as a free-standing and major topic that is worthy of proper analysis in its own right. This book addresses and fills that lacuna.

The authors begin, like all good storytellers, at the beginning. They point out that 'people have always moved, travelled, migrated' and that 'as an inevitable consequence, systems of criminal justice have always had to deal with the existence of, and claims by, other systems of criminal justice'. Covert (and not so covert) historians will enjoy finding an early example of harmonised, Europe-wide criminal procedure (trial by ordeal, in which the Church was an active institutional participant until Pope Innocent III decided otherwise at the Fourth Lateran Council in 1215) rubbing shoulders with references to the von Clausewitzean conception of a constant 'state of nature'[2] to describe relations between sovereign States in dealing with requests for inter-State cooperation such as applications for extradition or letters rogatory. It is likewise salutary to be reminded that the conventional division of criminal law systems in Europe into the adversarial and the inquisitorial is in fact a rather artificial classification that did not come about by conscious design and that is, in some respects, in the process of being broken down anyway as new national criminal laws borrow from the neighbours' good ideas. And I can only agree wholeheartedly with the proposition that as, when or if there is going to be a conceptual shift in the system of criminal justice, 'what one would wish is for it to be made consciously and with consideration given to the analytical consequences which necessarily flow from it'.

In successive chapters, the authors get down to business and present the institutional actors before moving on to police cooperation, judicial cooperation, external cooperation in matters of criminal justice and substantive criminal law (in respect of those offences for which EU law, rather than individual national criminal laws, provides the definition). The analysis is sharp, well-informed and thoughtful. To pick out examples from a good book is always slightly invidious, but the explanation offered of the travails of the European Arrest Warrant ('EAW'), the description of the long and ultimately fruitless attempt by the Commission to push through a framework decision on certain procedural rights applying in criminal matters throughout the European Union (the 'FDPR') as the logical counterbalance to other mutual recognition measures, and the critique of the Court's judgments in *Ship-source Pollution*[3] and *Environmental Crimes*[4] all make for compelling reading.

The authors conclude by trying to highlight some of the common threads and concerns that have pervaded the complex agenda for EU criminal law and justice. They make a strong case for thinking that 'the actual framing of the AFSJ suffers from a failure properly to consider the theoretical implications of providing the "good" of criminal justice at the EU level' and that:

> EU criminal law and justice currently uncomfortably straddles two not entirely compatible logics . . . the Member States and the EU institutions alike . . . fully subscribe to the view that the EU can provide practical benefits . . . on the other hand, these same actors seem to be of the opinion that ground-breaking advances in cooperative practices as a result of common EU legislation can be introduced without changing the classical concept of criminal justice as the sharp end of national sovereignty.

They are not likewise afraid to stick their necks out and offer some predictions as to what may, or should, be the future of criminal justice in the

EU. They plead eloquently for proper involvement of the European Parliament as the natural forum for discussions on the rationale of the system and on core issues such as how *real* mutual trust (the necessary underpinning for continued widespread reliance on the principle of mutual recognition rather than (more intrusive) harmonisation) is to be fostered, whilst emphasising that 'the most important effect of giving the European Parliament a decisive role in EC legislation in matters of criminal justice is that it would serve to balance the preponderance of executive power'. They highlight – sometimes, with disconcerting acuity – issues such as weak structures for judicial supervision, problems of competence and legal base, extra-EU cooperation subsequently integrated into the EU (Schengen in the past, Prüm in the immediate future) and what will (and will not) change if the Lisbon (Reform) Treaty is ratified. I hope that they are already earmarking time to monitor the breaking news on the AFSJ and that they have scheduled when they will need to sit down again together to write the second edition.

Many other Members of the Court are, like myself, not particularly specialist in criminal law or procedure (there are, of course, honourable exceptions, like Judge Cuñha Rodrigues and Advocate General Bot, whose experience before coming to the Court gives them a significantly better overview of the issues and the likely problems). Many EU law practitioners do few criminal cases. Many criminal law practitioners have had relatively little exposure to EU law. Academics working on EU law tend to have left criminal law behind with their undergraduate days (and vice versa). Civil servants working on AFSJ questions will tend to have in mind established national practice and immediate policy concerns rather than the wider picture. This book will therefore be immensely useful to a number of different readerships. The only prerequisite is, I think, that the reader must be willing to look thoughtfully at the subject-matter rather than merely wanting to look up a particular point in two minutes in order to stuff it into his draft.

Of course I have found places where I do not necessarily instantly agree with the authors' perspective. When does one not have that reaction, reading oneself into an area where law, sociology, moral philosophy and political theory overlap? I suspect my questions stem precisely from the fact that this is an imaginative, helpful and stimulating attempt to present EU criminal law 'in the round'. As such, it is warmly to be welcomed as an important and provocative contribution to a debate that is just beginning to gain real impetus about an area of law of fundamental importance. And those who – like myself – cannot resist the less serious moments in the middle of studying a serious subject will be enchanted, along the way, to discover little snippets such as that, every six months, at the last meeting in a presidency of the Comité de l'Article Trente-Six[5] (CATS), the outgoing presidency hands over two porcelain cats, one white and one black, representing the police and the judiciary (it has not been decided which is which) to its successor.

Eleanor Sharpston

NOTES

1. Or, as a younger colleague of mine has delightfully and memorably re-christened it, the 'area of peace, love and understanding' – currently Part IV of the EC Treaty.
2. C. von Clausewitz, *On the Nature of War* (first published 1832, re-published Penguin Books, London, 2005).
3. Case C-440/05 *Commission v Council (Ship-source Pollution)*, Grand Chamber, 23 October 2007.
4. Case C-176/03 *Commission v Council (Environmental Crimes)*, (Grand Chamber) [2005] ECR I-7879.
5. Named after the article of the TEU that makes provision for its existence.

Series editor's preface

When in 1991 the EC Member States negotiated the first Directive on money-laundering, they felt unable in the text of that Directive to make money-laundering a criminal offence; rather, they attached a statement that they would take all necessary steps to enact criminal legislation. Later that year, the Maastricht Treaty was negotiated, introducing an express competence in criminal matters not under the EC Treaty (the 'first pillar') but under a separate intergovernmental pillar of the EU Treaty on Home Affairs and Justice, largely outside the jurisdiction of the European Court of Justice, the so-called 'third pillar'. Under the Amsterdam Treaty, much of this pillar was transferred to the EC Treaty, leaving a third pillar concerned with Police and Judicial Cooperation in Criminal Matters, but under which framework decisions (rather like EC Directives) and decisions could be adopted, subject to the (limited) jurisdiction of the European Court. In the meantime, that Court has held that criminal penalties relating to matters governed by EC Law can (and should) be imposed under the EC Treaty itself; furthermore, the Lisbon Treaty signed in 2007 would largely eliminate the differences between the first and third pillars (subject to special treatment for the UK).

Against this constantly evolving background, there has been an exponential growth in EU and EC legislation concerned with criminal matters, partly reflecting the fact that an area without internal frontiers may increase the possibilities for cross-border crime, and also reflecting the growth of international terrorism. These developments are critically examined in the present book by Maria Fletcher, Robin Lööf and Bill Gilmore, which also studies the underlying principles. These include the way in which a concept of mutual recognition (akin to that used in internal market legislation) lies behind measures such as the European Arrest Warrant. This book represents an important contribution to the study of an area of growing importance in the context of EU law.

John A. Usher
Exeter, June 2008

Preface

Following the signing of the Lisbon Treaty the authors took a strategic decision to ring-fence discussions of the relevant changes in the book. If you read the 'boxed text' throughout this book, you will realise that the changes affecting the field of criminal law contained in the Lisbon Treaty are particularly important. The value of this ring-fencing approach was demonstrated when on Friday 13 June 2008 the legislation necessary to ratify the Lisbon Treaty by Ireland was rejected in a referendum. At present, the EU and Member State leadership are unsure whether and (if so) how to salvage at least some of the reforms contained in the Lisbon Treaty. For now, and for the second time in recent years, the EU is forced, somewhat embarrassingly, into a 'period of reflection'. Faced with the sometimes confused state of the texts in the current treaties and in the absence of Treaty reform, it is a legitimate question whether the European Court of Justice will step into the breach judicially to impose the coherence currently lacking. Whatever happens institutionally, with or without the Lisbon Treaty, the field of EU criminal law and justice will undoubtedly remain a dynamic policy area and thus a fascinating area to study.

As with any multi-authored work there are many, many people to thank. Maria Fletcher would like to thank Carol Gammie for her excellent research assistance and Robin Lööf for his inspiration and for agreeing to take part in this project! Conversely, Robin would like to thank Maria for trusting him to take part in this project. Colleagues, friends and family have been an incredible support to Maria – particular thanks to Noreen, Rosa, Jane, Mark F., Adam, Sarah, Maurizio, Bruce, Mark, Helen, Mum, Dad, Anna, Tom and Lucy, all of whom have offered invaluable encouragement in the last year or so. Robin would like to thank Katie for suffering their living room becoming a writers' nest for a couple of weekends. And Bill Gilmore would like to express his thanks to his co-authors who have shouldered the major burden in producing this volume and to acknowledge the contribution of numerous colleagues in Brussels and elsewhere who assisted with the research effort in important ways.

Maria would like to dedicate her stake in this book to the memory of her grandma, Kathleen Goddard.

All of the authors would like to acknowledge the professionalism, friendliness and support of the team at Edward Elgar.

The law in this book is intended to be up to date as at December 2007. Comments about the book may be addressed to Maria Fletcher at M.Fletcher@law.gla.ac.uk and are always gratefully received.

Maria Fletcher
Robin Lööf
Bill Gilmore

Florence, Glasgow, Edinburgh, London and Luxembourg, June 2008

Table of cases

Introduction

WHY 'EU CRIMINAL LAW AND JUSTICE'?

Within the confines of legal commentary on the EU institutions dealing with what has become known as EU Justice and Home Affairs (JHA) law, it can perhaps seem unduly limitative to restrict the ambit of the present book to EU criminal law and justice. However, there are two reasons why we feel that this approach is justified. First, the legislative achievements of the EU in the specific field of criminal law and justice are now significant both in scope and in depth and are in many ways revolutionising the day-to-day practice of criminal law in the EU. A field of such growing importance deserves separate and dedicated treatment. Second, there never was a logical or analytical necessity to link those topics dealt with within the confines of EU JHA law. Rather, their linking is a consequence of the history of the EU Treaties. When the EU Treaty was first drafted and signed in Maastricht in 1992, the EU was restructured into 'Pillars'. The traditional European Community (EC) was put in the 'first pillar' and retained those characteristics which had made the EC such a successful and innovative organisation: monopoly on legislative initiatives in the Commission, qualified majority voting in the Council of Ministers, extensive input from a supranational, popularly elected European Parliament (EP), and an effective and well-developed system of judicial oversight. So much for confirming and restating what was already a reality. The importance of Maastricht, however, was that there the Member States decided that there was a need for EU cooperation with respect to a number of politically more sensitive matters: defence and foreign policy, immigration and asylum, and criminal justice. But, as a result of their sensitive nature, the Member States were unwilling to organise their cooperation in these matters along the lines of the supranational 'Community method'. Therefore, these matters were put in separate pillars subject to separate institutional arrangements taking into account their close affinity with issues of national sovereignty. As it happens, it was deemed proper to put the provisions pertaining to immigration and asylum together with those pertaining to criminal justice in the 'third pillar'. EU JHA law was born. Whether this was a result of a conscious linking of immigration with criminal justice or whether it was simply the result of a political compromise which led to that similar institutional arrangements were deemed proper for decisions in the two fields we can leave to one side because these arrangements were drastically changed with the entry into force of the Treaty of Amsterdam. This treaty 'communitarised' that part of the third pillar dealing with immigration and asylum placing it in the first pillar, namely in Title IV EC. Left in the third pillar is now only criminal justice.

Even though the institutional arrangements which gave rise to the habit of dealing with EU activity in matters of immigration and asylum together with EU activity in matters of criminal justice no longer exist, the practice of dealing with them in conjunction nevertheless persists.[1] We believe that this approach needs revising. There is the practical consideration that the amount of normative output is now such that dealing with these two fields separately is convenient, both for the readers and, perhaps more critically, for the authors. More important, however, is the fact that these are fields which are fundamentally different and which, therefore, deserve to be dealt with separately. At least the field of EU criminal justice has now developed to a degree of complexity which makes it a field of study in its own right, where some of the difficulties and issues will be familiar from national criminal legislations but where, at the same time, the very particular context that is the EU gives rise to a plethora of challenges new to the field of criminal justice. The present book aims to provide an overview of the achievements of the EU in the field of criminal justice while at the same time highlighting and discussing some of the more important issues thrown up by the administration of criminal justice at the EU level. This is why we have chosen to call this book 'EU Criminal Law and Justice'. We want to indicate that, in addition to providing a reference guide to EU criminal legislation, in the positivist sense, we also aim to discuss the 'justice' of this legislation. In short, in addition to attempting to provide answers to the 'What?' and the 'How?', we also aim to deal with the 'Why?'

BOOK OUTLINE

The chapters in this book are organised so that the reader who wishes to get a quick insight into one particular aspect of EU criminal law can read them individually. However, all chapters build upon the general analyses and discussions in this introduction, as well as the first two chapters. It is therefore recommended for all readers to read these three parts before moving on to any of the more specific chapters.

The remainder of this Introduction seeks to put EU criminal justice in a broad historical context focusing on the age-old question of the link between state sovereignty and the provision of criminal justice. Chapter 1 discusses the possible justifications for the EU to get involved in matters of criminal justice and the objectives which the EU has set itself in this regard, notably the creation of the *Area of Freedom, Security and Justice*. In this chapter you will also find an outline of the institutional structure of the third pillar: competences, legal instruments and the available judicial interpretations of these instruments. Chapter 2 provides a review of the institutional actors in the field of EU criminal justice. Chapter 3, the first field-specific chapter, explains and discusses police cooperation in the EU. Chapter 4 is an essential chapter as it deals with what has become the normatively most emblematic aspect of EU criminal justice: judicial cooperation. Here you will find the discussion relating to the principle of *mutual recognition* and its applications, most notably the European Arrest Warrant (EAW). Chapter 5 discusses that aspect of EU criminal justice affecting the EU's relationship with the rest of the world, or, put simply, external cooperation in matters of criminal justice. Chapter 6 reviews and discusses the EU's efforts in the area of substantive criminal law, i.e. those offences for which the EU has provided the definition.

The Conclusion seeks to highlight some of the common threads and concerns that have pervaded the complex agenda that is EU criminal law and justice. Here we will also attempt to provide cautious predictions for the future of criminal justice in the EU.

BOX 1   REFORM TREATY – TREATY REFORMS

This book is published as the EU yet again tries to redraft its foundational legal documents. As the manuscript for this book was being finalised, on 18 October 2007, the heads of state and government of the 27 Member States agreed to the Treaty of Lisbon (known as the 'Reform Treaty') to be signed, again in Lisbon, on 13 December 2007.[2] This treaty significantly modifies the institutional set-up of the whole EU and one of the areas most affected is precisely EU criminal justice. During the next couple of years the Reform Treaty will be subjected to the various ratification procedures applicable in the 27 Member States with a view to its entry into force on 30 June 2009. Although it seems that the number of popular roforonda will bo lowor than for tho now dofunct Constitutional Treaty with, *inter alia*, France and the Netherlands both claiming that no referendum is necessary this time, the institutional concern is that, where referenda are held, they might again result in the blocking of the Reform Treaty and a continuation of the EU's institutional 'crisis'. All in all, the future of the Reform Treaty is very uncertain.

> Even if the Reform Treaty becomes a reality, most of what is said in this book remains valid: the instruments adopted to date will remain good law[3] and the more principled discussions as to the proper role of the EU in the provision of criminal justice will not be exhausted by the entry into force of the new treaty. However, matters of competence, legal instruments and institutional arrangements will of course be the subjects of sometimes fundamental change. In order to take these probable developments into account, we have gone through the provisions of the Reform Treaty applicable to EU criminal justice to try to predict the legal landscape after its potential entry into force. These discussions will be found highlighted throughout the book in the same manner as the present section.

We have included as a separate annex attached to the end of the book an explanation of the special position of the UK and Ireland in relation to EU criminal justice if the Reform Treaty enters into force.

It is worth explaining at this point that the Reform Treaty will amend both the existing EC and EU treaties. It will also rename the EC Treaty, the Treaty on the Functioning of the EU (TFEU) and all references to the 'Community' or 'European Community' will be replaced by references to the 'Union'. The Reform Treaty contains 11 Protocols which will be annexed to the EU Treaty, the TFEU, and where applicable, to the European Atomic Energy Community. As will become clear, several of these Protocols contain provisions that impact in some way upon EU criminal law.

In general structural terms the Reform Treaty shifts the entire current third pillar into the TFEU, thereby, in effect, putting an end to the existing situation whereby AFSJ matters are scattered across different pillars. Consequently, under the TFEU, the AFSJ becomes an umbrella Title IV under which are inserted four specific policy chapters:

- 'borders and immigration';
- '[j]udicial cooperation in civil matters';
- '[j]udicial cooperation in criminal matters'; and
- '[p]olice cooperation.'

With the undeniable extension of EU competence in criminal matters (as will be revealed later in the book), we would argue that EU criminal law will remain and grow an area worthy of specific academic attention, distinct from the other AFSJ policy areas in Title IV TFEU.

EU CRIMINAL LAW AND JUSTICE IN CONTEXT

It has already been hinted at that the provision of criminal justice including the enforcement of criminal law has traditionally been intimately tied to sovereignty in the sense that the right to punish according to more or less uniform criteria is among the defining features of an organised and independent polity. From the moment polities became sufficiently durable and bureaucratised to qualify as 'states', they have jealously guarded their exclusive right to exercise coercion to punish breaches of the rules of social interaction on their territory. Be that as it may, people have always moved, travelled, migrated and, as an inevitable consequence, systems of criminal justice have always had to deal with the existence of, and claims by, other systems of criminal justice. The traditional conception of the interaction and, sometimes, cooperation between systems of criminal justice has been as an aspect of international relations. Sovereign states have decided to assist other sovereign states with various aspects of the provision of criminal justice depending on purely political considerations. In his seminal work, *On the Nature of War*,[4] the Prussian theorist Carl von Clausewitz describes the relationship between sovereign states as a constant 'state of nature' in which no party can be said to be bound to any course of action but that which it itself deems it is in its own interest to pursue. In this conception, the only limit to a sovereign state's total freedom of action in relation to its neighbours in matters of international relations in general, and cooperation in matters of criminal justice in particular, is the risk of so angering a neighbouring state as to cause the outbreak of war. Of course, these days international relations are to a greater or lesser extent governed by various forms of international law, which at least tends to diminish the persuasive force of the von clausewitzean conception of international relations. This is certainly the case of Europe since World War II. However, one does not have to look very far back in the history books for examples testifying to the continued relevance of the von clausewitzean notion of international relations as a 'state of nature'. In fact, was it not the refusal of the Taleban leadership in Afghanistan to cooperate in the apprehension and bringing to justice of the masterminds behind the 9-11 attacks which provided the US with the *casus belli* for the invasion of Afghanistan and the forced displacement of the Taleban regime? Von Clausewitz no doubt smiles in his grave.

While the international cooperation in matters of criminal justice can thus seem an almost savage game played in the arena of the greater national interest, criminal justice, as it is most commonly perceived, on the ground, is very much a question of the *individual* interest. At the most basic level, the criminal law is justified by the existence of absolute individual interests which society has decided merit collective protection. Thus, for the most part, the substantive criminal law lays down those actions which constitute violations of certain individual interests such as our physical bodily integrity and our property interests.[5] It needs to be stated that there are many ways of viewing and justifying the criminal law. Some, more utilitarian-orientated, conceptions tend to emphasize the danger to society as a whole posed by individuals who commit crimes and will therefore conceive of the criminal law more as a way of protecting the future of a particular society than the vindication of a past violation of an individual interest. But whichever conception one adopts, at the very least it can be agreed by all that the starting point for most criminal processes is the violation of an individual interest. Further on, the criminal process itself is generally seen as a delicate structure designed to tutor and to restrain the punitive might of society in order to protect the interests of the not yet judged defendant. This confluence of individual interests which constitutes criminal justice in the Western world is thus made up of binding rules which apply *irrespective of any contrary national interest*. The eventual circumstances in which that is not the case are regarded with much suspicion and are generally both exceptional and temporary.

When looked at from the point of view of the interests protected, it seems clear that criminal justice *simpliciter* and international cooperation in matters of criminal justice belong to completely different disciplines. And just as there can probably be said to be a near-global agreement on the centrality of the individual interest in criminal justice, globally the traditional conception of international cooperation in matters of criminal justice remains the paradigm: an aspect of international relations and therefore a relationship purely between sovereignties in which the only principle of action is opportunity and in which the ultimate and sometimes only sanction is war. As we shall see, this traditional paradigm has been displaced as regards certain aspects of criminal justice and in certain parts of the world, in particular in the area with which we are concerned, Europe and the EU. Nevertheless, it is important to keep the basic starting point of the von clausewitzean 'state of nature' in mind when discussing the very recent developments in the EU. These developments are most definitely an improvement on what went before, but they are nonetheless a drastic change away from a system which has developed over centuries. Such weighty tradition, ingrained as it is in the institutional memories of governments everywhere, is difficult to displace. Add to this the additional difficulty that the various criminal justice systems in Europe have until relatively recently evolved according to very separate traditions and the complexity of the task the EU has set for itself becomes abundantly clear.

Criminal Justice and the Vagaries of History

It has become fairly standard, and somewhat populist, to point to the sometimes important differences between systems of criminal justice, and the deep, cultural meaning they supposedly have,[6] only then to conclude that harmonisation and sometimes even cooperation is neither possible nor desirable. Commonly, the main distinction is made between the systems inspired by the common law tradition, said to be 'adversarial', and the systems said to belong to the Continental, 'inquisitorial' tradition. To this it is probably proper to add the ex-socialist systems in Central and Eastern Europe because, while they will have been inspired by the two abovementioned traditions, it can only with difficulty be said that they are as ingrained culturally there as the 'adversarial' procedure is in England and Wales and the 'inquisitorial' is in, for example, France. However, while it is true that there are significant differences between the systems of criminal justice in existence within the confines of the EU, modern thinking tends to be sceptical of such cut-and-dried divisions.[7] It is pointed out, first, that it is difficult conclusively to settle which features are typical of an 'adversarial' or of an 'inquisitorial' system. Further, many systems of criminal justice have undergone quite extensive reforms which have tended to bring them closer together, especially under the influence of the ECHR and the case law of the ECtHR. As noteworthy examples of this latter trend can be cited *il Codice di Procedura Penale* adopted in Italy in 1988 and *le Nouveau Code de Procédure Pénale* adopted in France in 1992. Both these reforms incorporated significant elements traditionally associated with 'adversarial' procedures. In the UK, on the other hand, although the 'geography' of the legal system renders such sweeping reforms of the kind introduced in France and in Italy extremely difficult and therefore highly unlikely, recent discussions on restricting trial by jury, special counsel, etc. go in the direction, if not of 'inquisitorial' procedures, then at least away from some of the most emblematic facets of the 'adversarial' tradition.

In addition to this empirical argument that differences between systems of criminal justice are less a matter of kind than of degree, there is also the fact that the appearance of the two main traditions (the 'adversarial' and the 'inquisitorial') was by no means the result of a principled standpoint on how to organise a 'just' criminal procedure. Until fairly late medieval times, a criminal 'trial' looked pretty much the same all over the Christian world. *Ordeals* were the order of the day: by water, by iron, by combat. The pivotal idea was that, when the priest in charge of the 'ordeal pit' consecrated the event, God would intervene in the ordeal to show the guilt or the innocence of the accused. Then, at the Fourth Lateran Council in 1215, Pope Innocent III decided that Holy Mother Church would no longer participate in the organisation of ordeals. It is to be noted that this was not a decision which based itself on some idea that it was unduly harsh to expect guilt or innocence to be shown by throwing old ladies in ponds to see if they floated or by having people carry red hot irons around to see if they healed without infections. No, the decision was one based on purely theological grounds:

> For Christian theologians there was no doubt that God could work miracles. He could, for example, make a guilty man's body stay on the water's surface. The problem was, however, that the basis of the ordeal was that God was required to work a miracle every time he was asked to do so, but since a miracle was surely a free act of God, this was theologically unacceptable unless the ordeal was, like the Mass, a sacrament.[8]

It followed that, since ordeals were not a sacrament they constituted an abuse of God's time and the Church would have nothing to do with them.

At this point, the administration of criminal justice was in a pickle to say the least: the whole basis for the way guilt and innocence were determined was suddenly removed. Although the much less religious ordeal by battle continued to be used in some circumstances – in the UK, under certain circumstances, it remained a statutory option until 1819[9] – it was clear that new procedures would have to be invented. In the UK and in Denmark, some form of trial by jury was instituted, whereas on the continent the emphasis was placed on 'persuading' the accused to confess, something which usually involved what would today be referred to, somewhat euphemistically, as 'exceptional methods of interrogation'. But before we jump to the conclusion that the freedom-loving Britons placed their trust in the judgment of 'twelve good men and true' whereas the evil continentals were somehow predisposed to torturing people, we should remember that in the UK torture was permitted in proceedings for treason *and*, more commonly, in the guise of what was known as *peine forte et dure*: essentially slowly and incrementally crushing a recalcitrant defendant in order to make her or him 'choose' to put her- or himself before the jury of her or his peers in the first place.[10]

If the origins of the first divisions between the 'adversarial' and 'inquisitorial' traditions, however random and unprincipled they seem, can thus be traced some 800 years back, it was surprisingly late that they acquired some of their most emblematic features. For instance, in the common law tradition, prosecution and defence counsel only became a regular feature of criminal proceedings during the second half of the eighteenth century[11] and, unlike today, juries were generally 'self-informing' and therefore expected to have prior knowledge of the case. The present insistence on no previous bias in jurors and the jury's modern status as the passive representation of the people and objective trier of fact would have seemed very alien to Englishmen until relatively recently.

Nevertheless, there is no doubt that criminal procedure is an important part of how a society sees itself and relates to others. Whether or not such far-reaching conclusions are justified from a historical perspective, it is pointless to contest that the diversity in the systems of criminal justice in Europe are a present-day fact and that this became a distinct source of difficulties for cross-border cooperation in matters of criminal justice. Such cooperation was, as we have discussed, already rendered difficult by the conception of cross-border criminal cooperation as a facet of international relations.

Normative Convergence and Institutional Formalisation

Even after World War II, when it became the general consensus that one of the main objectives of the criminal procedure was to safeguard the rights of the individuals involved, this dichotomy between the individual-centred internal procedure, and the state-centred external procedure persisted. The CoE formalised the new consensus on the primacy of the individual in the post-World War II European legal culture. But even in the CoE conventions, the dichotomy appears clearly. On the one hand, the increasingly important ECHR very much places the individual at the heart of state action, in particular in matters of criminal justice. On the other hand, the many CoE conventions formalising the rules of international cooperation in matters of criminal justice very much retain the international relations approach. The obvious example is extradition, where the rule has always been that the ultimate decision of whether to extradite or not lies with the political authorities.[12] Those familiar with the now most common organisation of extradition proceedings will object that national courts have an increasing influence in these matters and that their rulings are generally followed by the political decision makers. This is true, but it should be recalled that the powers of the national courts are essentially negative in the sense that, while extradition can be effectively prevented by a court, in the alternative situation the court can only declare that the executive is free to extradite should it wish to do so. Thus, the positive decision to extradite is always one made by the executive in the national interest. The same goes for requests for mutual legal assistance and the system of letters rogatory sent between ministries of justice. In short, the ultimate decision on whether to provide assistance to another country in matters of criminal justice was made on the basis of considerations of political expediency rather than doing justice by the individuals concerned, which is the prime concern of a court of law. In this sense, although increasingly covered up in the clothes of international law in the form of international conventions, international cooperation in matters of criminal justice – even in Europe – in many ways still conformed to the von clausewitzean conception of a relationship between sovereignties well into the final years of the twentieth century.

When the EU first started to act in the field of cooperation in matters of criminal justice, it sought to build on and increase the effectiveness of the CoE achievements as between the Member States of the EU. This can be seen by observing that the instruments made available to the EU legislator in the Treaty of Maastricht, in what became known as the 'third pillar', were more reminiscent of traditional, international cooperation than the advanced integration of the EC. At this point of its development, in the field of cooperation in matters of criminal justice the EU seemed intent on becoming an area of enhanced cooperation within the system built up by the CoE.

The position in the EU as regards criminal justice in general and cooperation in matters of criminal justice in particular at the end of the twentieth century can thus be described as follows. As far as the objectives of the criminal procedure were concerned, there was a broad consensus that the main features of the system ought to be the safeguarding of the individual interests involved. On the other hand, while international cooperation was increasingly formalised through a network of conventions and special procedures, the fact that ultimate control over such cooperation rested with the political authorities ensured the continued predominance of the von clausewitzean theoretical position that international cooperation in matters of criminal justice belonged in the realm of international relations. This position was about to change dramatically.

The EU post-Amsterdam and beyond

In principle, there is little to criticise in the strict distinction of perspectives between criminal justice *simpliciter* and international cooperation in matters of criminal justice. Just as it seems entirely right that individual interests ought to be put front and centre of the criminal procedure in the purely internal context, it can easily be justified that those interests be subordinated to the interests of the state as a sovereign political entity when it comes to cooperating, or not, with other states. The protection of the identity and coherence of the national system of criminal justice *is* a political issue. This is not to say, however, that things could not be different. A system of criminal justice where the protection of individual interests is at the forefront also in those aspects relating to international cooperation is indeed conceivable. It would be a significant conceptual shift but, again, there would be little to object to in principle. If such a shift is to be made, what one would wish is for it to be made consciously and with consideration given to the analytical consequences which necessarily flow from it.

With the Treaty of Amsterdam, the EU was given more effective legislative instruments with which to pursue greater coordination between the systems of criminal justice of the Member States. Most notably, the framework decision was introduced which gave to the EU in the third pillar an instrument very similar to the first pillar directive; we all know how important an integrationist tool the EC directive has been. Parallel to this purely institutional development, there was a political development in that it became an established truth that the (for all practical purposes) disappearance of internal borders in the EU gave rise to a situation where intense supranational cooperation was required if crime was to be fought successfully. We will look into these justifications in some detail in Chapter 1 but, somewhat simplified, the logic was that the internal market created an open and borderless zone for legitimate business as well as for criminal organisations. It was thought that the combination of no borders for personal and business-related movement, with a system of cooperation in matters of criminal justice where borders still constituted significant obstacles to law enforcement authorities resulted in both an increase in cross-border criminality and the risk that astute criminal organisations use the differences in the various systems of criminal justice to their advantage. And so, at the JHA summit in the little Finnish town of Tampere in October 1999, the EU's highest political organ which sets the political direction for the EU as a whole, the European Council, declared that henceforth the principle of *mutual recognition* would be the 'cornerstone' of the EU's action to promote cooperation in matters of criminal justice.

Mutual recognition as such was not a new concept in the EU context; it had already played an important role in the 'new approach' to common market integration and the EC treaty already stated that it was to be the governing principle in judicial cooperation in civil and commercial matters. What made the Tampere declaration so remarkable was that it was a political declaration which became the guiding legislative methodology in the third pillar and as such rigorously applied by *all* the institutional actors of the EU. The flagship legislative example is the EAW[13] but perhaps more remarkable is the adoption by the European Court of Justice (ECJ) of mutual recognition as an interpretative tool not only when interpreting legislative acts, such as the EAW, adopted expressly under the mutual recognition agenda, but also when interpreting legislation ante-dating the Tampere declaration. Most notable in this respect is the rather substantive case law on Article 54 of the Convention Implementing the Schengen Agreement (CISA) on the principle of *ne bis in idem*.[14] The CISA itself was signed in 1990 to implement the original 1985 Schengen convention whereby Belgium, France, Germany, Luxembourg and the Netherlands agreed between them, and outside of the then EC framework, to implement the complete freedom of movement across their mutual borders. In 1990, the third pillar had yet to be instituted, let alone the principle of mutual recognition. At first glance then, it is at the very least eyebrow-raising that the ECJ uses mutual recognition as the concept with reference to which to interpret Article 54 CISA. The most plausible explanation for this course of action is the incorporation of the CISA into the EU treaty framework which was effected by a 1999 Council decision assigning third pillar legal bases to the CISA provisions.[15] From then on it is at least arguable that the CISA was to be interpreted using the same interpretative tool as applies generally to the third pillar, i.e. mutual recognition. Nevertheless, the complete success of mutual recognition as the methodological and conceptual centre of gravity for EU action in the context of EU criminal justice is fascinating.

Whether the abovementioned institutional effects of introducing mutual recognition to the third pillar had been predicted or not is difficult to tell. Simplifying ever so slightly, it can probably be said that the EU project has been propelled by political initiatives which the EU's own institutions have appropriated and built upon in ways which, with hindsight, seem entirely logical but which are unlikely to have been within the intentions of the original authors of the initiatives. It is the stuff of clichés but it still deserves mentioning that the arguably most important constitutional events in the history of the EU and which set it apart from public international law generally were the result of the ECJ drawing the logical conclusions from what the politicians had decided but which nevertheless seemed to catch those same politicians by surprise. We are of course referring to the famous decisions in *Costa* v. *E.N.E.L.* and *Van Gend en Loos* which instituted, respectively, the principles of primacy and direct effect. Today it is difficult to imagine the EU, or, rather, the EC without them. At the time however, the solutions these cases provided were not obvious. So, when the political leaders at Tampere decided to make mutual recognition the 'cornerstone' of EU action in the third pillar, the historically more astute of them probably had a hunch that they were letting a rather large cat out of the bag.

EU Criminal Law and Justice: between Legislative Pragmatism and Legal Consequentialism

Although there is considerable controversy over how to conceptualise the act of judicial interpretation, we will go out on a limb and claim that, when lawyers are faced with a legal issue, they seek to find a solution which is conceptually consistent with the guiding principles of the system within which they operate. Thus, no legal issue is 'an island' but needs to be approached as part of a larger whole. Usually, there is some sort of 'higher law' which serves as the reference for this 'larger whole'. If we imagine that a law were to be passed laying down that permanently depriving a person of her or his car is not theft if the keys were in it, we would, presumably, be upset not only because it would be a stupid and unfair law but also because it would have repercussions for the conception of property pertaining in that legal system. If then, as is usually the case, national constitutions (or, if all else fails, Article 1 of Protocol 1 to the ECHR) contain a provision protecting private property, we would have a reference by which to hold such a legislative provision unlawful. Thus the protection of private property acts as a higher law or principle which permeates a number of more specific legislative areas, one of which is the penal law of theft.

In the EU context, there are a certain number of principles which permeate the system as a whole and with which any individual piece of legislation needs to be in conformity. Some of these principles are formally higher law in that they are explicit in the treaties. One of the most important of these is the principle of non-discrimination on the grounds of nationality.[16] Others can only indirectly be linked to the treaties and are rather explicable on the grounds that no European judge could imagine giving effect to a legal system which does not respect them. Here the obvious example is the famous 'general principles of EU law' of which the ECJ has formulated a few. We expect judges applying EU law to respect these tenets of higher law in the sense that the outcomes in particular cases should be in conformity with the principles enshrined in them.

We cannot know to what extent the political leaders at Tampere were planning on introducing a new such higher principle into EU law when they decided to consecrate the principle of mutual recognition. It seems highly unlikely, however, that they predicted the paradigmatic shift which they had thereby set in motion. Mutual recognition, as defined in the guidance documents, implies that 'while another state may not deal with a certain matter in the same or even a similar way as one's own state, the results will be such that they are accepted as equivalent to decisions by one's own state'.[17] For the Commission, this implied a transfer of the ultimate responsibility for requesting of, as well as dealing with requests from, foreign authorities from the political to the judicial authorities. Before, as was briefly outlined above, a judge wanting a person extradited from a neighbouring country would have had to ask her or his national ministry of justice (or perhaps the ministry of foreign affairs) to send a request to the political counterparts in the requested country who would then have had to go through the inverse juridico-political procedure before deciding whether to accede to the request or not. Now, with the advent of mutual recognition, the idea was that a judge simply rules on a matter and that that ruling be recognised by her or his counterparts throughout the EU, and this without the cumbersome intervention of political authorities.

This change, again seen most clearly in the EAW, implies a much more fundamental change than a mere increase in efficiency and speed. As was discussed above, the 'science' of criminal justice had evolved to the point where internal criminal justice was animated by the concern for individual interests and cooperation in criminal matters was animated by the concern for the systemic sovereignty and coherence of the national system of criminal justice. This was reflected in the institutional actors ultimately responsible for the two aspects of criminal justice. In the Western legal tradition, courts are the ultimate guarantors of individual rights and freedoms, whereas national executives are the ultimate guarantors of the national interest. Shifting the responsibility for international cooperation in matters of criminal justice from national executives to national judiciaries not only shifted administrative burdens from one governmental power to another. More than anything it also shifted the whole rationale of the system. With courts responsible for international cooperation in matters of criminal justice, the individual interest is put front and centre also in this facet of criminal justice *and* it is consequently aligned with the principles animating internal criminal proceedings.

When a court is faced with an EU instrument based on the principle of mutual recognition, that instrument cannot be treated as 'an island'. It needs to be read in conformity with the principle of which it is a subspecies. Now, the principle of mutual recognition does not figure in the EU treaty, nor has it been declared a general principle of EU law by the ECJ. Nevertheless, the ECJ treats it much as it does other principles of higher law in that it serves as the prism through which more specific legislative instruments are read, interpreted and applied. In this way, the ECJ has adopted the logic of the new conceptual paradigm that was ushered in with the adoption of mutual recognition as the guiding principle of EU action in the field of cooperation between the Member States in matters of criminal justice: the primacy of the individual interest over the national interest. On the other hand, the EU legislator does not seem to have realised that the adoption of the principle of mutual recognition as the guiding principle in this field had this implication. The result is that we have a legal logic applied and reinforced by the ECJ and, unfortunately somewhat inconsistently, by the Commission and the European Parliament (EP), while the true masters of the EU's legislative agenda in matters of criminal justice, the Member States and the Council, seem to continue to reason as though it were possible to combine mutual recognition with the continued primacy of the national interest.

BOX 2

Perhaps by way of recognition that that had not always been the case, Article 2F TFEU lays down that '[t]he Union shall ensure consistency between its policies and activities, taking all of its objectives into account and in accordance with the principle of conferral of powers'.

The consequence of this conflict is that EU action in matters of criminal justice can sometimes appear somewhat schizophrenic. The EAW is a perfect example of this. The framework decision itself is a very coherent application of the principle of mutual recognition under which the judge in the executing state is to do little more than to make sure that the certificate sent to her or him by her or his counterpart in the issuing state is correctly filled out. No investigation into the merits, no objections based on national standards of evidence or procedure should prevent the surrender of an individual who is suspected of having committed a crime over which the authorities in the issuing state have recognised jurisdiction. Simple and straightforward. Despite the fact that these were principles unanimously agreed to in Council, it proved a vain hope that the transposition of the framework decision in the various Member States should follow the same simple and straightforward pattern. As will be discussed at greater length in Chapter 4, the transposition of the EAW in the legislation of the Member States has been anything but simple and straightforward.

The EAW is an example of a discrepancy between Member State action as part of the Council and Member State action as national legislator. Unfortunately, there are also examples of persisting inconsistencies at the EU level. One example is Article 54 CISA mentioned above which, again, will be the subject of lengthier discussions in Chapter 4. In its first part, this article lays down the principle that 'a person whose trial has been finally disposed of in one Contracting Party may not be prosecuted in another Contracting Party for the same acts'. In a system of mutual recognition, this is very easy to understand: a final judgment in a criminal trial in one Member State should be recognised as final in the other Member States in the same way as a final judgment from one of their 'own' courts. This is also the manner in which the ECJ has interpreted this provision which has resulted in a series of judgments clearly stating the consequences of the practical application of the principle of mutual recognition.[18] The problem is that the second part of Article 54 CISA qualifies the principle in a manner rather difficult to understand. It states that the principle of one prosecution per set of facts applies 'provided that, if a penalty has been imposed, it has been enforced, is actually in the process of being enforced or can no longer be enforced under the laws of the sentencing Contracting Party'. What this means is that a fugitive and even, in all probability, a person awaiting execution of her or his sentence, can be tried again for the same facts in a different Member State. It is very hard to see how this can be anything but inconsistent with the principle of mutual recognition. What if the latter court reaches a different result? Which Member State's judicial authorities are then obliged to recognise the other's final decision? Especially after the adoption of the EAW under which the first Member State could have the convicted person surrendered whenever it wants, it is difficult to avoid the conclusion that the only interest this provision serves is some national interest of a Member State retaining as much power as possible over individuals on its territory. In any case, however narrowly interpreted, this provision can cause nothing but conflict with the general logic of the principle of mutual recognition. This was seen in the recent case of *Kretzinger*.[19]

As we hope to have shown with this brief discussion, there are many aspects of EU criminal law and justice which offend against the legal sense of consistency in principle. We would argue that one of the main reasons for this is the general failure to understand that the adoption of mutual recognition as the guiding principle of EU action in matters of criminal justice constituted a massive conceptual shift in the realm of international cooperation in this area. With the autonomous EU institutions doing their best to consolidate the principle of mutual recognition and the Member States and Council still clinging on to the old von clausewitzean conception of cooperation in matters of criminal justice, there is a tension at the heart of the EU project as it relates to criminal law and justice. Again, we would argue, this is why the identity of the EU as an institutional actor in this field is so difficult to grasp. Starting with the Tampere Declaration, the EU seems to have expressed an implicit wish to change paradigms for its internal system of cooperation in matters of criminal law and justice. But having done this without properly discussing the theoretical justifications and ramifications of this choice, the EU is now hovering somewhere in between, with the result that legislative action, policy statements and implementation practices quite often betray a fundamental confusion of what kind of system it is that the EU is constructing.

In this book we will not attempt to provide the theoretical justification for EU action in matters of criminal law and justice which is so sorely lacking. We merely seek to point to the fact that no such justification has been provided and that the roots of many of the difficulties besetting the EU's efforts to construct a strong and coherent *Area of Freedom, Security and Justice* (AFSJ) can be traced to this basic theoretical *lacuna*. In this interinstitutional 'struggle' between the old, international relations-inspired view of cooperation in matters of criminal justice, and the new, individual-centred principle of mutual recognition, there are no absolutes. Each system brings with it consequences (advantages and drawbacks) which need to be compared, assessed and evaluated. What needs to be understood, however, is that these are two conflicting paradigms, each with its own theoretical justifications and history.

It can of course be said that this development is in line with the EU's earliest ambitions to be a legal system which applies directly to the individual citizens, bypassing the eventual hurdles set up by the narrower, national interests of the Member States. That is probably correct and, in any case, lest any of our readers misunderstand, we welcome this development; in an area of complete freedom of movement, it seems almost perverse that a person could not be brought to justice, that a central witness could not be heard, or, consequently, that a victim of a crime (or the victim's family) could not receive the solace and comfort of knowing that justice had been done simply because of a red line on a map of no consequence to anyone but to law enforcement authorities. However, and this is the central point, that does not mean that the old system was completely erratic and incomprehensible. There *was* a logic to the old 'order' and that was that, in matters central to national sovereignty, individual interests in justice had to take a step back in favour of the national interest. The common argumentations used to justify, first, the EU's initial involvement in matters of criminal justice and then, second, to justify mutual recognition, all focus on the practical consequences of the old 'order': the internal market is said to have caused increases in cross-border crime, terrorism is a cross-border problem, the CoE instruments lack teeth, etc.[20] While these may certainly be valid arguments, nowhere do they acknowledge that dealing with this problem meant changing the normative logic of the cooperation between EU Member States in matters of criminal justice. The prime concern of the political decision makers was with increasing the effectiveness of their national law enforcement authorities. Mutual recognition certainly achieves this objective but it also entails the important normative changes described above. In short, no one seemed properly to have grasped that such massive changes to the very foundations of the way the system is run necessarily imply, in order to function, significant shifts at the level of principle as well as on the level of application.

From an institutional perspective, this debate on the conceptualisation of EU criminal justice can seem a simple variant of the traditional cooperation versus integration debate. Superficially, this may indeed be the case. There are, however, some aspects of the present debate which set it apart.

A traditional move from cooperation to integration will start with an argument for integration being necessary or desirable, followed by the introduction of the institutional instruments necessary to effect the change. In
the context of the third pillar, this natural order of things seems to have
been reversed. While the third pillar is still referred to as an 'intergovernmental pillar', to distinguish it from the 'supranational' EC pillar, the institutional reality of the third pillar is very much supranational. This
discrepancy between the integrationist potential of the third pillar's institutional framework and the almost automated intergovernmentalist
justifications offered for it has turned EU criminal justice into a field of
extreme constitutional uncertainty. There is, from a legislative perspective,
precious little theoretical direction. In this context, the fact that the third
pillar has a certain, if incomplete and unsatisfactory,[21] judicial autonomy
again leaves the field open for the interplay between the national courts and
the ECJ to provide some of the answers the legislative organs of the EU
seem unable to deliver. The available indications from the ECJ seem to
point in the direction of conceptual and therefore institutional harmonisation as between the first and third pillars, i.e. the introduction into and use
of concepts in the third pillar which are already familiar from the first,
Community pillar. For these reasons, the study of the justifications for and
the development of EU criminal justice should be of interest to those interested in the institutional development of the EU as a whole.

It is very possible that inter-Member State cooperation in matters of
criminal justice could not be rendered more effective within the confines of
the old, von clausewitzean system. Perhaps greater effectiveness could only
be achieved via a complete change of the theoretical bases and the institutional reform of the system. We would argue that that was the case, but that
the general tendency not to deal with matters of criminal law in theoretical
terms has deprived the EU as a political entity of the vocabulary and thus
the instruments necessary to construct a theoretically coherent and practi-
cally just system of criminal justice. Without an understanding of these
theoretical starting points, which will be further developed in Chapter 1, it
is very difficult to make sense of EU criminal law and justice as a project
and we would ask our readers to keep these difficulties in mind when
reading the subject-matter specific chapters in this book.

NOTES

1. Not only in academic writings. At the European Commission, the two issues share a
    directorate general (DG *Justice, Liberté et Sécurité*) and their in-house counsel at the
    Commission Legal Service are also in the same unit.
2. OJ C 306, 17.12.2007, p. 1 et s.

3. Note that a new Protocol on Transitional Provisions confirms at Article 9 that the legal effects of pre-existing third pillar instruments 'shall be preserved until those acts are repealed, annulled or amended'. Article 10 clarifies that for a five year period after the entry into force of the Treaty of Lisbon the pre-existing limits on the powers of the Commission (vis-à-vis infringement proceedings) and the ECJ (vis-à-vis jurisdiction) shall continue to apply in respect of pre-existing third pillar measures. The extent to which there will be a conversion of third pillar instruments into appropriate 'first pillar' instruments during this transitional period remains to be seen, as does the extent to which this will be used as an opportunity to renegotiate the wording of existing instruments.
4. C. von Clausewitz (2005), *On the Nature of War*, London: Penguin Books.
5. We say 'for the most part' because, traditionally, parts of the criminal law also protect the national interest. Offences such as treason, espionage and desertion have only a contingent link to the individual interest. More recently, the criminal law has also been called upon to protect certain 'policies' which a society may adopt. This is also a facet of EU criminal law and will be dealt with fully in Chapter 6.
6. For a historical, now perhaps slightly quaint example, see C.J. Hamsoun and R. Vouin (1952), 'Le procès criminel en Angleterre et en France', *Revue Internationale de Droit Pénal*, **23**, 177–90.
7. See, e.g., J.D. Jackson (2005), 'The effect of human rights on the criminal evidentiary process: towards convergence, divergence or realignement?', *Modern Law Review*, **68**(5), 737–64.
8. D. Danziger and J. Gillingham (2003), *1215 – The Year of Magna Carta*, London: Hodder and Stoughton, at p. 196.
9. Ibid.
10. Ibid.
11. See J.H. Langbein (1977), 'The criminal trial before the lawyers', *The University of Chicago Law Review*, **45**(2), 263–316; also J.H. Langbein (1999), 'The prosecutorial origings of defence counsel in the eighteenth century: the appearance of solicitors', *Cambridge Law Journal*, **58**(2), 314–65.
12. See, e.g., M. Mackarel and S. Nash (1997), 'Extradition and the European Union', *International and Comparative Law Quarterly*, **46**, 948–57.
13. See below, Chapter 4.
14. See below, ibid.
15. Council Decision 1999/436/EC of 20 May 1999 (OJ L 176, 10.7.1999, pp. 17–30).
16. Article 12 EC.
17. Mutual Recognition of Final Decisions in Criminal Matters, COM(2000) 495 final, 26.7.2000.
18. See, e.g., joined cases C-187 and 385/01, *Gözütok and Brügge*, judgment of 11 February 2003.
19. C-288/05, judgment of 18 July 2007.
20. For a more extensive discussion, see Chapter 1 below.
21. See below, Chapter 1.

1. Justifications, competences and principles

As will have been understood from the reasoning in the introduction, the highly emotive evocation of an 'Area of freedom, security and justice' by the EU Treaty was probably not the result of any deeper probing into what the theoretical foundations of a novel, EU system of criminal justice ought to be. As a matter of rhetoric it is a pleasing triplet and it can probably be placed in that tradition of aspirational taglines which can trace its lineage back to the 'Life, liberty and the pursuit of happiness' of the American revolution and the '*Liberté, égalité, fraternité*' of its French counterpart. It is of course true that the American and French slogans were meant to encapsulate the hopes and aspirations of, respectively, a newly born and a reborn nation-state whereas the EU's AFSJ is more limited in scope. Nevertheless, a comparison can prove enlightening. Precisely as it was with its historically illustrious counterparts, the AFSJ is capable of serving as support for the hopes and aspirations of a great number of very varied ideologies, all claiming to interpret and give voice to its 'mandate'. In this vein, a multitude of academic criticisms of the development of the AFSJ with reference to a perceived lack of 'balance' between the three foundational concepts in the normative output of the EU has emerged. Again, however, precisely as with the American and French slogans, very little in terms of legal rights and obligations can be said to derive directly from the words 'freedom, security and justice': this despite the fact that they figure prominently in the foundational legal documents of the EU. We may say that, as a matter of political philosophy, a system of criminal justice *ought* to provide a certain balance between 'freedom, security and justice', but then again, we might as soon disagree.

Be that as it may, the existence of the terminology of 'freedom, security and justice' is significant precisely because of its aspirational character. The fact that it has become synonymous with the EU's efforts to construct a system of criminal justice linking the systems of criminal justice of its Member States makes it an interesting starting point for any attempt to organise and to make sense of what is happening in the EU's third pillar. This chapter seeks to do just that. These three concepts serving as the rhetorical and aspirational basis for EU criminal justice will be used to highlight the justifications, objectives and competences providing the impetus and basis for its development. They will also be used to highlight some question marks surrounding this development.

FREEDOM

In the context of EU criminal justice, 'freedom' can be read in a multitude of ways. Here it will be attempted to identify that version of 'freedom' which can be taken to have served as an objective of the AFSJ and which, consequently, constituted one of the justifications for its creation.

Freedom in Criminal Justice: the Traditional Interpretation

In the theory of criminal justice, the term 'freedom' is most commonly associated with the relationship between the individual and the state. The individual is entitled to a significant degree of freedom from excessive state intervention in her or his activities. The exact scope and nature of this freedom will vary depending on the particular situation in which the individual finds her- or himself with respect to the state. Again in the theory of criminal justice, the central relationship is that between the individual as suspect of a crime and the state seeking to punish the individual responsible for that crime. The defining concept of this relationship is the presumption of innocence. National systems of criminal justice will have extensive provisions guaranteeing the freedoms of suspects and defendants while they remain unconvicted and thus presumed innocent. These provisions prevent state authorities from abusing their monopoly on violence.

A cursory look at the provisions of the EU Treaty reveals that the protection of 'freedom' in this sense was not something which overly preoccupied the contracting parties. In later chapters it will be discussed further whether that initial impression is necessarily accurate when all the relevant considerations are taken into account. For present purposes, however, it is important to note that, while national systems of criminal justice tend to place significant emphasis on the protection of freedom in this sense (it could even be claimed that they define themselves through the modalities of this protection) the text of the EU Treaty is silent on this aspect of freedom. Given that a system of criminal justice which does not provide rigorous protection of the freedoms of suspects and defendants is perhaps the defining characteristic of tyrannical government, the absence of express provisions for it in the context of the AFSJ necessitates comment.

The essential starting point for this discussion is that the freedoms of suspects and defendants in criminal proceedings are the necessary counterparts of the coercive powers of the organs of the state. It is precisely because the organs of state constitute a potential threat to the physical integrity of individuals involved in criminal proceedings that these freedoms need to be institutionalised. In this sense it is clear that all the national systems of criminal justice in the EU constitute such potential threats to the individuals under their jurisdiction. The EU, however, does not. Currently, there are no EU organs capable of constituting a threat to the physical integrity of individuals in the EU. Even when EU instruments are being enforced, such enforcement is effected by organs of the various Member States. From this perspective, the EU Treaty's silence on the protection of 'freedom' in this sense is understandable and justifiable: sufficient protection of this most fundamental value exists in the national laws governing the actions of the organs posing the actual threats to individual integrity reinforced, of course, by the European Convention of Human Rights.

Recently, this traditional view of freedom in criminal justice has been challenged. The last couple of years have seen a rise to prominence of a school of thought which seeks to promote the freedom from fear as one of the main objectives of criminal justice. The proponents of this school of thought switch perspectives and focus on everyone not involved in any particular criminal proceedings. The idea is that the state has a responsibility to all law abiding individuals under its jurisdiction to provide them with an environment where they can go about their daily business free from the fear of being the victims of crime. The proponents of this interpretation are often politicians seeking to justify reforms of criminal justice which are difficult to justify with reference to the traditional conception of freedom.[1] The eventual merits and demerits of this interpretation of freedom in the context of criminal justice will not be discussed here. Suffice to say that it is unlikely that this was the version of 'freedom' which motivated the AFSJ. This is because the 'freedom from fear' school has become important in conjunction with the so-called 'war on terrorism' and thus ante-dates the institutional settlement which gave rise to the AFSJ with the Treaties of Maastricht and Amsterdam. We will come back to the importance of this school of thought in its more proper guise of 'security' when we discuss this concept and its influence on the character of the normative output of the AFSJ.

The AFSJ, the Four Freedoms and Spillover

Given that the traditional interpretation of freedom in the context of criminal justice sits uneasily with the institutional set-up of the AFSJ, one is tempted to look outside of criminal justice in order to find that version of 'freedom' which can be said to be one of the inspirational components of the EU's AFSJ. In fact, the word 'freedom' has a very precise connotation in EU law or, to be more precise, *EC* law. The most important achievement of the EU to date is (arguably) the realisation of the single internal market: the so-called 'four freedoms'. These are of course the free movement of persons, goods, services and capital. With this in mind, it is not an unreasonable supposition that the 'freedom' in the AFSJ refers back to these four traditional freedoms of EC law which should be enjoyed in better 'security and justice'. This supposition is further strengthened by the fact that, in the preamble to the EU Treaty, the contracting parties affirm their resolve 'to facilitate the free movement of persons, while ensuring the safety and security of their peoples, by establishing an area of freedom, security and justice, in accordance with the provisions of this Treaty'. However, this formulation is not conclusive in that the implied link between the free movement of persons and the safety and security of the peoples of the EU is not clarified. It can be read so as to say that the reality of free movement of persons makes the EU as a whole responsible for the safety and security of these persons. But that does not necessarily imply that free movement of persons in itself is a cause of increased unsafety and insecurity. As we shall see, this ambiguity is at the very core of the discussion of the supposed effect of the four freedoms on the creation and the development of the AFSJ.

There is a lot of academic writing justifying the conferral of legislative competences on the EU in matters of criminal law starting from the realisation of the four freedoms. The fundamental idea is that the realisation of the four freedoms gave rise to a situation where criminal elements could benefit from the practical disappearance of intra-EU borders. If, the argument goes, the EU has the competence to create a situation the necessary side-effect of which is increased crime, it should have the competence to counter those negative effects of the exercise of its initial competences. In the context of the debate on the competences to be attributed to the EU, this is known as 'spillover'.[2] Thus, the completion of the single market is assumed to have had and continues to have significant consequences for the nature and extent of crime in the EU:

> The abolition of the remaining obstacles to cross-border economic activities and the full implementation of the 'four freedoms' generated *de facto* a common internal security zone encompassing all Member States in which free movement, increased economic interpenetration and the facilitation of cross-border financial activities rendered borders between the Members States increasingly ineffective both as instruments of control and obstacles to the movement of asylum-seekers, illegal immigrants and crime.[3]

The regulation of the economic and to some extent social consequences of the single market is generally seen as the natural remit of the institutions at the European level. According to the proponents of 'spillover' in the field of criminal justice, it follows that to deny the EU competence to deal with the single market-effects on crime amounts to artificially separating one set of logical and predictable consequences of the four freedoms from another. The fact that 'criminals, and terrorists in particular, do not respect national borders' and that, in addition, 'the Single Market has made it very easy for them to travel freely across the EU – more freely than national police forces', all amounts to 'a compelling need for action at supra-national level'.[4]

Superficially, these claims are compelling in that they seem logically sound. When analysed closely, however, it is difficult to ascertain what exactly is claimed. Has the single market merely caused a qualitative shift in already existing criminal structures? Has there been a quantitative increase in crime levels? Both? Are criminals really, and literally, outrunning the police by using some Member States with more 'favourable' systems of criminal justice as 'safe havens' for pan-European criminal activities?[5] Are they really able to forum-shop? That organised, transnational crime is a serious problem and a challenge for us all is beyond doubt.[6] But while, in some places in the world, 'criminal organizations are able to defy government authority, suborn or even partially supplant it',[7] as far as the EU pre the 2004 enlargement was concerned, 'in virtually none of the Member States does organized crime pose a real threat to the democratic constitutional state and the free market economy. Rather, it represents a greater or lesser challenge to the authorities'.[8] The question is, of course, whether this remains the case or whether the expansion of the single market following the latest rounds of enlargement in 2004 and 2007 has led to a deterioration of the situation. Although they make for sobering reading, pure crime statistics[9] are not very helpful in this regard and, by way of example, Mueller admits that 'we do not know how many of the businesses we frequent daily have been infiltrated, or are actually owned, by transnational organized crime groups'.[10] Consequently, we have no way of knowing the organisational structure and reach of these groups. Fijnaut has remarked that 'for all intents and purposes, it is impossible to have an overview of the nature, scope, and development of (organized) crime in the EU and its neighbouring countries'.[11]

This lack of reliable statistics is probably to a large extent due to the fact that the information we are looking for is empirically elusive: how would one go about verifying the claim that the single market engenders crime? How could we control for other factors such as the general process of internationalisation of economic activity, licit as well as illicit? The existence of organised, transnational criminal networks in parts of the world where borders remain very much a part of economic life lends credence to Bruggeman's assertion:

the internationalisation of the major criminal organisations has come about regardless of the treaties on the free movement of goods and persons. They have been helped in this internationalisation process by the gaps in, and inadequacy of, international treaty rules and by the difference in national legislation and by the gaps in, and incompleteness of, the criminal laws of many countries.[12]

What Bruggeman alludes to is the effect of globalisation on pre-existing 'criminogenic asymmetries'. The notion of a criminogenic asymmetry refers to any type of disparity (asymmetry) between the life situations of individuals or economically independent geographical entities which create circumstances in which there is a potential gain in exploiting the asymmetry through illicit means. Thus an example of an economic criminogenic asymmetry would be the different levels of taxation on tobacco products in various parts of the EU, not to mention the world, which has resulted in a very lucrative trafficking industry. An example of a social criminogenic asymmetry would be differing living standards in geographically relatively proximate locations. This is the main driving force behind the extensive trafficking in human beings into the EU. Further, the idea is that certain criminogenic asymmetries – economic, social, power and influence related, etc. – are accentuated by the increase in international exchange.[13] This intensification is due to a combination of several factors: globalisation arguably facilitates massive accumulation of wealth and, some would say, accentuates economic inequalities. Further, it renders inequality more visible to more people. Finally, whereas the exercise of economic power is now virtually unconstrained by national borders, the exercise of, for want of a better expression, 'disciplining power' is still very much constrained by red lines on the map. At the other end, 'asymmetries provide the catalyst for globalization to produce criminal opportunities, motives to take advantage of those opportunities and weaker controls'.[14] Finally, in these times of increasing speed and intensity of human interaction in all fields of activity, differences which previously would not have had criminogenic potential, because too distant spatially or temporally, are becoming increasingly proximate which in turn increases their criminogenic potential: '[t]he time–space compression activates the criminogenic potential of existing power and economic asymmetries too'.[15] In short, 'criminogenesis increases significantly as a result of the dynamic of globalization, which multiplies, intensifies or activates asymmetries'.[16]

The only reasonable conclusion to be drawn from all this is that organised, transnational crime is a side-effect of the increasingly organised and transnational nature of all economic activity, and that, while it is not an unreasonable assumption that the single market and its four freedoms do have an effect in this regard, there is no reliable empirical data either to

confirm or to quantify this assumption. The Europol Organised Crime
Reports (OCR) and, since 2006, the Organised Crime Threat Assessments
(OCTA) confirm this conclusion. The 2005 OCR states that 'OC
[Organised Crime] takes advantage from the increasing mobility, urbanisa-
tion, anonymity and diminishing social control which are characteristic of
modern society' in general while, in relation to specific crime, exploiting the
'discrepancies between EU laws and national legislations in committing
among others environmental crime and high technology crime, and [. . .]
gaps in EU procedures for example in VAT and other fraud'.[17] The 2005
OCR also states that enlargement does not seem to have had a qualitative impact on organised crime. The 2006 OCTA paints a picture of a
great diversity of organisational models in the world of organised
crime, but especially of a degree of regional integration within Europe.[18]
As for the factors creating the 'market' for organised crime, Europol
points to a number of sources of criminogenic asymmetries mainly to
do with remaining regulatory differences between Member States, for
example in alcohol taxation, and various EU budgetary schemes more or
less open to fraud. Consequently, it is very difficult to isolate the impact
of the single market on organised crime. While the organisational
integration of the various operators certainly seems to be facilitated by
increased integration in Europe, that very integration seems to do away
with some of the criminogenic asymmetries on which those same operators
thrive.[19]

Nevertheless, despite the inconclusive nature of the available data, the
'[e]uropeanization of Justice and Home Affairs was seen as part of a series
of flanking measures intended to compensate for the security deficit
arguably arising from the abolition of internal border control',[20] and
this, seemingly, without addressing the fundamental issue of 'whether
organized crime was actually starting to pose such a threat to the EU
that structural intervention in relationships just created was urgently
required'.[21] The consensus seems to be that, correctly or not, the 'spillover'
argument was instrumental in bringing about the inclusion of criminal
justice in the EU treaty framework. Thus the *freedom* of movement of
persons, goods, services and capital was clearly central to the creation of
the AFSJ and arguments based on 'spillover' have been and remain central
to the continued development of the EU in general, and of the AFSJ in
particular.

If the empirical claims inherent in arguments based on 'spillover' are very
tenuous, the confusion as to the *theoretical* nature and, consequently, the
strength of such argumentation is probably even more patent. In order to
address this issue we need to analyse in greater detail what 'spillover'
actually entails. The concept of 'spillover' was coined by Lindberg in his

1963 book, *The Political Dynamics of European Economic Integration*. There it is presented as a methodological concept aimed at identifying areas where political integration can be justified consequentially from the initial objective of the integration process:

> '[S]pill-over' refers to a situation in which a given action, related to a specific goal, creates a situation in which the original goal can be assured only by taking further actions, which in turn create a further condition and a need for more action, and so forth . . . . [T]he initial task and grant of power to the central institutions creates a situation or series of situations that can be dealt with only by further expanding the task and the grant of power.[22]

What often appears to be lost in the discussion is the absolutely central role played by the 'goal' of the central institutions in the concept of 'spillover'. The goal of the central institutions is in fact the reference against which the validity of a 'spillover' argument must be gauged. In other words, it is essential always to keep separate the *descriptive* and the *prescriptive* parts of a 'spillover' argument. For *only if* there is a common definition of the goal of the central institutions (description) can the further grant of power to reach that goal (prescription) be justified on the basis that it is necessary to achieve that goal.[23] 'Spillover' only applies within a certain ideological framework and, before that ideological framework has been established, 'spillover' arguments are virtually devoid of persuasive force. It is very likely that some of the confusion stems from the transfer of the concept of 'spillover' from the realm of economic integration, where Lindberg found and analysed it, to a policy area such as criminal justice where the goals of the EU are (even?) less agreed. While the goal of the internal market can be described with some accuracy with reference to the EC Treaty, it is difficult to say the same with reference to the provisions on the AFSJ in the EU Treaty's third pillar.

In discussions on the future development of the AFSJ, this is a very live issue. Arguments are often made that there is an objective *need* for one development or another, backed up or not, as the case may be, by empirical data. But as Fijnaut points out in discussing the *Corpus Iuris* project,[24] which is justified predominantly in terms of 'spillover', in reality 'this is largely an ideological question'.[25] For our purposes this must be read to mean that the neutral terminology of 'spillover' is used to hide what in reality is an argument on what the goals of the EU *ought to be*. It follows that it is incorrect to say, as is often done, that the potential effects of the four freedoms, as a matter of 'spillover', need to become a subject of EU intervention.

In reality, it would be very difficult to give an example of a social process which does not have any knock-on effects on other social phenomena. It is very likely that the four freedoms have had a profound effect on a large number of aspects of social organisation beyond crime patterns. If the very fact that the exercise of EU competences in one area has effects on other areas were to entail an extension of EU competences to cover those areas, the fundamental principle of attributed competences would cease to make sense. The results of the realisation of the four freedoms cannot, as a matter of 'spillover' theory, be used as a justification for the creation of the AFSJ since the goals of the four freedoms never included the struggle against criminality. This was the result of the ideological position discussed in the introduction: criminal justice is traditionally seen as being part of the core of national sovereignty.

The fact that it is theoretically erroneous to use 'spillover' arguments to justify the creation of the AFSJ has not prevented exactly that from happening. The AFSJ is now a reality and as such it is to be welcomed. So what, it may be asked, is the problem? The answer to that links up with what was discussed in the introduction: the lack of a proper discussion of the theoretical justifications for the EU's involvement in criminal justice. 'Spillover' is an ideologically neutral argument in that it presents one development (the AFSJ) as being a simple consequence of another (the four freedoms). But, as we have seen, 'spillover' cannot be used in this way. The further development, the area 'spilt-over', cannot itself constitute the goal which justified the 'initial task and grant of power'. The point of 'spillover' as a methodological device is to identify further developments in integration which are devoid of ideological contention as being necessary continuations in order to further a pre-established objective. Put differently, the correct application of 'spillover' entails a pre-established goal (X) which remains the same and only acts as the reference with respect to the grants of power, or competences (A, B, C, etc.) necessary in order to achieve it. The essential question in a 'spillover' argument is whether, having agreed to the objective X, the exercise of competence A gives rise to a situation in which competence B is necessary in order to further objective X, and then whether the exercise of competence B gives rise to a situation in which competence C is necessary, still in order to further objective X, and so on. 'Spillover' presupposes that all ideological contention was evacuated when the initial objective or goal was decided. The consequence of the use of 'spillover' in the context of the AFSJ is that what is in fact a highly ideological development – the EU's involvement in matters of criminal justice – is hidden behind arguments of administrative effectiveness, perfecting the internal market. Applying our formula, it is easy to see how this argument must fail. The internal market is non-contentious objective X for the achievement of which the EU, simplifying somewhat, has been granted competences A and B. The AFSJ, however, is *contentious* objective Y for the achievement of which competences C and D would be necessary. What the proponents of 'spillover' argue is that the conferral of competences C and D is justified with reference to the achievement of objective X thus avoiding the rather more difficult discussion involved in settling objective Y. In analytical terms, what the proponents of 'spillover' in this area do is to blur the distinction between the consequentialism of proper 'spillover' which directs the further action necessary to reach an already agreed objective, and the existence of mere consequences of any particular course of action. Any principled (or opportunistic) position comes at a certain cost which, it has to be assumed, is an acceptable price to pay for the holder of that particular position. We can refer to this as 'choice cost'. It is certainly the case that the EU may seem less desirable equipped with an internal market without the AFSJ and that the EU would be better with an internal market alongside the AFSJ. However, this is merely an argument in favour of making the EU responsible for achieving objective Y. The choice cost of not doing so may be less effective crime enforcement. On the other hand, the choice cost of making the EU responsible for objective Y is that competences C and D will pass from the Member State legislatures to the EU.

The problem is that, when it comes to the subject-matter of the AFSJ, the choice cost is tallied in blood rather than in money. However that still does not change the fundamental fact that, as Walker points out, 'security policy is never *compelled* by external events'.[26] External events are an indicator as to what the choice cost of one policy option may be, but they are in no way conclusive as to the correctness of that policy option. A statement which at first glance may seem devoid of ideological controversy becomes very problematic if it is to provide the basis for institutional reform. To say that 'because of the cross-border nature of terrorism, the EU is an appropriate forum to deal with it',[27] is only true if certain ideological preconditions pertain, namely that effective repression of terrorism trumps national sovereignty over criminal justice (assuming that terrorism is considered a problem of criminal justice). Likewise, simply to say that '[t]he task is to diminish or eradicate undesirable asymmetries and to reduce the criminogenic effect of those we wish to preserve or cannot do much about'[28] in the context of international cooperation in fact seeks to bypass a large number of very controversial issues. The argument which needs to be made and won in order to justify the internationalisation, or, in this case, europeanisation of criminal justice, must relate to the weight attributed to national sovereignty *contra* repressive effectivity.[29] A policy position incorporating a strong defence of national sovereignty in criminal justice may or may not come at a choice cost in human lives. That is an as yet unanswered empirical question. In turn, that may or may not be considered a reason to modify this underlying policy position. It is, however, always logically erroneous to deduce the correctness of one policy option from the eventual choice cost of another. 'Spillover' is *always* ideologically contextual. In the context of the creation of the AFSJ, the *ideological* nature of the development is illustrated by the absence of empirical data to substantiate the claims as to the choice cost relating to cross-border criminal activity. This very strongly indicates that the empirical reality, if there is such a thing, was very much subordinated to ideological considerations.

This question is addressed at length by von Bogdandy in his partial and guarded endorsement of human rights as the new 'axis of the European legal system'.[30] He very correctly identifies the ideological roots of that agenda: 'Given the strong centralizing effects, a forceful human rights policy will, nevertheless, be advocated by those who wish courageous steps to be taken to strengthen the European federation.'[31] What needs to be forcefully resisted, not least from a political perspective, is the notion that the EU is inexorably and almost uncontrollably moving towards universal centralisation. As Monar has pointed out, '[m]ajor political projects, once launched on a sufficiently broad scale and backed by an effective legitimizing political discourse, can become a driving force of their own'.[32] However, this is only true as long as it is not remembered that 'spillover' is ultimately based on agreed *goals* which, in turn, are based on ideological choices.

In conclusion, it seems evident that 'spillover' arguments, however flawed, have been absolutely central to the creation and further development of the AFSJ. The above criticism of the way the arguments have been made should not be read as a general criticism of the direction of the EU's development. In fact, it probably *is* a forceful argument in favour of further europeanisation of criminal justice that law enforcement must undergo structural modification in order to deal with criminal entities operating in a virtually borderless world.[33] And, as Walker very correctly points out, 'no sensible security policy can be blind to gradual or sudden environmental changes'.[34]

Let us assume for a moment that there were solid data to support the position that the realisation of the four freedoms in fact led to both a quantitative and a qualitative increase in criminal activity in the EU. Pointing to this fact, it is, as we have already seen, incorrect to state that as a matter of 'spillover' the EU needs to have the competences to combat crime. The correct use of these data would be to ask whether the Member States of the EU, in view of this new evidence as to the choice costs associated with the realisation of the four freedoms, would not be inclined to modify the goals and objectives of their cooperation. This, however, presupposes a preparedness to discuss the ideological foundations of both criminal justice in general and the role of the EU as distinct from its Member States in its production. But here we move away from 'freedom' as an original justifying concept for the AFSJ and move towards the second of the three foundational concepts: 'security'. In our fictitious discussion about the ideological foundations of an EU understanding of criminal justice, the Member States of the EU would rather have been swayed by arguments relating to the security of its citizens. Those arguments have also been, and continue to be, made in order to justify the creation and further development of the AFSJ, respectively. The argument here is that the EU, since it is a political actor subject to popular opinion, needs to react to sudden and often traumatic events in the lives of its citizens. As we will see, individual events have sometimes had a determinate effect on developments in the AFSJ.

SECURITY

The very existence of the EU compels it to relate somehow to specific events, whether their remedy would normally be considered within EU competence or not. This is emphasised not least by popular clamour for 'action' and a consequential wish on behalf of the EU to benefit from this way of improving its popular appeal. From a PR perspective this makes a lot of sense: 'What is beyond dispute is public support for the objectives of the Third Pillar. A Eurobarometer Report in 2000 showed that the European public regarded fighting organized crime and drug trafficking as the second equal highest priority of the EU.'[35] In this way, the EU can benefit from increases in what is often referred to as 'output legitimacy'.[36] The levels of democratic legitimacy in any given political community can be measured in terms of 'input legitimacy' as well as 'output legitimacy'. Input legitimacy is derived from the level of popular participation in the decision-making process, most commonly through the election of representatives. Output legitimacy measures the extent to which the achievements of government (or governing powers) correspond to popular desires. The EU is often criticised for lacking democratic legitimacy in both senses. Whether or not that is true will here be left to one side, but, given the persistence of this criticism, it should come as little surprise that the EU should try to benefit from the obvious output legitimacy it stands to gain in responding forcefully to popular demands in the field of internal security. In relative terms, the AFSJ is not old as a policy area, but already this outspoken wish to 'deliver the goods' has set it apart from the other areas of EU action: 'One striking characteristic of the development of Justice and Home Affairs (JHA) has been the extent to which it has taken the form of a *reaction* to current events or to secular trends, *or at least has been presented in these terms.*'[37]

It is probably at this intersection of arguments based on the new European reality following the realisation of the four freedoms and the development of a new internal security situation – which may or may not have been precipitated by the internal market – that the key to understanding the justifications and the objectives of the AFSJ is to be found. Before we move on to discuss the effect of specific security-related events on the development of the AFSJ, and as a reference for the discussion of specific areas later on in the book, an outline of the institutional set-up which has actually resulted from these developments is necessary.

Substantive Competences and Institutional Arrangements

In addition to the mention in the preamble to the EU Treaty, the AFSJ figures in two articles more precisely setting out the objectives of the EU. First, Article 2 EU lays down that the EU shall set itself as an objective 'to maintain and develop the Union as an area of freedom, security and justice, in which the free movement of persons is assured in conjunction with appropriate measures with respect to external border controls, asylum, immigration and the prevention and combating of crime'. Then, in Title VI EU dedicated to 'Police and judicial cooperation in criminal matters', Article 29 EU restates the objective already set out in Article 2 EU. Later on in that same article, the EU Treaty specifies the methods by which the AFSJ is to be achieved. These are 'closer cooperation' between the operational law enforcement organisations and between the judicial authorities of the Member States, and 'approximation, where necessary' of aspects of criminal law.

Article 29 EU also refers to the further articles of Title VI EU which lay down the detailed provisions on how to achieve these objectives. The detailed provisions on closer cooperation between operational law enforcement organisations are essentially found in Article 30 EU, which mentions cooperation in matters of 'the prevention, detection and investigation of criminal offences', information gathering and exchange, and training and development. Article 30 EU also states that cooperation through Europol[38] should be promoted. In keeping with what was said earlier in this chapter – that the EU does not constitute a threat to the physical integrity of its citizens – it is worth mentioning that the framers of the EU Treaty had no intention of letting that change. The vision is that the operational, and thus potentially threatening, powers of national police forces are enhanced and coordinated via the use of EU-based cooperation agencies. Article 33 EU specifies that the provisions of Title VI EU 'shall not affect the exercise of the responsibilities incumbent upon Member States with regard to the maintenance of law and order and the safeguarding of internal security'.

Cooperation between judicial authorities and harmonisation of aspects of criminal law are dealt with in Article 31(1) EU. It is in this article that the core of the EU's competences in matters of criminal justice is set out. Article 31(1) EU provides a legal basis for EU intervention in five fields of action:

(a) cooperation between institutional actors;
(b) the facilitation of extradition between Member States;
(c) 'ensuring compatibility' of applicable rules 'as may be necessary to improve such cooperation';
(d) the prevention of conflicts of jurisdiction; and
(e) common definitions of offences and their penalties 'in the fields of organised crime, terrorism and illicit drug trafficking'.

Article 31(2) EU then states that cooperation through Eurojust[39] should be encouraged.

As can be readily understood, while some of the legal bases in Article 31(1) EU provide a fairly clear and unambiguous mandate for EU action, others are less clear than is perhaps ideal and are thus open to significant interpretation. Chief among these is Article 31(1)(c) EU which states that '[c]ommon action on judicial cooperation in criminal matters shall include . . . *ensuring compatibility in rules applicable in the Member States, as may be necessary to improve such cooperation*' (emphasis added). It will be fairly obvious that the scope of this provision very much depends on the view one takes of the cooperation instituted in Title VI EU. This will be the subject of extensive discussions in further chapters. It should also be borne in mind that, following the ECJ's ruling in *Environmental crimes*,[40] the legal bases in Title VI EU can no longer be said to exhaust the EU's competences in criminal justice. This will also be the subject of discussions later on.

In order to give effect to its mandate the EU has a number of legislative instruments at its disposal. The details of these and the procedures involved in their adoption are found in Article 34 EU. Before elaborating upon the various legislative instruments, Article 34(2) establishes three aspects of the legislative process in general which need to be mentioned. First, unlike the standard position in EC law, the Commission shares the legislative initiative with the Member States. Second, the EP has no actual power over the drafting of legislative instruments. Its only input, by all means obligatory, is organised in Article 39(1) EU which enjoins Council to 'consult' the EP before adopting any decision, framework decision or convention and to give the EP at least three months in which to prepare its opinion. Council is *not* obliged to take the EP's opinion into account. Third, the adoption of legislative instruments require *unanimity* in Council. This is to be contrasted with the default position in EC law which currently has the Council acting with a qualified majority. The effects of these institutional arrangements will be discussed later on.

Article 34(2) then goes on to enumerate the four legislative instruments which the EU may choose from in order to adopt a measure in the area of criminal justice:

(a) *common positions* which serve to '[define] the approach of the Union to a particular matter';
(b) *framework decisions* which may be adopted 'for the purpose of approximation of the laws and regulations of the Member States';
(c) *decisions* which may be adopted 'for any other purpose consistent with the objectives of this title, excluding any approximation of the laws and regulations of the Member States'; and
(d) *conventions*.

The first comment which needs to be made is that there seems to be no formal constraint on Council in choosing between the four instruments when it seems that two or more of them could be used to achieve the same goal. Addressing this particular issue, the ECJ has held as follows:

> *Article 34(2) EU . . . does not establish any order or priority between the different instruments listed in that provision, with the result that it cannot be ruled out that the Council may have a choice between several instruments in order to regulate the same subject-matter, subject to the limits imposed by the nature of the instrument selected.*[41]

Nevertheless, despite the fact that this collection of instruments only exists since the 1997 Treaty of Amsterdam when the framework decision was added, there can already be observed trends in the use of the various instruments by Council. First of all there seems to be very little interest in using conventions at all. This is hardly surprising given that this is essentially the traditional convention of public international law fame given an EU law flavour. Consequently, it incorporates all the delays and tergiversation traditionally associated with ratification by national parliaments. It was quickly realised that this 'EU convention' hardly had the potential to promote the objectives of the AFSJ. Not many conventions have been adopted, of which the Europol convention[42] and the Convention on mutual assistance in criminal matters[43] are the only ones of any lasting impact. The 1995 Convention on simplified extradition procedures between the Member States of the European Union[44] was rendered obsolete by the EAW and the remaining ones are not much spoken of.[45] Only the 2000

Convention on mutual assistance in criminal matters was adopted after the entry into force of the Treaty of Amsterdam. In the same vein, after the introduction of the framework decision, very little interest is devoted to the common position. In most instances, if a 'common approach' is called for, it is far more effective to approximate national laws using a framework decision. In fact only four common positions have ever been adopted.[46] That leaves the decision and the framework decision. Without putting too much weight on the comparison, the division of labour between the decision and the framework decision can be said to be akin to that between the EC law instruments: the regulation and the directive. Decisions are mainly used to legislate in matters which concern the EU itself or its institutions necessitating no direct action from the Member States. Thus the setting up of Eurojust was done by way of a decision[47] and discussions are well advanced on transcribing the pre-Maastricht Europol convention into a decision.[48] Like the directive in EC law, in the AFSJ the framework decision has proved the most important instrument. Institutionally, the framework decision bears more than a passing resemblance to its EC cousin. Echoing the formulation in Article 249 EC, Article 34(2)(b) EU states that framework decisions 'shall be binding upon the Member States as to the result to be achieved but shall leave to the national authorities the choice of form and methods'. However, in this most sensitive field of criminal justice, the Member States were very concerned not to leave any scope for a repeat of the judicial developments which gave the directive such integrationist clout. With a very clear formulation – framework decisions 'shall not entail direct effect' – Article 34(2)(b) EU excludes the possibility of a *Van Duyn*[49] in the context of Title VI EU.

This leaves framework decisions with a similar problem to what we had with directives before their direct effect had been recognised, namely that their effectiveness is dependent solely on the willingness of Member States to implement them, correctly or at all. In this context it needs to be remembered that in EU law there is no equivalent to Article 226 EC: the Commission cannot bring a Member State before the ECJ for a failure to comply with its obligations under Title VI EU which would include the correct and timely implementation of framework decisions. This problem was soon put to the ECJ and, in the case of *Maria Pupino*,[50] the Grand Chamber of the ECJ gave to the framework decision what effectivity it could. The case concerned the Council Framework Decision 2001/220/JHA of 15 March 2001 on the standing of victims in criminal proceedings. The question posed to the ECJ by the *Tribunale di Firenze* was whether this act, which remained unimplemented in Italian law, affected the interpretation to be given to provisions of the Italian code of criminal procedure on when special procedures could be used for particularly vulnerable victims giving evidence. The prevailing interpretation of the relevant provisions was that the special procedures were not available for victims of the offences charged. Somewhat controversially, the ECJ held as follows:

> *the principle of interpretation in conformity with Community law is binding in rela-tion to framework decisions adopted in the context of Title VI of the Treaty on European Union. When applying national law, the national court that is called upon to interpret it must do so as far as possible in the light of the wording and purpose of the framework decision in order to attain the result which it pursues and thus comply with Article 34(2)(b) EU.*[51]

The ECJ established two limits to this obligation. First, the duty of con-forming interpretation could not result in violations of *'general principles of law, particularly those of legal certainty and non-retroactivity'*.[52] Second, national courts cannot use their duty of conforming interpretation to inter-pret national legislative provisions *contra legem*.[53]

Subject to those limitations, national courts are obliged to give effect to framework decisions through the conforming interpretation of national law. The duty of conforming interpretation is also sometimes referred to as the duty of consistent interpretation or, simply, as indirect effect. In *Maria Pupino* the ECJ also implicitly ruled that this obligation arises from the date of adoption of the framework decision, and not, as would have been con-ceivable, from the date at which the framework decision should have been implemented in national law. Interestingly, this is a clarification which had not yet been made with respect to EC directives and, when the Grand Chamber of the ECJ had the opportunity to make that clarification in the case of *Adeneler and Others*,[54] its ruling was not entirely consistent with the findings in *Maria Pupino*. In the latter case the offences with which the defendant had been charged were alleged to have taken place during January and February 2001. The request from the prosecution for special procedures with which the *Tribunale di Firenze* grappled came in August of that same year. The framework decision was adopted on 15 March 2001 and the date by which it had to be implemented was 22 March 2002. It is clear that *all* the potentially relevant events occurred prior to the date by which the relevant framework decision had to be implemented in national law. Without even mentioning the time aspect, the ECJ went on to hold as has been described above. When, in *Adeneler and Others*, the ECJ was faced with employment contracts concluded prior to the date by which the direc-tive in question had to be implemented, it provided a much more compli-cated and detailed reply. Without going into the details of that case, suffice to say that, in relation to EC directives, the ECJ found that the full duty of conforming interpretation only applied *after* the date by which the direc-tive had to be implemented in national law.[55]

Given that *Maria Pupino* is the one case in which the ECJ has had the opportunity to express itself on the effects of framework decisions in national law in the absence of proper implementation, caution is called for in extrapolating from it. This is especially the case when comparing it to the very detailed case law on the duty of conforming interpretation of directives. Even so, given that that duty is the EU's one instrument for post-adoption discipline *vis-à-vis* the Member States, it is not inconceivable that the ECJ should feel the need to give it a much stricter interpretation in the context of Title VI EU than under EC law. Unless the Reform Treaty becomes a reality with the significant institutional changes envisaged for the AFSJ, it is very likely that the ECJ will have to come back to the issue of the impact of unimplemented or wrongly implemented framework decisions.

Finally, mention needs to be made of the EU's competence under Title VI EU to conclude international agreements. In fact, the main provision on this is found in Title V EU – Provisions on a common foreign and security policy. There, Article 24 EU lays down the procedure applicable for the EU to 'conclude an agreement with one or more States or international organisations in implementation of this title'. Article 24(4) EU specifies that 'the provisions of this Article shall also apply to matters falling under Title VI'. To make absolutely sure that this last provision is not forgotten, Article 38 in Title VI EU repeats the cross-reference in Article 24(4) EU but the other way: '[a]greements referred to in Article 24 may cover matters falling under this title'. A later chapter of this book is dedicated to the external dimension of EU criminal justice.

BOX 1.1

Already with the now defunct Constitutional Treaty, it became apparent that criminal justice was one of the areas in which the most far-reaching reforms could be expected. The text of the new TFEU confirms this to some extent while in some respects it still treats criminal justice as an area requiring additional safeguards for the Member States.

Article 2 C(2) TFEU entails a 'conceptual promotion' for the AFSJ. There it is listed as one of the areas in which the EU shares competence with the Member States. It is true that factually that was in many ways already the case, *but* Article 2 C(2) TFEU puts the AFSJ on a conceptual par with such areas of established EC competence as the 'internal market', 'environment' and 'transport'. The present argument over the status of the AFSJ – supranational or intergovernmental – can thereby be overcome.[56]

The EU's substantive competences in matters of criminal justice under the TFEU are expressly organised around the two sometimes competing methodologies of mutual recognition and approximation of laws. As will be discussed later on, 'mutual recognition' does not figure in the current Title VI EU. To rectify the anomaly that what has become such a central reference for EU legislative action in the field of criminal justice has no express basis in the Treaties, Article 61(3) TFEU formalises the status of mutual recognition in criminal matters by establishing that '[t]he Union shall endeavour to ensure a high level of security [. . .] through the mutual recognition of judgments in criminal matters and, if necessary, through the approximation of criminal laws'. This provision would seem to consecrate the view of mutual recognition as a first option and preferred alternative to harmonisation/approximation.

The provisions enumerating the EU's specific competences in matters of criminal justice operate a clear distinction between criminal procedure and substantive criminal law. Article 69 A TFEU deals with criminal procedure and Article 69 B TFEU with substantive criminal law. Article 69 A TFEU operates a further rough distinction between procedures to coordinate the criminal justice systems of the Member States (Article 69 A(1) TFEU) and what can be referred to as 'forensic' criminal procedure, i.e. aspects of criminal procedure applicable in a specific trial (Article 69 A(2) TFEU). This latter division also reflects the hierarchical conception of the relationship between mutual recognition and the approximation of laws. Article 69 A(2) TFEU in fact states that minimum rules shall only be approximated in the areas it enumerates '[t]o the extent necessary to facilitate mutual recognition of judgments and judicial decisions and police and judicial cooperation in criminal matters having a cross-border dimension'.

As concerns the specific competences to coordinate the criminal justice systems of the Member States, Article 69 A(1) TFEU enumerates four areas of EU action:

(a)   the blanket mandate to 'lay down rules and procedures for ensuring recognition throughout the Union of all forms of judgments and judicial decisions';
(b)   to 'prevent and settle conflicts of jurisdiction between Member States';
(c)   to 'support the training of the judiciary and judicial staff'; and

(d) to 'facilitate cooperation between judicial or equivalent authorities of the Member States in relation to proceedings in criminal matters and the enforcement of decisions.'

Article 69 A(2) TFEU then goes on to enumerate the areas where EU action may intervene, if necessary to give effect to mutual recognition, to approximate specific aspects of forensic criminal procedure:

(a) 'mutual admissibility of evidence between Member States';
(b) 'the rights of individuals in criminal procedure';
(c) 'the rights of victims of crime'; and
(d) 'any other specific aspects of criminal procedure which the Council has identified in advance by a decision; for the adoption of such a decision, the Council shall act unanimously after obtaining the consent of the European Parliament'.

The combination of the express consecration of mutual recognition and the division between procedures to coordinate the criminal justice systems of the Member States and forensic criminal procedure gives the system under the TFEU a clarity which the present Article 31 EU lacks. The competence basis in Article 69 A(1)(a) TFEU is written as, and clearly intended to be, a catch-all basis for the implementation of the principle of mutual recognition. Approximation of forensic criminal procedure is thus only justifiable if the simple mutual recognition of the different laws and procedures is for some reason unacceptable. This ought to ensure maximum coordination while according maximum respect to national traditions. It should be pointed out, however, that, given the lack of criteria by which to assess whether mutual recognition would be acceptable, the new provisions are unlikely to settle the argument as to the proper division of labour between the two methodologies in criminal procedure generally.

Also of note is Article 69 A(1)(b) TFEU which gives the EU express competence not only to prevent conflicts of jurisdiction – which is the present mandate under Article 31(1)(d) EU – but also to *settle* such conflicts.

When it comes to substantive criminal law, the criteria governing EU intervention are *a priori* unrelated to mutual recognition. Instead, the criteria provided by the TFEU depend on a division of criminal legislation into 'core' or traditional criminal law, and what can be called 'regulatory' criminal law.[57] In the case of the former, Article 69 B(1) TFEU lays down that EU action is limited to approximating legislation in the following areas: 'terrorism, trafficking in human beings and sexual exploitation of women and children, illicit drug trafficking, illicit arms trafficking, money laundering, corruption, counterfeiting of means of payment, computer crime and organised crime'. This list can be expanded by unanimous decision in Council and with the consent of the EP. Article 69 B TFEU justifies the selection of these specific areas because they are 'areas of particularly serious crime with a cross-border dimension resulting from the nature or impact of such offences or from a special need to combat them on a common basis'. Presumably, any area which the Commission or Council propose to add to this list will have to fulfil this general criterion. In the case of regulatory criminal law, Article 69 B(2) TFEU provides an independent legal basis for the harmonisation of provisions of criminal law sanctioning the breach of EU regulation in other policy fields. This distinction will be dealt with in Chapter 6.

The article dedicated to Eurojust may be a disappointment to some. Absent is a provision for Eurojust to be able to initiate prosecutions on its own accord. On the other hand, Article 69 E TFEU lays down a special procedure for the establishment of a European Public Prosecutor 'from Eurojust' and '[i]n order to combat crimes affecting the financial interests of the Union'.

Police cooperation is given a specific chapter under Title IV TFEU. Substantially, the only addition of note is that operational cooperation between law enforcement authorities may be organised directly by a unanimous Council. Europol is given a specific Treaty article (Article 69 G TFEU). Finally, an important addition is Article 69 H TFEU which provides for a special procedure whereby a unanimous Council, having consulted the EP, may posit the conditions under which judicial and law enforcement authorities from one Member State may operate on the territory of another.

Of horizontal importance for all EU action, and in particular for EU criminal justice, is the fact that new Article 6(2) EU provides that '[t]he Union shall accede to the [ECHR]'. However, this is unlikely to be as simple as that, given that Article 188 N(8) TFEU specifies that Council shall adopt the act of accession unanimously. New Article 6(3) EU also formalises the ECJ's case law on the role of the ECHR by providing that '[f]undamental rights, as guaranteed by the [ECHR] and as they result from the constitutional traditions of the Member States, shall constitute general principles of the Union's law'.

One of the most welcome aspects of the new TFEU is that it does away with the specific legislative instruments found in Article

34(2) EU. Henceforth, legislation in the area of criminal justice is done by way of regulations, directives, regulations and opinions. The definitions of these instruments currently found in Article 249 EC remain essentially the same and will be found, conveniently, in Article 249 TFEU. As to the matter of the choice of instrument, Article 253 TFEU establishes that '[w]here the Treaties do not specify the type of act to be adopted, the institutions shall select it on a case-by-case basis, in compliance with the applicable procedures and with the principle of proportionality'. If at present there could potentially be some overlap between framework decisions and conventions, it seems unlikely that these difficulties will remain under the new arrangement. The principles governing the use of the instruments now found in Article 249 EC have been developed during decades of legislative practice and it seems unlikely that it will cause much difficulty when applied to matters of criminal justice. If anything, Article 253 TFEU seems to indicate that, when in doubt, the least restricting instrument should be chosen. It is however unlikely that the ECJ will change its present non-interventionist position on this eminently political matter.

The legislative procedure is modified dramatically and aligned with the standard legislative procedure henceforth applicable to most areas of EU action. This 'ordinary legislative procedure' is defined in Article 249 A TFEU as 'the joint adoption by the European Parliament and the Council of a regulation, directive or decision on a proposal from the Commission'. However, in the 'General provisions' of the AFSJ, Article 61 I TFEU provides a blanket derogation from this ordinary procedure as applicable to criminal justice and police cooperation in that it ensures that the right of initiative continues to be shared between the Commission and the Member States. It is difficult to see what the rationale for this derogation is, especially in the context of a supranational decision-making structure. Given that the exercise of this power has caused nothing but hassle in the past, it is a shame that it could not be agreed to do away with it.

The 'ordinary legislative procedure' itself is modelled on the present co-decision procedure and is laid down in Article 251 TFEU. For EU criminal justice the two crucial changes are that henceforth Council will legislate with qualified majority[58] and that, with the exception that no legislation can originate there, the EP will have complete legislative equality with Council. It is difficult to enumerate all the advantages, in principle as well as in practice, it is likely or, at the very least, hoped that these changes will bring about. We would emphasise the disciplining effect of parliamentary scrutiny in terms of both the proposals actually made and the quality of legislation adopted. Notably, parliamentary scrutiny is likely to entail a considerably lower risk that a Member State government can 'hijack' the EU agenda by placing on it an issue which is concerning it.[59]

A few specified decisions, some of which have been outlined above, are subject to a special decision-making procedure. This is modelled on the present system with unanimity in Council and mere consultation of the EP. In addition, if a measure approximating laws is contemplated and a member of Council is of the opinion that it would 'affect fundamental aspects of its criminal justice system', the ordinary legislative procedure can be suspended for up to four months for discussions in the European Council. At this point, one of two things can happen. Either the European Council reaches a consensus and the matter is referred back to Council for decision or, in the absence of consensus and if at least nine members of Council wish to proceed, the measure will be adopted as a measure of enhanced cooperation. The exact procedure of enhanced cooperation is then laid down in Article 280 D TFEU.

On the one hand, this system raises the spectre of the normative fragmentation of EU criminal justice. On the other hand, it is to be hoped that the political pressure will be such that mere opportunistic blocking of approximation measures is minimised. It should also be pointed out that measures implementing mutual recognition are not subject to this special procedure. In addition to approximating measures which are adopted using the ordinary legislative procedure, whenever a special legislative procedure is provided for, so is generally the possibility of enhanced cooperation. This will prevent unanimity from constituting an automatic block to EU action although, again, there is likely to be considerable political reticence to too frequent recourse to enhanced cooperation.

Article 188 L TFEU empowers the EU to conclude international agreements with third countries or international organisations

'where the Treaties so provide or where the conclusion of an agreement is necessary in order to achieve, within the framework of the Union's policies, one of the objectives referred to in the Treaties, or is provided for in a legally binding Union act or is likely to affect common rules or alter their scope'.

Under Article 188 N(8) TFEU, the voting arrangements in Council for the conclusion of such acts mirror those applicable in the substantive policy area. This will be expanded upon in Chapter 5 below.

Judicial Oversight in Title VI EU

As has already been stated, there is no equivalent of the Article 226 EC infringement procedure in Title VI EU and, as concerns the other main judicial tool in the EU toolbox, the preliminary reference, in the context of the AFSJ this has been considerably blunted. There are in fact two levels of voluntarism, which considerably weakens the jurisdiction and thus influence of the ECJ in the AFSJ.

The powers of the ECJ in Title VI EU are detailed in Article 35 EU. The principle of the ECJ's competence to give preliminary rulings is set out in Article 35(1) EU but sub-paragraph (2) conditions that principle on the prior acceptance of such jurisdiction by Member States. Sub-paragraph (3) then goes on to require that, if and when a Member State accepts the jurisdiction of the ECJ under sub-paragraph (2), it has further to declare whether that acceptance entails the possibility for *all* its courts and tribunals to make preliminary references, or whether that possibility is limited to courts and tribunals 'against whose decisions there is no judicial remedy under national law'. The distinction between courts and tribunals of last instance and others is not new and is found in Article 234 EC which sets out the traditional preliminary reference procedure. There, however, the distinction has a very different implication. In EC law, Article 234 EC specifies that, whereas any court or tribunal 'may' refer a question of interpretation of EC law to the ECJ for a preliminary ruling, courts and tribunals of last instance faced with such a question 'shall' make a reference. By way of comparison, whether a Member State opts to give all of its courts and tribunals or just those of last instance the power to request preliminary rulings, Article 35(2) EU uniformly uses the less onerous modal verb 'may'.[60] There is thus no scope for the case law on the obligations of national courts to make preliminary references and the related doctrine of *acte clair*[61] to apply in the context of Title VI EU. However, the parallel with Article 234 EC is intact as far as the principle established in the 1987 case of *Foto-Frost*[62] is concerned: Member State courts have no jurisdiction to declare an EU instrument invalid. Only the ECJ can do that, either when dealing with a preliminary reference or as a result of a direct challenge under Article 35(6) EU. The jurisdiction of the ECJ to give preliminary rulings is thus subject to two levels of variable geometry. First, not all Member States have made the requisite declaration under Article 35(2) EU.[63] Second, of those which have, there is no uniformity in the choices made between the extensive and restrictive options. For clarity, it is important to point out that any ruling under Article 35 EU on the interpretation of an act adopted under Article 34(2) EU has effect *erga omnes*, i.e. it binds also courts and tribunals in Member

States which have not made the declaration under Article 35(2) EU. The UK House of Lords seems to have implicitly recognised this in the recent ruling on the interpretation of the 2003 Extradition Act in view of the EAW.[64]

Subject to these particularities, the principles applicable in relation to Article 234 EC are applicable to preliminary references under Article 35 EU. This results from the text of the EU Treaty which, in its Article 46, states that

> [t]he provisions of the Treaty establishing the European Community . . . concerning the powers of the Court of Justice of the European Communities and the exercise of those powers shall apply only to the following provisions of this Treaty . . .
> (b) provisions of Title VI, under the conditions provided for by Article 35.

By way of example, in applying these provisions the ECJ has held that '*the case-law of the Court of Justice on the admissibility of references under Article 234 EC is, in principle, transposable to references for a preliminary ruling submitted to the Court of Justice under Article 35 EU*'.[65]

There are two further ways in which the ECJ can be seized of a question of interpretation of acts adopted under Article 34(2) EU. Article 35(6) EU states that the ECJ has jurisdiction to hear actions brought either by a Member State or by the Commission questioning the legality of framework decisions or decisions. Given that instruments are adopted by a unanimous Council, it is unlikely that a Member State would then have an interest in attacking the legality of an instrument. Perhaps ironically, the major use of the provision thus far has been to enable the Commission to safeguard the integrity of *EC* law. It was this provision which enabled it successfully to attack the Council's choice of placing the criminal law provisions of the directive on the protection of the environment in a separate framework decision under Title VI EU[66] on the basis that the provisions of the framework decisions ought to have been included in an EC directive. The consequence was that the framework decision fell foul of Article 47 EU which provides that 'nothing in this Treaty shall affect the Treaties establishing the European Communities or the subsequent Treaties and Acts modifying or supplementing them'. A similar ruling was handed down by the ECJ with respect to a framework decision imposing criminal sanctions against ship-source pollution.[67] The substantive implications of these decisions will be discussed in a later chapter.

The last avenue for seizing the ECJ of a question arising in relation to a legislative act adopted under Article 34(2) EU is the provision in Article 35(7) EU enabling the Court to settle a dispute between two or several

Member States as to the interpretation of such an act. The article stipulates that Member State(s) must first give Council six months in which to mediate. As yet there are no examples of such actions being brought, perhaps unsurprisingly given the political stigma attached. The equivalent EC treaty provision has rarely been activated.

BOX 1.2

The TFEU makes few substantial amendments to the text of those articles in the EC Treaty which establish the traditional and emblematic judicial enforcement mechanisms of EC law. The general restructuring of the treaty framework, however, brings with it a sea change as far as EU criminal justice is concerned. Henceforth, the Commission will be able to introduce infringement proceedings for Member State failure to fulfil their obligations under the new Title IV TFEU (Articles 226–228 TFEU), the direct action against legislative acts is opened up to include acts adopted under Title IV TFEU (Article 230 TFEU), and the preliminary rulings procedure is generalised (Article 234 TFEU). With regard to the preliminary rulings procedure, a paragraph of great principled importance for criminal proceedings is added: 'If such a question is raised in a case pending before a court or tribunal of a Member State with regard to a person in custody, the Court of Justice of the European Union shall act with the minimum of delay.'

The above advances are, however, somewhat reduced by the provisions of Article 10 of the Protocol on Transitional Provisions. This article essentially says that with respect to legislative acts adopted under Title VI EU, the above changes to the system of judicial enforcement mechanism are suspended – the old Article 35 EU system persisting – until five years after the entry into force of the TFEU. Article 10(2) specifies that any measure adopted under Title VI EU but *amended under the TFEU* will immediately after the amendment be subject to the new scheme. Barring any amendments this means that, for instance, it will be until late 2014 at the earliest before the Commission can bring proceedings for erroneous transposition of the EAW. All legislation adopted under the TFEU is immediately subject to the new scheme of judicial enforcement.[68]

Internal Security, Output Legitimacy and Exceptional Circumstances

The above overview of the institutional arrangements for EU action in the field of criminal justice clearly shows the centrality of preoccupations with internal security to the framers of the EU Treaty's provisions on criminal justice. At the same time, it seems clear that these framers did not aim primarily to turn the EU into an independent actor in the field of internal security. Provisions such as Articles 33 EU (ensuring continued Member State responsibility for 'the maintenance of law and order and the safeguarding of internal security') and Article 35(5) EU (no jurisdiction of the ECJ over Member State law enforcement operations) clearly show that the Member States wish to retain the monopoly on the physical protection of the EU citizenry and the material provision of criminal justice. The competence catalogue with its emphasis on the facilitation of cross-border cooperation between national law enforcement authorities also reflects what can probably be described as the animating philosophy of Title VI EU: a wish on behalf of the Member States to use the EU to increase the effectiveness of their own systems of internal security in dealing with threats to public order. The EU is thus seen as a qualitative addition to the repressive branch of the national systems of criminal justice.

While this vision of Title VI EU probably dominates in the national capitals, it must be kept in mind that the EU is by now an advanced and autonomous political actor in its own right and independent of its Member States. The very same events which test the popular legitimacy of governments in the Member States also place pressure on the popular legitimacy of the EU, perhaps to an even greater extent. So if considerations of 'security' were probably very important, possibly central, in the framing of the provisions of criminal justice in the EU Treaty, they have been even more so in the ulterior development of the AFSJ *acquis*. External events which have rattled citizens' sense of security have reinforced an already security-orientated competence catalogue even further in that repressive direction by way of the initiatives actually taken.

Sadly, recent years have suffered no lack of instances where events with an internal security dimension, within the EU as well as without, have caused a perceived popular clamour for 'action'. There is little doubt that events such as 9-11, the commuter train bombings near Madrid's *Atocha* station on 3 March 2004, and the 7 July 2005 bus and underground bombings in London as well as the general, global security situation, have had a profound impact on criminal justice in the Western world. As far as the EU is concerned, many have pointed out that the legislative output of early 2002, spectacular in terms of both quantity and added value/quality, was to a large extent due to the Council feeling the need to show that the EU could adequately respond to these traumatic events.[69] It is this period which saw the advent of such pivotal legislative acts as the Council Framework decisions on the EAW,[70] the common definition of terrorism,[71] and the Council Decision setting up Eurojust.[72] While it is true that most of these measures 'had been in the pipeline prior to September 11',[73] the political will which had been lacking before that fateful date was now overabundant.

At this point, a distinction needs to be made. If the world can be said to have entered a new mindset after 9-11 and that the legislative achievements of the EU post-9-11 definitely reflects this, it must also be emphasised that the EU institutions in the field of criminal justice remain essentially the same since the Treaty of Amsterdam signed in 1997. To put this another way: there have been no constitutional changes in EU criminal justice since the beginning of the 'war on terrorism'. What seems clear is that external events which provide an otherwise lacking political will in the EU Council have revealed the actual potential of the existing institutional set-up. The legislative reaction to the international trauma of 9-11 could be seen as a very positive demonstration that the EU, despite the criticisms often levelled at its institutional set-up, can make significant progress. On the other hand, the very fact that the EU could take action *this* swiftly and *this* forcefully can be seen as a cause for concern. One of the characteristics of the institutional settlement in this area is that, not only does the Council need to be unanimous when legislating, but the Commission shares the legislative right of initiative with the Member States. This must be seen in addition to the fact that the *European* Council already controls the *political* direction of work in the third pillar through the adoption of documents guiding the legislative agenda. The Tampere declaration was the first such initiative and now the most recent one is the Hague programme from 2004.[74] The result is that the Council is the true supremo of the EU legislative process in the field of criminal justice by first setting the goals for the legislative agenda and then by implementing this agenda. In a field which has as one of its main objectives to discipline the exercise of coercive force by the executive, it is patently concerning that the executive has a near monopoly on the legislative process. The story of the post-9-11 legislative achievements provides us with an interesting insight into the possible consequences of this institutional situation. As Douglas-Scott has noted, the lack of democratic accountability enabled a Council unanimously convinced that action was necessary to jump to it in a way which would have been impossible 'had democratic controls been in place [. . .] the checks and balances of the democratic process tend[ing] to get in the way of efficiency'.[75] Thus, contrary to the usual way of things, lack of democratic accountability may, under special circumstances, operate as a catalyst for action in the AFSJ. However, lack of democratic accountability can also be seen as the *result* of such swift action by the Council. So while the present situation, under certain circumstances, could be said to promote output legitimacy, it does so at the price of increased deficiencies in input legitimacy. The absence of any identifiable opposition makes it extremely difficult to hold anyone to account for the decisions once they have been made. The Council as such is not accountable before the electorate and a unanimous vote by members of numerous political persuasions is a very effective screen against attacks by domestic opposition.

BOX 1.3

Article 61 B TFEU is very direct testimony to the special importance of input legitimacy in matters of criminal justice and its effects on individual liberty. That article makes a specific link between the policy areas of 'judicial cooperation in criminal matters' and 'police cooperation', and the Protocols on 'on the role of national parliaments in the European Union' and 'on the application of the principles of subsidiarity and proportionality' respectively. However, this article would appear to be of symbolic importance only because the procedures established in the Protocol 'on the role of national parliaments' apply to *all* legislation and those in the Protocol on subsidiarity and proportionality to *all legislation in areas of shared competence*. Article 61 B TFEU thus imposes no special obligation either on the EU institutions or on national parliaments in relation to legislative proposals in the policy areas it mentions. While it is certainly likely that national parliaments will be more zealous in the application of their new powers of scrutiny in relation to these sensitive topics, it is equally unlikely that they needed to be told to be so by a dedicated Treaty article.

The lack of democratic accountability is a serious concern in both of its incarnations, as catalyst and as result. Its catalytic effect raises concerns over issues of opportunity and quality of legislation, while from the point of view of it *qua* result, the lack of any real possibility to hold the responsible politicians to account surely menaces the core of democratic government. Faced with an extraordinary event which can be construed as an emergency situation, we have now seen that the very institutional design which was perceived and construed to hinder and slow down EU action – unanimity – can in fact facilitate precipitous action. These situations can be compared to that which many national constitutions call a 'state of emergency'. The EU is, strictly speaking, not empowered to deal with 'states of emergency' in this sense, but it has nevertheless become clear that the EU, in its own way, *does* deal with them. In the case of 9-11, the actual, if not formal, state of emergency which followed served to justify and to rally support for EU action. The problem is that the measures justified and brought in to deal with an emergency situation related to terrorism 'go far beyond the terrorism field, seeping into the criminal law generally, intruding on individual rights'.[76] It might be contended that this was necessary in that the world is now in something of a 'permanent state of emergency'.[77] The problem is that generally in national constitutions, parliament defines or acknowledges a state of emergency and also verifies that the measures adopted during the state of emergency are limited to that period.[78] In any case, the executive cannot declare a state of emergency and act upon it unilaterally.[79] This is, however, precisely what seems to be the case in the EU context: national executives, acting as the EU legislature, use a perceived state of emergency to push through measures which, at the very least, can be qualified as controversial. In addition, these measures extend beyond the context of the perceived emergency, both temporally *and* substantively.[80]

JUSTICE

The perhaps best argument against placing any great weight on the three foundational concepts of the AFSJ is that an exhaustive discussion of the first two – 'freedom' and 'security' – seems to leave little to place under the banner of 'justice'. Perhaps somewhat artificially, and to justify the subdivisions of this chapter, we will discuss 'justice' in the sense of distributive justice between the fundamental aspects of criminal justice in general. This type of reasoning is important in that it has significant bearing on discussions on the real extent of the EU's competences under Title VI EU.

'Secondary Spillover'

Once the AFSJ was in place and there had been enough legislative output to confirm the fears of many commentators that the EU criminal justice would be a security-orientated, repressive policy area, this perceived imbalance gave rise to argumentation which can be referred to as 'secondary spillover', in view of the fact that many of the same authors are proponents of the principle of EU intervention in criminal justice on the basis of the classic 'spillover' argument discussed above. In essence, this is the argument which starts from the basic premise that criminal justice is an area which combines a number of inseparable aspects. These are most commonly described as some sort of weighing-exercise of the interests of the majority in high levels of security and the duty to respect the rights of individuals caught up in the criminal justice process, as defendants but also as witnesses.[81] From there, the proponents of 'secondary spillover' insist that, if the EU has started to concern itself with the enforcement side of criminal justice, it can no longer ignore the other aims and values served by criminal justice. In commenting on the EAW, Alegre and Leaf have provided a clear example of this type of reasoning: 'As judicial and police cooperation are enhanced to meet the mounting problem of cross-border crime and the issue of fugitives from justice taking advantage of freedom of movement in the EU, all elements of criminal justice in Member States must become a matter of concern for the EU as a whole.'[82] The feeling is that thus far EU cooperation in matters of criminal justice has been very repression-orientated and the elements perceived as lacking are those relating to procedural safeguards and the rights of the defence. In this regard, Peers is categorical: '[A]ny further legal integration must strike the right balance between prosecution and defence interests.'[83] The role of procedural safeguards in the nascent European criminal justice will be the focus of discussions in further chapters, so for now suffice to say that the concern is that the balance of the criminal process perhaps best described using the French procedural expression *égalité des armes*,[84] albeit struck differently in each individual legal system, has become imperilled by this one-sided development of the European dimension of criminal procedure. To those advocating EU action in the field of procedural safeguards, it is simply a matter of a symmetrical imperative: no system of criminal justice, at whatever stage in its development, is complete without addressing the issue of procedural safeguards. To put it bluntly, 'if we are developing common powers and policing at the EU level, then we must also develop the "European safeguards" necessary for the defence of civil liberties'[85] simply because these operate 'as an indispensable counterweight in the context of a "checks and balances" theory in the field of judicial cooperation in criminal matters'.[86]

Inspired by the successful use of the concept in the construction of the single market, at a special Justice and Home Affairs Council in Tampere, Finland, in October 1999, the European Council declared that *mutual recognition* was to be the 'cornerstone' of the building of the AFSJ.[87] Executing this declaration, the Commission elaborated on the concept, explaining it to mean an acceptance by every national jurisdiction that, 'while another state may not deal with a certain matter in the same or even a similar way as one's own state, the results are accepted as equivalent to decisions of one's own state'.[88] For the Commission, mutual recognition required 'mutual trust': 'not only trust in the adequacy of one's partners' rules, but also that these rules are correctly applied'.[89] Implicitly espousing the 'secondary spillover' argument, the Commission concludes that 'it must therefore be ensured that the treatment of suspects, and the rights of the defence, would not only not suffer from the implementation of the principle [of mutual recognition], but that the safeguards would even be improved through the process'.[90] In a 2001 document outlining a Programme for the implementation of the principle of mutual recognition, the Commission and Council included the following statement of principle:

> Implementation of the principle of mutual recognition of decisions in criminal matters presupposes that Member States have trust in each other's criminal justice systems. That trust is grounded, in particular, on their shared commitment to the principles of freedom, democracy and respect for human rights, fundamental freedoms and the rule of law.[91]

For the Commission, this reasoning necessarily implied a mandate to take action in the field of procedural safeguards. This resulted in a 2003 Green Paper,[92] followed by a concrete proposal for a framework decision in 2004.[93] The proposal argued that Article 31(1)(c) EU implicitly provided a legal basis for minimum harmonisation of procedural rights in criminal proceedings on the basis that it would improve mutual trust which, in turn, was necessary for mutual recognition and thus 'necessary to improve such cooperation'. This proposal will be discussed later on but we will signal here that the controversy over the adequacy of argumentation based on 'secondary spillover' is likely to continue. Despite the eventual failure of the proposal, the Commission remains committed to the principle and, if declarations in Council negotiations are anything to go by, it is supported by a large number of Member States.

One difficulty with 'secondary spillover' when used as an argument to justify implied legal bases in Title VI EU is that it takes as its starting point a concept (mutual recognition) which itself does not figure in Title VI EU, let alone as a legal basis for EU legislative action. Mutual recognition is probably best seen as the methodological device chosen to realise the 'closer cooperation' spoken of in Article 31(1)(c) EU. As such it is, in our opinion, justified both in theory and, as is attested by its by now proven track-record, in practice. However, given its dominance in the debate, it is easy to lose sight of the fact that 'mutual recognition' as such is absent from the text of Title VI EU and that every legislative initiative needs to be attached to one of the express legal bases actually provided in the Treaty: 'every promotion of this principle, as long as the proposed regulations cannot be based on other provisions of the treaties, constitutes an excess of power from the organs of the Union, as the powers of the latter are given, special and restricted'.[94] The principle of conferred powers, fundamental to EU law generally and thus, *a fortiori*, also to the third pillar, needs to be respected. Mutual recognition is not a legal basis as such but a methodological device used to interpret the substantive legal bases contained in the text of the Treaty. In this sense, mutual recognition is a concept once removed from the text of Title VI. Consequently, *mutual trust*, a concept which does not figure in the text of Title VI either and which is considered necessary for the operation of mutual recognition, must be a concept *twice removed* from the text of Title VI EU. A very shaky foundation indeed for any implied competences.

As the above discussion of the justifications, objectives and competences of the EU in matters of criminal justice have made clear, the questions as to the theoretical foundations of the AFSJ raised in the introduction are far from resolved. Although very much open to criticism from a variety of perspectives, it is nevertheless the case that issues of 'security' can at least be said to have provided an analytically coherent justification for the creation of the AFSJ and, as will have become clear, it has become the supreme objective of EU action in the framework provided by the AFSJ. In that latter context, the concept of 'security', in addition to acting as a freestanding justification for action, also reinforces arguments based on 'freedom' as discussed above. But although this is probably the best explanation of how we got to where we are and why Title VI EU looks the way it does, it is still unsatisfactory as a justificatory account. This is because arguments based on both 'freedom' and 'justice' share the claim to objectivity and apolitical rationality. Developments are presented as natural and uncontroversial consequences following from objectively ascertainable facts. This we find to be deeply problematic. Criminal justice constitutes the ultimate power in society whereby the collective justifies the use of physical force on individual citizens. As such its organisation and implementation need better justifications than at best weak and at worst patently erroneous inferences from empirically very doubtful premises. This screen of objectivity hides a reality which is very much ideological, be it in the implicit understanding of what the 'goals' of the EU are in the case of 'spillover', or the determination of what constitutes a state of emergency in the case of 'security'-based argumentation.

Perhaps despite appearances, we are not opposed to current developments in EU criminal justice. We merely wish to highlight some problems with the premises of the current debate and suggest that other justificatory avenues need to be explored even though, repeating what was already stated in the introduction, it is not within the scope of this book to do so in any greater detail. As we now propose to examine various substantive aspects of the AFSJ in detail we encourage readers always to keep these very tenuous theoretical foundations in mind as they will help to explain many of the problems and inconsistencies besetting EU criminal justice.

NOTES

1. See, for example, T. Blair (2006), 'I don't destroy liberties, I protect them', *The Observer*, London.
2. This model is usually traced back to L.N. Lindberg (1963), *The Political Dynamics of European Economic Integration*, Stanford: Stanford University Press.
3. J. Monar (2001), 'The dynamics of justice and home affairs: laboratories, Driving factors and costs', *Journal of Common Market Studies*, **39**(4), 747–64, at p. 754.
4. S. Douglas-Scott (2004), 'The rule of law in the European Union – putting the security into the area of freedom, security and justice', *European Law Review*, **29**(2), 219–42, at p. 222. See also L. Ferola (2002), 'The fight against organized crime in Europe – building an area of freedom, security and justice in the EU', *International Journal of Legal Information*, **30**(1), 53–91.
5. See, e.g., A. Weyembergh (2004), *L'harmonisation des législations : condition de l'espace pénal européen et révélateur de ses tensions*, Bruxelles: Editions de l'Université de Bruxelles, at p. 180.
6. See generally contributions in P. Williams and D. Vlassis (eds) (2001), *Combating Transnational Crime – Concepts, Activities and Responses*, London: Frank Cass.
7. Roy Godson and Phil Williams (2001), 'Strengthening cooperation against transnational crime: a new security imperative', in P. Williams and D. Vlassis (eds), *Combating Transnational Crime – Concepts, Activities and Responses*, London: Frank Cass.
8. Cyrille Fijnaut (2001), 'Transnational organized crime and institutional reform in the European Union: the case of judicial cooperation', in P. Williams and D. Vlassis (eds), *Combating Transnational Crime – Concepts, Activities and Responses*, London: Frank Cass, at p. 278. Along the same lines, see also Europol's EU Organised Crime Threat Assessment 2006, at p. 10.
9. See, e.g., A. Alvazzi del Frate (2004), 'The international crime business survey: findings from nine Central-Eastern European cities', *European Journal on Criminal Policy and Research*, **10**(2–3), 137–161; C. Lewis, G. Barclay et al. (2004), 'Crime trends in the EU', *European Journal on Criminal Policy and Research*, **10**(2–3), 187–223; and H. Brady and M. Roma (2006), 'Let justice be done: punishing crime in the EU' (policy brief), London: Centre for European Reform.
10. Gerhard O.W. Mueller (2001), 'Transnational crime: definitions and concepts', in P. Williams and D. Vlassis (eds), *Combating Transnational Crime – Concepts, Activities and Responses*, London: Frank Cass, at p. 16.
11. Cyrille Fijnaut (2004), 'Police co-operation and the area of freedom, security and justice', in N. Walker (ed.), *Europe's Area of Freedom, Security and Justice*, Oxford: Oxford University Press, at p. 267.
12. Willy Bruggeman (2004), 'Policing in a European context', in J. Apap (ed.), *Justice and Home Affairs in the EU: Liberty and Security Issues after Enlargement*, Cheltenham, UK and Northampton, MA, USA: Edward Elgar, at p. 164.
13. See Nikos Passas (2001), 'Globalization and transnational crime: effects of criminogenic asymmetries', in P. Williams and D. Vlassis (eds), *Combating Transnational Crime – Concepts, Activities and Responses*, London: Frank Cass.
14. Ibid., at p. 33.
15. Ibid., at p. 34.
16. Ibid., at p. 28.
17. Europol's EU Organised Crime Report 2005, at p. 8.
18. Cyrille Fijnaut, above n. 8.

19. Ibid., especially at p. 22.
20. Paul de Hert (2004), 'Division of competencies between national and European levels with regard to justice and home affairs', in J. Apap (ed.), *Justice and Home Affairs in the EU: Liberty and Security Issues after Enlargement*, Cheltenham, UK and Northampton, MA, USA: Edward Elgar, at p. 71.
21. Cyrille Fijnaut, above n. 8, at p. 287.
22. L.N. Lindberg, above n. 2, at p. 10.
23. This reasoning coincides with that of the ECJ on Article 308 of the EC Treaty in *Opinion 2/94* (EC accession to the ECHR) [1996] ECR I-1759.
24. See M. Delmas-Marty (1997), *Corpus juris: introducing penal provisions for the purpose of the financial interests of the European Union*, Paris: Economica.
25. Cyrille Fijnaut (2001), above n. 8, at p. 293. See also, on the proposed European Public Prosecutor, Christine Van den Wyngaert (2004), 'Eurojust and the European Public Prosecutor in the Corpus Juris Model: Water and Fire?', in N. Walker (ed.), *Europe's Area of Freedom, Security and Justice*, Oxford: Oxford University Press.
26. Neil Walker (2004), 'In Search of the Area of Freedom, Security and Justice: a constitutional odyssey', in N. Walker (ed.), *Europe's Area of Freedom, Security and Justice*, Oxford: Oxford University Press, at p. 13.
27. S. Douglas-Scott, above n. 4, at p. 220.
28. Nikos Passas, above n. 13, above, at p. 46.
29. See, e.g., Roy Godson and Phil Williams, above, n. 7; Willy Bruggeman, above n. 12; and B. Gruszczyńska (2004), 'Crime in Central and Eastern European countries in the enlarged Europe', *European Journal on Criminal Policy and Research*, **10**(2–3), 123–36.
30. A. von Bogdandy (2000), 'The European Union as a human rights organization? Human rights and the core of the European Union', *Common Market Law Review*, **37**, 1307–38.
31. Ibid., at p. 1337.
32 J. Monar, above n. 3, at p. 758.
33. See, e.g., Raymond E. Kendall (2001), 'Responding to Transnational Crime', in P. Williams and D. Vlassis (eds), *Combating Transnational Crime – Concepts, Activities and Responses*, London: Frank Cass; and N. Gerspacher (2005), 'The roles of international police cooperation organizations – beyond mandates, towards unintended roles', *European Journal of Crime, Criminal Law and Criminal Justice*, **13**(3), 413–34.
34. Neil Walker, above n. 26, at p. 12.
35. Denza, E. (2002), *The Intergovernmental Pillars of the European Union*, Oxford: Oxford University Press, at pp. 286–7.
36. See, e.g., K. Lenaerts and M. Desomer (2002), 'New models of constitution-making in Europe: the quest for legitimacy', *Common Market Law Review*, **39**, 1217–53. More generally on 'input legitimacy', see Fritz W. Scharpf (1999), *Governing in Europe. Democratic and Efficient?* Oxford: Oxford University Press
37. Neil Walker (2003), 'Freedom, security and justice', in B. De Witte (ed.), *Ten Reflections on the Constitutional Treaty for Europe*, Florence: European University Institute and Robert Schuman Centre for Advanced Studies and Academy of European Law, at p. 164.
38. See Chapters 2 and 3, below.
39. See Chapter 2, below.
40. C-176/03 *Commission* v. *Council*, judgment of 13 September 2005.
41. C-303/05 *Advocaten voor de Wereld*, judgment of 3 May 2007, at para. 37.
42. Council Act of 26 July 1995 drawing up the Convention on the establishment of a European Police Office (OJ C 316, 27.11.1995, p. 1).
43. Council Act of 29 May 2000 establishing the Convention on Mutual Assistance in Criminal Matters between the Member States of the European Union (OJ C 197, 12.7.2000, p. 1–2).
44. Council Act of 10 March 1995 drawing up the Convention on simplified extradition procedure between the Member States of the European Union (OJ C 78, 30.3.1995, p. 1).

45. Council Act of 26 July 1995 drawing up the Convention on the protection of the European Communities' financial interests (OJ C 316, 27.11.1995, p. 48); Council Act of 26 July 1995 drawing up the Convention on the use of information technology for customs purposes (OJ C 316, 27.11.1995, p. 33); Convention of 26 May 1997 on the fight against corruption involving officials of the European Communities or officials of Member States of the European Union (OJ C 195, 25.6.1997, p. 2–11); Council Act of 18 December 1997 drawing up, on the basis of Article K.3 of the Treaty on European Union, the Convention on mutual assistance and cooperation between customs administrations (OJ C 24, 23.1.1998, p. 1).

46. Common Position 97/661/JHA of 6 October 1997 on negotiations in the Council of Europe and the OECD relating to corruption (OJ L 279, 13.10.1997, p. 1–2); Common Position 1999/364/JHA of 27 May 1999 on negotiations relating to the Draft Convention on Cyber Crime held in the Council of Europe (OJ L 142, 5.6.1999, p. 1–2); Council Common Position 2000/130/JHA of 31 January 2000 on the proposed protocol against the illicit manufacturing of and trafficking in firearms, their parts and components and ammunition, supplementing the United Nations Convention against transnational organised crime (OJ L 37, 12.2.2000, p. 1–2); Council Common Position 2005/69/JHA of 24 January 2005 on exchanging certain data with Interpol (OJ L 27, 29.1.2005, p. 61–62).

47. Council Decision 2002/187/JHA of 28 February 2002 setting up Eurojust with a view to reinforcing the fight against serious crime.

48. See Chapter 3.

49. 41/74, judgment of 4 December 1974.

50. C-105/03, judgment of 16 June 2005. For comment, see M. Fletcher (2005), 'Extending "Indirect Effect" to the Third Pillar: The Significance of Pupino', *European Law Review*, **30**(6), 862–77.

51. At para. 43.

52. At para. 44.

53. At para. 47.

54. C-212/04, judgment of 4 July 2006.

55. On this, see R. Lööf (2007), 'Temporal aspects of the duty of consistent interpretation in the First and Third Pillars', *European Law Review*, **32**(6), 888–95.

56. It needs to be remembered that this statement needs to be issued with a major caveat with respect to the effect of the AFSJ on the UK which is governed by a special protocol.

57. This division will be developed in Chapter 6.

58. It should be noted that the rules on qualified majority are complicated. Until (at least) 31 October 2014, the procedures outlined in Article 3 of Protocol (No 10) on transitional provisions apply. Between 31 October 2014 and 31 March 2017, a Member State may request that an act be adopted under the rules of the protocol. It is only after 31 March 2017 that the 'standard' rules on qualified majority laid down in new Article 9c(4) EU and Article 205(1) and (2) TFEU take full effect.

59. See the discussion on 'jumping of scales' in Chapter 6.

60. Note that yet different provisions apply to preliminary references under Title IV EC – immigration asylum – where only courts of final instance can request preliminary rulings but 'must' do so.

61. See 283/81 *Cilfit*, judgment of 6 October 1982.

62. 314/85 *Foto-Frost*, judgment of 22 October 1987.

63. In 2005, 10 Member States (Germany, Austria, Belgium, France, Hungary, Italy, Luxembourg, Netherlands, Czech Republic and Slovenia) had voluntarily aligned their practice in relation to preliminary references under Article 35 EU with the provisions of Article 234 EC. Four Member States (Finland, Greece, Portugal, Sweden) had opted to allow *all* national courts to make preliminary reference, and one Member State (Spain) had opted to limit the possibility of making a preliminary reference to courts of last instance. Ten Member States (Cyprus, Denmark, Estonia, Ireland, Latvia, Lithuania, Malta, Poland, Slovak Republic and the United Kingdom) did not allow any preliminary references to be made at all. (*Source:* 'Report on the situation of fundamental rights

in the European Union and its Member States in 2005: Conclusions and recommendations', EU Network of Independent Experts on Fundamental Rights, 2005.)

64. *Dabas* v. *High Court of Justice, Madrid*, [2007] UKHL 6.
65. *Pupino*, above n. 50, at para. 29.
66. C-176/03, above n. 40.
67. C-440/05 *Commission* v. *Council* ('ship-source pollution'), judgment of 23 October 2007.
68. Article 10(4) and (5) of Protocol No 10 makes special provision for the UK in relation to the powers of the ECJ under the TFEU. These issues are dealt with in the Annex dedicated to the special position of the UK and Ireland at the end of the book.
69. See, e.g., Joanna Apap and Sergio Carrera (2004), 'Progress and obstacles in the area of justice and home affairs in an enlarging Europe: an overview', in J. Apap (ed.), *Justice and Home Affairs in the EU: Liberty and Security Issues after Enlargement*, Cheltenham, UK and Northampton, MA, USA: Edward Elgar; Z. Deen-Racsmány and R. Blekxtoon (2005), 'The decline of the nationality exception in European extradition?', *European Journal of Crime, Criminal Law and Criminal Justice*, **13**(3), 317–63; S. Douglas-Scott, above n. 4.
70. Council Framework Decision 2002/584/JHA on the European arrest warrant and the surrender procedures between Member States (OJ L 190, 18.7.2002, pp. 1–20).
71. Council Framework Decision 2002/475/JHA on combating terrorism (OJ L 164, 22.6.2002, p. 3).
72. D. Flore (2002), 'Le mandat d'arrêt Européen: première mise en Oeuvre d'un Nouveau Paradigme de la Justice Pénale Européenne', *Journal des tribuneaux* (6050), 273–81.
73. S. Douglas-Scott, above n. 4, at p. 220.
74. The Hague Programme: strengthening freedom, security and justice in the European Union' (OJ C 53, 3.3.2005, pp. 1–14). We were slightly puzzled as to how best to solve the grammatical conundrum that the city is called 'The Hague' while the document which came out of the summit held there *also* takes the definite article. Having chosen what we consider the lesser of two evils, we decided that the slight grammatical error of 'the Hague programme' was preferable to the correct but cumbersome 'the The Hague Programme'.
75. S. Douglas-Scott, above n. 4, at p. 221.
76. Ibid., at p. 228.
77. See, e.g., T. Blair (2006), above n. 1.
78. See, e.g., Article 36 of the French Constitution of 1958.
79. See reasoning of the UK House of Lords in *A.* v. *Home Secretary* [2004] UKHL 56.
80. The Italian philosopher Giorgio Agamben identifies as one of the main features of the 'state of emergency' the weakening of the legislative and judicial branches of government to the advantage of the executive (see G. Agamben (2003), *Stato di eccezione*, Torino: Bollati Boringhieri). Given what has been said about the institutional set-up of the third pillar, the EU seems well adapted to deal with self-proclaimed states of emergency.
81. See discussion under 'Freedom', above.
82. S. Alegre and M. Leaf (2004), 'Mutual recognition in European judicial cooperation: a step too far too soon? Case study – the European arrest warrant', *European Law Journal*, **10**(2), 200–217, at p. 215.
83. S. Peers (2000), *EU Justice and Home Affairs Law*, Harlow: Pearson Education, at p. 187.
84. 'Equality of arms' denotes the idea that the prosecution and the defence have had equal procedural means to build their cases. On the notion in the ECHR context, see, e.g., S. Stavros (1993), *The Guarantees for Accused Persons Under Article 6 of the European Convention on Human Rights: An Analysis of the Application of the Convention and a Comparison with other Instruments*, Dordrecht, Boston and London: Martinus Nijhoff Publishers, and Université Robert Schuman de Strasbourg (report) (1996), *Les nouveaux développements du procès équitable au sens de la Convention européenne des droits de l'homme*, Bruxelles: Bruylant.
85. Sarah Ludford (2004), 'An EU JHA policy: what should it comprise?', in J. Apap (ed.),

     Justice and Home Affairs in the EU: Liberty and Security Issues after Enlargement, Cheltenham, UK and Northampton, MA, USA: Edward Elgar, at p. 27.

86.   M. Jimeno-Bulnes (2004), 'After September 11th: the fight against terrorism in national and European law. Substantive and procedural rules: some examples', *European Law Journal*, **10**(2), 235–53, at p. 252.

87.   Tampere European Council conclusions, 15–16 October 1999, at para. 33.

88.   Mutual Recognition of Final Decisions in Criminal Matters (COM(2000) 495 final), 26.7.2000, at p. 4.

89.   Ibid.

90.   Ibid., at p. 16.

91.   Programme of measures to implement the principle of mutual recognition of decisions in criminal matters (OJ C 12, 15.1.2001, pp. 10–22), Introduction, at p. 10.

92.   Green Paper on procedural safeguards for suspects and defendants in criminal proceedings throughout the European Union (COM(2003) 75 final).

93.   Proposal for a Council Framework Decision on certain procedural rights in criminal proceedings throughout the European Union (COM(2004) 328 final).

94.   Submission of Professor Kaiafa-Gbandi to 'Procedural rights in criminal proceedings', Session 2004–2005, HL Paper 28, 7.2.2005.

2. The institutional framework of EU criminal law and justice

This chapter explores the current 'institutional framework' of EU police and judicial cooperation in criminal matters, understood in its widest sense. As such it begins with a discussion of the role of the formal EU institutions, followed by the various bodies and networks in the fields of judicial cooperation and police cooperation, respectively. Most prominently, the increasingly important European agencies of Eurojust and Europol will be examined in some detail. An effort is made to refer to the wide range of other actors that have emerged in this field, some of which have a clear basis in EU law (e.g. European Judicial Network, Liaison Magistrates, European Crime Prevention Network) and others of which do not (e.g. European Judicial Training Network and the European Police Chiefs Task Force); however, we make no claims to having been exhaustive.[1] The proliferation of semi-autonomous special agencies and bodies in the field of justice and home affairs has been described as a 'special characteristic' of its governance, illustrating the 'dynamism of this field of cooperation'.[2] Given the diversity of actors and networks at play, a key challenge is to ensure that the objectives of each individual entity remains pertinent to achieving the collective goal and that the relations and synergies between them are clear and effective. Where appropriate, and where not dealt with elsewhere in the book, Reform Treaty boxes will be inserted to highlight institutional amendments and developments.

THE EU INSTITUTIONS

Council

The Justice and Home Affairs (JHA) Council brings together Justice ministers and Interior ministers about once every two months to discuss the development and implementation of cooperation and common policies in this sector. In addition, it has become customary to hold an informal Council meeting during each presidency, to enable a less constrained and, consequently, often more fruitful discussion of strategic issues. Any progress achieved in these informal sessions can be formalized in binding or non-binding texts afterwards. For example, following the terrorist attacks in London in July 2005, the JHA Council convened an extraordinary meeting in order to discuss and adopt a Declaration on the EU response to the London bombings. The JHA Council is mandated to deal with all policies that might be said to contribute to an area of freedom, security and justice and therefore it deals with relevant policies in both the first pillar (Title IV EC) and the third pillar. In the field of criminal law cooperation, where the adoption of measures requires a unanimous vote in Council, there is no doubting that the Council retains a powerful role. The Council has only to consult the European Parliament before adopting a measure. It need not act on the European Parliament's proposals nor explain its reasons for not doing so.

A cumbersome multi-level system of decision making lies beneath the ministerial Council level, to prepare its work and to ensure that national positions on proposed measures can be represented and where possible compromised, in order to achieve unanimous approval of a legislative text. Agendas for JHA Councils are prepared by Coreper II which meets on a weekly basis. Coreper II comprises the EU's permanent representatives, that is national ambassadors who almost invariably come from national ministries of foreign affairs. An additional layer of consultation between the usual working groups and Coreper lies in the form of a senior coordinating committee, known as the Article 36 Committee (named after the provision of the EU Treaty that provides for its existence. Prior to the Treaty of Amsterdam this was known as the K.4 Committee).[3] The Article 36 Committee comprises senior officials from national ministries of justice or interior affairs. The influence of this 'expert' group in practice on decision making is perhaps not as great as that of Coreper II for several reasons. First, it meets less regularly than Coreper, on a monthly basis, which means it takes longer to consider documents before it. Second, the knee-jerk reaction of officials within the Committee is to protect their own legal systems against changes, thereby limiting their room for manoeuvre in negotiations. Such a focused dynamic rarely allows for the consideration of broader policy objectives as defined by the European Council or the identification of potential problems of principle and implementation.[4] Finally, any deficit of specialised expertise in Coreper II was filled by the attachment of special JHA Advisers from the relevant national ministries to the permanent representations.

The four-tier working structure of the JHA Council (working groups, Article 36 Committee, Coreper II and the ministerial Council) may appear rather clumsy and complex. It certainly requires extensive management, which falls in practice to the presidency of the EU with now considerable assistance from the Council's Secretariat-General. Coordination can be particularly problematic where an issue engages aspects of both the first and third pillars, since working groups operate under different structures and pursuant to different decision-making rules in each of the pillars.[5] This is the case, for example, with regard to illegal immigration and human trafficking, the law enforcement aspects of which are covered by the third pillar, while the common approaches and border control issues are covered by Title IV EC.

While some streamlining of the system would be clearly desirable, the most significant influence upon the working practices of the Council system is the requirement for a unanimous vote. Securing unanimity in such a politically sensitive field is an arduous task. It requires very significant and often lengthy preparatory work to broker acceptable compromises and achieve full consensus. At times this task has appeared almost impossible and it is hardly surprising that 'lowest common denominator' legislation emerges from this procedure.

BOX 2.1

Article 61 D TFEU mandates that a 'standing committee shall be set up within the Council in order to ensure that operational cooperation on internal security is promoted and strengthened within the Union'. Its role and composition appears to be as wide as it is unclear. Article 61 D TFEU merely states that 'it shall facilitate coordination of the action of Member States' competent authorities' and the only reference to its composition is that '[r]epresentatives of the Union bodies, offices and agencies concerned may be involved in the proceedings of this committee'. Moreover, the European Parliament and national Parliaments will merely be 'kept informed' of its proceedings. The absence of any real parliamentary scrutiny or control is worrying bearing in mind the potentially seminal role of this committee.

It is noteworthy that a Standing Committee on Internal Security (COSI) was first proposed in the now defunct EU Constitutional Treaty in Article III-261. An 'interim' COSI was even set up, called for by the Hague Programme. Since then there have been different views on what the precise role and composition of the body should be, ranging from a purely coordinating body to a high-level grouping with strategic and even legislative functions.[6] The wording of the relevant provision in the Reform Treaty suggests that an absence of clarity persists.

Commission

Directorate-General for Justice, Freedom and Security of the Commission (DG FSJ) has a relatively high-profile and active role in the field of EU criminal matters. One of the four directorates which make up DG FSJ is dedicated to 'Internal Security and Criminal Justice' matters. Unlike the case in most areas of Community policy, the Commission *shares* a right of legislative initiative with the Member States in third-pillar matters. Despite this, the Commission has produced the lion's share of the many legislative proposals in criminal matters – testament to the work rate of the Commission's smallest and newest Directorate-General. The quality of legislative proposals is generally high as its in-house expertise increases and its consultation procedures improve, although there is still room for improvement here.[7] It is now making more systematic and effective use of pre-proposal consultation mechanisms such as the regulatory impact assessments and public hearings, and its recent commitment to spend more resources on pre-legislative scrutiny and expert consultations is a most welcome development.

In addition to its legislative role the Commission has played an important role in managing and shaping policy direction. It has, for instance, through the publication of communications, imposed an order and timetable for the adoption of legislation,[8] 'fleshed out' key political endorsements such as the principle of mutual recognition,[9] and offered its interpretation of, and proposed policy following, an ECJ judgment.[10] Finally, and in the absence of an infringement procedure mechanism similar to that found in Article 226 EC, the Commission's 'watchdog' role in the third pillar is somewhat limited. Essentially, it is confined to monitoring the adoption and implementation of legislation and producing evaluation reports. So, for instance, it produces and regularly updates a 'scoreboard' recording the *acquis* on all AFSJ matters and it produces annual reports on the implementation of individual framework decisions. The latter offer at least some degree of political scrutiny and play an important 'naming and shaming' role. More recently, in response to calls made in the Hague Programme, the Commission has proposed the establishment of a more comprehensive and strategic evaluation mechanism in the AFSJ field.[11] This mechanism comprises three stages; the setting up of a system for information gathering and sharing, a reporting mechanism which allows this information to be consolidated and analysed and, finally, the carrying out of targeted and in-depth strategic evaluations of policies or institutions as appropriate.

European Parliament

The European Parliament (EP) has a formal right to be consulted on all third pillar proposals that would lead to a legally binding act (framework decisions, decisions, conventions). However, there is no obligation for the Council to take account of its suggested amendments and it has no powers to amend or block legislation. The EP's Committee on Civil Liberties, Justice and Home Affairs (LIBE) works hard to provide effective scrutiny in the face of a burgeoning legislative agenda and information deficits that sometimes exist during the consultation procedure. The president of LIBE is regularly invited to attend the informal meetings of JHA ministers, and Council representatives regularly visit the EP in the framework of interinstitutional dialogue.[12] Nevertheless, relations between these bodies remain contentious and the practical impact of the EP on final decisions remains limited, which represents a worrying and unacceptable democratic deficit in the field of EU criminal law. At the broader strategic level, the EP is not consulted on influential strategy documents adopted by the Council and the European Council.

European Council

The primacy of executive power and influence in the development of EU criminal law and policy is further emphasised by the role of the European Council. Although not currently an official EU institution, this high-level political body has played an increasingly prominent role in European governance in recent years. In fact, matters concerning the creation of an area of freedom, security and justice have appeared on almost every single European Council summit agenda since the mid-1990s. Extraordinary European Councils dealing exclusively with AFSJ have also been held (Tampere, 1999; The Hague, 2004) in order to map out longer-term strategies. A 'futures group' has already been established to begin work on drawing up the next five-year AFSJ plan, which will run from 2009. The extraordinary summits combined with the on-going discussion of parts of this agenda at regular summits is indicative of the high profile this agenda now assumes in the EU. Heads of state and government have clearly asserted their considerable authority over the field and have provided both direction and impetus. The influential 'road-map' Tampere and Hague documents have provided important reference points for those involved and interested in the development of AFSJ policy. The Tampere Conclusions were particularly transformative in the field of judicial cooperation, most notably by declaring mutual recognition to be the underpinning methodological principle.

In 2004, the Hague Programme, which provides the AFSJ 'road-map' from 2004 to 2009 was a seemingly more conservative document. In fact European leaders had less direct input into the text of this document, which was largely prepared by justice and interior ministries ahead of the European Council summit.[13] Perhaps the most significant development in the Hague Programme affecting criminal law cooperation is the endorsement of the 'principle of availability' as the underpinning approach to securing more effective operational cooperation between national law enforcement agencies. According to this principle, which was to be operational from 1 January 2008, information held by an agency in one Member State is to be made available to another national agency for law enforcement purposes upon request, with the minimum of fuss, but subject to certain conditions (mostly relating to securing confidentiality and data protection standards). The full, practical and legal ramifications of the endorsement of the ordering principles of mutual recognition and availability are discussed elsewhere in the book. Suffice to say here that high-level political rhetoric and commitments, while clearly influential, are often not respected or implemented as easily as they are endorsed.

BOX 2.2

Two developments in the Reform Treaty in respect of the European Council are noteworthy for our purposes. First, the Reform Treaty stipulates that the European Council will be one of the official institutions of the EU (new Article 9 EU) and details of its broad functions and composition are laid down in new Article 9 B EU. Second, its strategic role in respect of AFSJ matters is formally acknowledged – Article 61 A TFEU states that '[t]he European Council shall define the strategic guidelines for legislative and operational planning within the area of freedom, security and justice'.

European Court of Justice

The limited and disparate jurisdiction of the European Court of Justice (ECJ) in the third pillar was highlighted in Chapter 1. Despite this, a small but significant body of case law has emerged from the Court in respect of the third pillar since 2003.

It would seem that the unique and contested legal and political environment within which the Court finds itself acting reveals both constraints and opportunities. Besides the formal limits on the judicial competence imposed by Title VI EU, the wider institutional characteristics of the third pillar and the politically sensitive nature of the subject-matter arguably point to a more conservative and constrained role for the court in exercising its powers of review and interpretation. In certain *Community* policy fields, traditionally sensitive from a national perspective, such as social and economic policy, the Court has shown itself more willing to defer to national policy choices, at least where they have acted in a non-discriminatory and proportionate manner. Or indeed, the Court might avoid establishing a Community solution altogether where a comparative analysis of an issue reveals profound contradictions or disparities between national legal systems.[14] Conway argues that the continuing sensitivity of national sovereignty in this area calls for a more cautious interpretive approach in relation to third pillar matters and that the widely accepted principles of criminal law, such as legality and specificity, also militate against a creative (and therefore less predictable) interpretation of criminal provisions.[15] On this view, one might expect the Court to show a high degree of deference to the will of the national governments as expressed in the EU Treaty and the emergent legislation and to interpret EU powers restrictively to prevent any further diminution of or 'encroachment' on national competences.

And yet, the reality, at least to date, appears somewhat differently. The Court has not shied away from its role as the independent judicial authority over the third pillar, at times adopting what might appear bold and controversial rulings. It has, contrary to the wishes of the EU Council, stated that the Community has the power to require Member States to establish criminal penalties for a breach of EC law[16] and, in the face of opposing submissions from seven of the then 15 EU governments, it ruled in the *Pupino* judgment that framework decisions can indeed have significant legal effects in national legal systems, thereby lessening the negative impacts of the existing institutional and legal settlement and highlighting the conceptual and constitutional similarities as between the first and third pillars. Moreover, its case law on the CISA principle of *ne bis in idem*[17] has not only produced a consistent and welcome definition and interpretation of that principle but, in so doing, has also revealed a certain conception of the AFSJ and clarified some of the legal implications that flow from the politically-endorsed principle of mutual recognition.[18] These early 'identity-forming' and 'parameter-defining' cases on EU criminal law and justice have lead to parallels being drawn with the early activism of the Court in the context of shaping the Community legal order.[19] Certainly, to the extent that limiting the jurisdiction of the Court over third pillar matters can be interpreted as a political attempt to stifle the EU judiciary, this strategy appears to have failed.

It may well be the case, then, that the institutional environment of the third pillar, combined with the absence of a clear theoretical underpinning for the development of the EU criminal law and justice agenda as a whole, provides a greater window of opportunity for the ECJ – and indeed national courts – in this field. Perhaps these features even encourage a bold and dynamic jurisprudence from the Court. Whatever the expectations, the Court must ensure that its case law is consistent, coherent and rational: this might lend a degree of 'social' legitimacy to the EU criminal law project to 'make up for' the absence of formal legitimacy in the legal settlement. However, concerns about the effectiveness of judicial oversight, legal certainty and coherence will surely persist until such time as the full 'Community jurisdiction' is extended to the Court in these matters.[20]

INSTITUTIONS AND BODIES ASSOCIATED WITH JUDICIAL COOPERATION IN CRIMINAL MATTERS

Eurojust

Eurojust, based in The Hague, is the European Judicial Co-operation Unit of the European Union. Its role is to facilitate and coordinate judicial cooperation by assisting national prosecuting authorities with serious cross-border criminal cases. The decision to create Eurojust was a political rather than a legal one. The Tampere European Council in 1999 called for the establishment of an EU judicial cooperation body in order to reinforce the fight against serious organised crime. Eurojust was formally established by a Council Decision of 28 February 2002[21] (the 'Eurojust Decision') following the insertion of a specific legal basis in the EU Treaty by the Treaty of Nice (see Articles 29 and 31(2) EU). It had, however, been in operation on a provisional basis prior to that following the setting up of a Provisional Judicial co-operation Unit known as 'Pro-Eurojust'.

Eurojust is composed of 27 national members, seconded from each of the EU Member States in accordance with their legal systems. Each of the national members will be either a 'prosecutor, judge, or police officer of equivalent competence', their precise status, including conditions of office and judicial powers in the territory of the Member State, being determined by national law (Articles 2 and 9 of the Eurojust Decision). National members may be assisted by one or several others. Together, the 27 national members form the Eurojust 'College', which is responsible for the organisation and operation of Eurojust. The College must elect a President and two Vice-presidents from among its members. In order to fulfil its tasks, Eurojust can act through one or several of its national members concerned (Article 6 of the Eurojust Decision) or, in specific cases, as a College (Article 7 Eurojust Decision.)

The general powers of Eurojust are laid down in Article 31(2) EU and fleshed out further in Article 3 of the Eurojust Decision.

Article 31(2) EU reads:

The Council shall encourage cooperation through Eurojust by:

(a) enabling Eurojust to facilitate proper coordination between Member States' national prosecuting authorities;

(b) promoting support by Eurojust for criminal investigations in cases of serious cross-border crime, particularly in the case of organised crime, taking account, in particular, of analyses carried out by Europol;

(c) facilitating close cooperation between Eurojust and the European Judicial Network, particularly, in order to facilitate the execution of letters rogatory and the implementation of extradition requests.

Article 3 of the Eurojust Decision provides that Eurojust will:

(a) stimulate and improve the coordination, between the competent authorities of the Member States, of investigations and prosecutions in the Member States, taking into account any request emanating from a competent authority of a Member State and any information provided by any body competent by virtue of provisions adopted within the framework of the Treaties;

(b) improve cooperation between the competent authorities of the Member States, in particular by facilitating the execution of international mutual legal assistance and the implementation of extradition requests;

(c) support otherwise the competent authorities of the Member States in order to render their investigations and prosecutions more effective.

The main role of Eurojust therefore is to assist with investigations and prosecutions in bilateral and multilateral cases. However, under certain specific circumstances, it may assist where only a single Member State and a non-Member State are concerned or where the investigation concerns only one Member State and the Community.

In terms of material scope, Eurojust's competence is defined by reference to specific types of serious crime. According to Article 4 of the Eurojust Decision it is competent to act in relation to the same types of crime and offences for which Europol is competent to act (in accordance with Article 2 of the Europol Convention of 26 July 1995). This now constitutes a broad category of crimes including crimes against property or public goods and crimes against life, limb, or personal freedom. In addition to the 'Europol crimes', Eurojust can exercise its powers in respect of computer crime, fraud and corruption and any offence affecting the EC's financial interests, money laundering, environmental crime, participation in a criminal organisation and 'any other offences committed together with the types of crime and offence previously mentioned'. Moreover, at the request of a competent authority of a Member State, and in accordance with its objectives, Eurojust may assist in investigations and prosecutions relating to any other offence.

Despite this seemingly broad mandate, Eurojust has no powers of direct action on the territory of the Member States.[22] It cannot require a national authority to investigate or to prosecute in any particular case, nor can it take binding decisions on choice of forum for prosecution.[23] It can only make requests of Member State authorities, although such authorities are required to give reasons for refusal when such requests are made by the College. In practice the absence of formal powers and sanctions is not a major concern for Eurojust at present, the sanction of 'naming and shaming' of a recalcitrant Member State in its annual report usually sufficing to discourage refusals to cooperate. However, Eurojust has voiced its concerns about the failure of Member States fully to implement the Eurojust Decision which prevents the national members, upon whom it depends, from exploiting its full potential. As long as Eurojust remains an EU-level body whose role is to enhance cooperation and coordination at the horizontal level between national authorities, the 'real' players remain national investigative, prosecutorial and judicial authorities.[24] It is therefore not surprising that Eurojust has echoed calls by European leaders at the Hague Summit for Member States effectively to implement the Eurojust Decision and ensure the full cooperation of their national authorities.[25] Furthermore, Eurojust has called for a common minimum level of powers to be drawn up at the EU level to be imposed by Member States upon their national members.[26]

A shift towards a more direct, vertical and enforceable role for Eurojust, including the possibility for it to be able to initiate its own investigations, has been mooted for some time at the EU level and has provoked highly disparate responses. For some Member States Eurojust is simply the embryo of what should eventually become a fully-fledged 'EU public prosecutor' while, for others, Eurojust offers the ideal means to put paid to any such ambitious designs. It is significant in this regard that the Constitutional Treaty enabled the establishment of a European Public Prosecutor's Office 'from Eurojust' subject to the unanimous agreement of the Member States in Council.[27] The purpose of such an office would in the first instance be to prosecute, investigate and bring to justice crimes affecting the financial interests of the European Union. An extension of its powers to cover 'serious crime having a cross-border dimension' would be possible, again subject to a unanimous agreement of Council. The failure to adopt the Constitutional Treaty put this controversial suggestion on hold and the lack of any reference to a European Public Prosecutor in the Hague Programme testifies that strong doubts remain as to its desirability and necessity. However, as has been mentioned above, the idea has been resurrected in the Reform Treaty.

Certainly any future support for such a role for Eurojust would imply a considerable transfer of sovereign powers from the national to the EU arena (which in many cases would require the amendment of national constitutions) and a fundamental shift in thinking with regard to the concept of a European Judicial Space and the meaning of 'closer judicial integration'.[28] However, it may be that such a shift will emerge over a period of time as the realities associated with the effective combating of cross-border crime and effective protections of suspects and defendants and victims within that context emerge. For now, though, ambitions are more muted. Most recently, attention has turned to the role Eurojust might play in deciding where best to prosecute cross-border offences in the event of positive conflicts of jurisdiction. In the absence of a full-fledged harmonisation of criminal justice systems, criminal prosecutions are brought before national courts, in accordance with national laws and procedures. The choice of forum for criminal prosecution indicates which laws and procedures are to apply and therefore this is an important decision that is likely to have an impact upon all parties in a criminal proceeding: police, prosecutors, suspects, witnesses and victims. The Commission Green Paper on criminal jurisdiction[29] suggests that Eurojust might play a pivotal role here as a 'mediator', offering a dispute resolution function where conflicts of jusrisdiction arise, thus building upon its current *facilitative* role in this regard. The prospect of an EU body having the power to issue *binding* decisions on choice of jurisdiction is presented in the Green Paper only as a complex option that might be considered 'in the long run'. The Commission acknowledges the possibility for Eurojust to take on such an interventionist role if it receives the requisite additional powers, but points out that this would 'change its nature considerably'. As yet, no draft legislation has emerged from the Green Paper.

Eurojust does not exist in an institutional vacuum. On the contrary, the Eurojust Decision and Rules of Procedure provide for specific relations with the formal political EU institutions[30] as well as for 'close cooperation and privileged relations' with other bodies whose work intersects or complements that of Eurojust: Europol, European Judicial Network (EJN) and OLAF (European Anti-Fraud Office).[31] Eurojust national members may also cooperate on a case-by-case basis with Liaison Magistrates and

Eurojust is mandated to conclude operational cooperation agreements with third States.[32] While some good progress has been made with expanding and formalising cooperation arrangements, Eurojust has made clear its view, ahead of a forthcoming Commission Communication on the future of Eurojust and the EJN, that its full potential is not being tapped into and that a strengthening of its role combined with full implementation of existing arrangements (such as the Eurojust Decision) and a greater integration between it and other actors would improve the efficiency of the fight against transnational crime.[33]

Some good progress in formalising cooperation arrangements with Europol has been recorded. On 9 June 2004, following lengthy negotiations, Eurojust and Europol signed an agreement which allows both parties to establish a closer cooperation in the fight against serious forms of international organised crime. Accordingly, and for instance, both parties may participate in the setting up of joint investigation teams (JITs).[34] Moreover, Eurojust may provide Europol with information for the purpose of its Analytical Work Files (AWFs) or even present requests to Europol to open an AWF. Similarly, Europol may supply Eurojust with required analysis data and results. Such exchanges of information and intelligence mean that Eurojust and Europol are able more usefully to support Member States' criminal investigations and prosecutions on a day-to-day basis. The close geographical proximity of the two institutions in The Hague assists cooperation efforts, so that meetings are commonplace. National members of Eurojust are developing joint approaches with their national counterparts in Europol on issues such as marketing, information sharing and developing joint links back to relevant national authorities. However, while these efforts are to be applauded, the institutions themselves acknowledge that further improvements are possible. Eurojust, in particular, has called for an element of compulsion to be introduced into mutual reporting and information exchange possibilities and for structural reforms that will allow for a more rapid flow and exchange of information.[35]

Finally on this point, it is notable that the nature of the relationship between the two bodies is currently horizontal and complementary, such that Eurojust is regarded as the 'judicial counterpart of Europol'. However, as police and judicial cooperation in Europe becomes increasingly interconnected,[36] and as the prospect of Europol gaining operational powers of investigation increases,[37] it has been questioned what implications this would have for the relationship with Eurojust, as a European judicial body at the EU level. For instance should Europol be subject to some form of direct judicial control by Eurojust? It is surely right that, if Europol acquires operational powers at the European level, it should be subject to monitoring and control, not only by national prosecution authorities but also by a relevant authority at the European level (be it Eurojust, the ECJ, a newly created 'special panel' or a European Public Prosecutor).[38] Such judicial control is necessary to ensure that criminal investigation practice is lawful and does not breach individual rights relating to a fair trial and privacy, as protected by Articles 6 and 8 of the European Convention on Human Rights.

Cooperation between Eurojust and its sister organisation, the European Judicial Network (EJN) is particularly strong. According to Article 26(2) of the Eurojust Decision, Eurojust will maintain 'privileged relations . . . based on consultation and complementarity' with the EJN. As such Eurojust has access to centralised information from the EJN, members of Eurojust may attend EJN meetings and vice-versa and the EJN secretariat is integrated fully into the Eurojust Secretariat. Both Eurojust and EJN are fundamentally concerned with facilitating judicial cooperation in criminal matters in the EU. There are some overlaps regarding specific objectives (for instance the speeding up of mutual legal assistance requests) but the distinctive roles and structures have thus far been recognised and maintained so that the work of EJN and Eurojust as separate entities might be regarded as mutually supporting. The distinctive composition of the European Judicial Network, that of direct personal contacts between practitioners (national contact points) 'on the ground', means that it is well-placed to facilitate cooperation in bilateral cases, while providing invaluable assistance to Eurojust, a centralised and permanent agency, in more complex, multilateral cases. However, a change of heart has occurred within Eurojust more recently. It is now of the view, presumably based upon practical experience over time, that the partial overlap in mandate between the two structures is confusing for 'users' and results in a certain amount of competition and duplication of work. It therefore suggests that the two structures be merged into a single organisation, whereby the EJN would be 'integrated' into Eurojust.[39] It remains to be seen whether this radical suggestion will be taken up.

Relations between Eurojust and OLAF have been more strained, largely owing to the tension caused by the potential overlap in their mandates concerning fraud against the Community's financial interests. Some progress has been recorded with the signing of a Memorandum of Understanding by the institutions in April 2003 that envisages practical procedures for mutual communication of information and cooperation.[40] However, 'suspicion' and 'antagonism'[41] continue to hamper an effective cooperative relationship between the two bodies and Eurojust has recently acknowledged that 'overall, the cooperation cannot yet be considered as sufficient and satisfactory'.[42] Among its suggestions to enhance the 'synergy' between them is the adoption of a formal and clear mutual obligation to inform one another of cases falling within their respective competences and the appointment of contact points from each of the agencies.

Briefly on Eurojust's relationship with non-EU States, it continues to encourage cooperation through the development of a network of contact points and more formally through the negotiation of agreements.[43] Europol has even expressed its goal as becoming a 'one-stop shop' for multinational cooperation on cases within the EU with an external international dimension.[44]

Besides progress and ambitions in respect of Eurojust's relations with other bodies, some general points of progress should be highlighted. According to Eurojust's own annual reports the number of case referrals from national authorities has increased year on year, with an increasing proportion of those being multilateral cases and more complex in nature.[45] The 2004 Annual Report also reveals that a higher proportion of cases were referred for assistance at an earlier stage in international investigations, enabling Eurojust to save resources and add real value to the fight against international crime. The number of coordination meetings hosted by Eurojust increased from 26 in 2003 to 52 in 2004. In addition to its priority role of dealing with casework, Eurojust is playing a more strategic function by hosting high-level meetings on specific topics such as terrorism, VAT fraud, drug trafficking and the appropriate forum for criminal prosecution of cross-border offences. Moreover, it has created a specialist 'terrorism team' comprising several of its national members, to improve the facilitation and coordination efforts that Eurojust may offer in respect of this form of organised crime.

However, despite this progress, it is perhaps still too soon to offer a more comprehensive and definitive evaluation of Eurojust's contribution to the EU's fight against crime. It is clear that challenges to its success persist. First, the Eurojust College still feels it is being underexploited in respect of its capacity to deal with complex and multilateral cases. The main role of Eurojust to date has been in the *facilitating* of requests for legal assistance between national authorities (for example assisting the speedy execution of letters of request) rather than the *coordination* of investigations and prosecutions.[46] The reluctance to ask Eurojust for coordination assistance in complex cases may simply be attributable to an inevitable 'bedding-in' period. Awareness and confidence building at the level of national authorities is likely to take some time, especially following the recent enlargements of the EU. Additionally, Eurojust suggests that the lack of complex case referrals might be partly attributed to the low levels of support that some Member States offer to their Eurojust national members. As a result, considerable differences persist in the powers given to national members across the EU, which inevitably has an impact upon the efficiency and success of

Eurojust. Some Eurojust national members simply have the power to ask a national competent authority to bring a particular criminal prosecution while others have the full powers of a national prosecutor and are therefore able to initiate criminal proceedings themselves in their own Member States. Certainly a common minimum level of powers conferred on national members would be advantageous, but, in the absence of such, Member State political authorities are urged to confer such powers upon their national members as to enable them to fulfil their duties under the Eurojust Decision. Ideally they should also retain at least the powers they held under their own jurisdictions. Moreover, given the coordinating role of Eurojust, failure to implement or implement correctly other key third pillar instruments, such as the EAW framework decision and the Mutual legal Assistance Convention of 2000 and its Protocol, also has a detrimental impact upon its effectiveness. More generally, national political authorities should pay closer attention to the conditions and practice of the administration of justice and encourage practical measures to increase the awareness and use of the coordination assistance provided by Eurojust.

It will be interesting to see how this European agency evolves in future years. Certainly it would seem that its role will be enhanced rather than reduced: on the back of the Hague Programme the Commission's Action Plan suggests that 'Eurojust [. . .] be considered as the key actor for developing European judicial cooperation in criminal matters'.[47] Certainly Eurojust has been vocal about how to enhance its own capacity for improved coordination on criminal investigations and prosecutions in Member States. First, it recognised that its success as a 'horizontal' coordinating agency will depend upon the willingness of Member States to embrace the letter and spirit of judicial cooperation to which they have formally committed themselves. Allowing them less room for flexibility on this may be the best solution. Next, it is clear that improved relations with other agencies, networks and third states will facilitate effective coordination. The key challenges here may well relate to operational capacities and the need to supervise effectively the increased flows of data between agencies.[48] Third, Eurojust has asked for increased responsibilities. It has expressed a view that all requests made by it have a more binding character and that its tasks should be extended to include, *inter alia*, the issuing of European arrest warrants (EAWs),[49] the issuing and answering of letters rogatory, the initiation and lead of JITs, the monitoring of all JITs and a dispute resolution function in EAW, mutual legal assistance and conflict of jurisdiction cases. Finally, the development of the EU legislative *acquis* in the field of judicial cooperation in criminal matters is likely to have an impact upon the functioning of Eurojust. For instance, one can see how the harmonisation of criminal law, although by no means a prerequisite for the practical operation of Eurojust, might have an impact upon its operation in practice.[50] It is clear that an approximation of substantive criminal law (in the form of common offences) may be helpful to the functioning of Eurojust, whose powers are defined in respect of certain serious offences. Likewise, one can envisage that common procedural rules would improve the efficiency and effectiveness of Eurojust.

BOX 2.3

The Reform Treaty envisages a more prominent role for Eurojust in securing judicial cooperation in criminal matters. Article 69 D(1) TFEU lays down Eurojust's 'mission' in this regard. It is 'to support and strengthen coordination and cooperation between national investigating and prosecuting authorities in relation to serious crime affecting two or more Member States or requiring a prosecution on common bases, on the basis of operations conducted and information supplied by the Member States' authorities and by Europol'. The tasks of Eurojust *may* include:

(a) the initiation of criminal investigations, as well as proposing the initiation of prosecutions, conducted by competent national authorities, particularly those relating to offences against the financial interests of the Union,

(b) the coordination of investigations and prosecutions referred to in point (a)

(c) the strengthening of judicial cooperation, including by resolution of conflicts of jurisdiction and by close cooperation with the European Judicial Network.

Task (a) above would be a new addition to the existing 'coordinating' powers of Eurojust. In order to confer this task and indeed any tasks upon Eurojust, regulations must be adopted by the European Parliament and the Council acting in accordance with the ordinary legislative procedure. Similarly, regulations shall also determine Eurojust's structure, operation, field of action and, notably, 'arrangements for involving the European Parliament and national Parliaments in the evaluation of Eurojust's activities'.

Controversially, Article 69 E TFEU establishes a separate legal basis for the establishment of a European Public Prosecutor's Office 'from Eurojust' in order to 'combat crimes affecting the financial interests of the Union'. For such a development to take place, a unanimous vote in Council would be required after obtaining the consent of the European Parliament. A special procedure may be activated in the absence of unanimity and at the request of at least nine Member States. It involves suspending the procedure in Council and enlisting the assistance of the political body to obtain a consensus on the draft regulation within a period of four months. Where a consensus still cannot be reached, a minimum of nine Member States may activate the enhanced cooperation mechanism laid down in new Article 10(2) EU and Article 280 D(1) TFEU to adopt the regulation amongst themselves.

Broadly the European Public Prosecutor's Office 'shall be responsible for investigating, prosecuting and bringing to judgment' perpetrators of, and accomplices in, offences against the Union's financial interests . . . It shall exercise the functions of prosecutor in the competent courts of the Member States in relation to such offences.' The regulation establishing a European Public Prosecutor's Office would determine both general rules and more precise arrangements concerning for example the admissibility of evidence and judicial review and presumably the extent to which it can instruct national authorities to begin investigations.

Article 69 E(4) provides for the possibility of extending the powers of the European Public Prosecutor's Office beyond financial crimes against the EU to include any serious cross-border crimes. Any such extension would require the adoption of a decision by the European Council acting unanimously after obtaining the consent of the European Parliament and after consulting the Commission.

European Judicial Network and Liaison Magistrates

The European Judicial Network (EJN) was established by a Council Joint Action in 1998[51] and, as such, became the first structured mechanism of EU judicial cooperation to become truly operational. As its name suggests, it is not a permanent EU-level agency like Eurojust, but rather a network consisting of national experts or judicial 'contact points' and the Commission. The aim of the Network is to facilitate and expedite judicial cooperation between the Member States, provide judicial and practical cooperation to national authorities and to ensure the proper execution of mutual legal assistance requests. The national contact points are tasked to meet these aims by acting as intermediaries in cases. National contact points are designated by each Member State among central authorities in charge of international judicial cooperation, judicial authorities and other competent authorities with specific responsibilities in the field of international judicial cooperation. Today, there are around 250 national contact points throughout the 27 Member States. As already mentioned, the EJN maintains 'privileged relations' with Eurojust, its Secretariat even forming part of the Eurojust Secretariat. This special relationship is enshrined in the EU Treaty at Article 31(2)(c). However, the bodies remain autonomous and their roles are largely complementary rather than overlapping. The operation of the EJN is assessed every three years by the Council on the basis of a report drafted by the Network.

A separate, but again related, mechanism for facilitating legal cooperation is the posting of national liaison magistrates to other Member States. Liaison magistrates 'translate' the legal principles of their Member State to the judicial authorities of the host Member States in order to facilitate judicial cooperation and the execution of letters of request for mutual legal assistance.[52] France was the first country to use a liaison magistrate, when it sent one to Rome following the assassination of two Italian judges in Sicily in May and July 1992.[53] Following further informal arrangements of this nature, the Council adopted a Joint Action in 1996 to formalise this voluntary cooperation mechanism.[54] Where the duties of liaison magistrates overlap with those of the European Judicial Network Contact Points, the latter may be linked to the EJN by the Member State appointing the liaison magistrate in each case, in accordance with national procedures.[55]

European Judicial Training Network

The European Judicial Training Network (EJTN)[56] was founded in 2000 and is registered under Belgian Law as a Non-Profit International Association. It comprises those institutions within EU Member States that are responsible for the training of the professional judiciary. It aims to promote training programmes with a genuine European dimension for members of national judiciaries and as such seeks to encourage the exchange of experiences and knowledge between judges and prosecutors of the Member States of the EU. Its objectives are therefore directly linked to the attainment of the EU goal of creating an area of freedom, security and justice even if it is not, as such, an EU network. Some of its activities are however co-funded by the EU. In 2005, approximately 900 judges and prosecutors (representing a 40 per cent increase compared to 2004) from almost 30 European countries participated in training, organised (at least in part) by the EJTN.[57] The recent endorsement of a strategy of non-legal

measures such as confidence building and policy learning to complement
the adoption of EU legislation is likely to secure an important role for the
EJTN in the future.[58]

Network of European Prosecutors (Eurojustice)

Eurojustice was established in order to foster and improve cooperation
between law-enforcement authorities across Europe and to encourage
mutual understanding of the different legal systems in existence in Member
States. The Eurojustice annual conference provides a forum for Heads of
Prosecution Services and top-level prosecutors across Europe to discuss
issues relating to European criminal law policy, management and best practice. It can identify problems, offer solutions from the prosecutors' point of
view and stimulate discussions that are going on within the different
European Union organisations. The first Eurojustice conference was held
in Noordwijk, Netherlands in 1998. A Eurojustice website has been developed, with financial support from the Commission's Agis programme.[59]
This website provides a useful source of information, including country
reports on the relations between the prosecutor and the police, the prosecutor and the Ministers of Justice and the role of the prosecutor in court
and in the execution of sanctions.

INSTITUTIONS AND BODIES ASSOCIATED WITH POLICE COOPERATION IN CRIMINAL MATTERS

Europol

Europol, the European Police Office, is the EU law enforcement organisation that handles criminal intelligence. It has its headquarters in The Hague
and a staff of approximately 700. Broadly, its mission is to assist the law
enforcement authorities of Member States in their fight against serious
forms of organised crime. Its role is therefore limited to facilitating the
cooperation of competent authorities in the Member States in 'preventing
and combating terrorism, unlawful drug trafficking and other serious forms
of international organised crime',[60] although its remit has been extended in
various ways over time, as we will see below. With its roots in the European
Drugs Unit set up in 1993, Europol came into operation in July 1999 as the
organisation we know today, following the entry into force of the Europol
convention.[61]

The institutional organisation and framework of Europol is complex. It
is composed of a Management Board comprising one representative from

each Member State but daily management is carried out by the director and deputy directors. A Joint Supervisory Body, comprising two data protection experts from each EU country, ensures the proper use of all personal data held by Europol. A whole range of implementing rules and regulations have been adopted (including staff and confidentiality rules) by the Management Board and director in addition to numerous Council decisions amending these rules. The Europol Convention has itself been supplemented by five Protocols, some of which have extended or seek to extend the competence of the agency. For example, a 2003 Protocol confers power upon the Council, acting unanimously, to give Europol competence over any other forms of serious international crimes over which it is not already competent. From April 2007 it is also authorised to participate in JITs and it is empowered to request individual states to initiate, conduct or coordinate investigations in specific cases. The entire Europol *acquis* amounts to well over 80 legal acts. In order to simplify matters, in 2006, the Commission called upon the Council to adopt a decision to replace the entire Europol *acquis*.[62] The Council agreed to this and in June 2007 it said that the Council decision would be finalised by 30 June 2008. It also called on the Commission and Europol to draw up an 'implementation plan (roadmap)' in order that Europol can operate on its new legal basis from 1 January 2010.[63] Key milestones to be achieved prior to that date have been identified and include the replacement of the existing Europol *acquis*, the establishment of a budget for Europol from the Community budget and the transfer over to EC Staff Regulations from the existing distinctive staff administration system.

Pursuant to the existing Treaty settlement, Europol is explicitly endorsed as a body through which to achieve police cooperation in the EU, one of the key strands of achieving a high level of safety for persons in an area of freedom, security and justice.[64] Article 30 EU expands on the role of Europol. In Article 30(1)(b) EU Europol is identified as the agency through which relevant information from, *inter alia*, national law enforcement agencies might best be collected, stored, processed, analysed and exchanged, 'subject to appropriate provisions on the protection of personal data'.[65] Article 30(2) EU then tasks the Council to promote cooperation through Europol in the following ways within a period of five years after the date of entry into force of the Treaty of Amsterdam (i.e., by 1 May 2004): it should

(a) enable Europol to facilitate and support the preparation, and to encourage the coordination and carrying out, of specific investigative actions by the competent authorities of the Member States, including operational actions of joint teams comprising representatives of Europol in a support capacity;

(b) adopt measures allowing Europol to ask the competent authorities of the Member States to conduct and coordinate their investigations in specific cases and to develop specific expertise which may be put at the disposal of Member States to assist them in investigating cases of organised crime;

(c) promote liaison arrangements between prosecuting/investigating officials specialising in the fight against organised crime in close cooperation with Europol.

Europol's main tasks, as is clear from both its Convention and the EU Treaty, are to facilitate the exchange of information between Member States and to analyse the data and intelligence it collates in order to assist national investigations. In this regard Europol supports Member States by facilitating the exchange of information between Europol and Europol Liaison Officers (ELOs). These ELOs are seconded to Europol by the Member States as representatives of their national law enforcement agencies and act in accordance with their national law. Additional roles for Europol include providing operational analysis and supporting Member States' operations, providing expertise and technical support for investigations and operations carried out within the EU, under the supervision and the legal responsibility of the Member States, and generating strategic reports (e.g. the annual Organised Crime Threat Assessments, or OCTAs) and crime analysis on the basis of information and intelligence supplied by Member States or gathered from other sources. In order to carry out its tasks Europol maintains its own computerised information system and analysis files.

In terms of scope, Europol can act where 'an organised criminal structure is involved and two or more Member States are affected' but only for specified crimes. In fact the list of crimes has grown considerably pursuant to various Council decisions. Most notably the Council in 2001 exercised its power to extend Europol's competence to the many forms of crime mentioned in the Annex to the Convention.[66] This includes terrorism, drug trafficking, immigration offences, human trafficking including child pornography, forgery of money and other means of payment, and trafficking in radioactive and nuclear substances.

With all of this intelligence and information exchange capacity at its disposal, Europol has the potential to exercise a seminal role in the effective combating of cross-border organised and serious crime. However, concerns have been raised about the degree of reluctance on the part of national law enforcement authorities to provide good quality information to Europol in a timely manner. A strong sense of national ownership of information and a reluctance to work with colleagues abroad has been observed.[67] The absence of a common culture and mutual trust among police authorities naturally undermines Europol's potential. Moreover, it undermines the 'principle of availability' which is based on the idea of sharing relevant law enforcement data. It has been suggested that the adoption of the proposed decision on Europol will help to stabilise the work of Europol and instil a degree of trust among national authorities.

Another problem associated with Europol is the extent to which it is shielded from external scrutiny and evaluation. From an *internal* perspective, the management structures of Europol, which include a management board and the joint supervisory body, led Fijnaut to describe Europol as 'perhaps the most controlled police agency in Europe'.[68] There are also various reporting obligations to be fulfilled by the Management Board to the Council, and the Council must then submit an annual report to the European Parliament.[69] But, from an *external* perspective, there is currently no provision for any parliamentary or judicial oversight of Europol's activities. While it is arguable that judicial scrutiny is not necessary as long as Europol does not acquire direct executive/enforcement powers, the absence of political oversight is more worrying. Disappointingly, the proposed Europol decision provides for only a limited role for the European Parliament in this regard. This is to be contrasted with the more strongly worded provision of the Reform Treaty, for which, see the box below.

It is fair to say by way of conclusion that Europol's role has developed and, indeed, increased over time. The terrorist attacks of 11 September 2001 were particularly instrumental in this regard. Following these appalling events, there was a renewed political impetus to consolidate and strengthen almost all aspects of criminal cooperation both at the EU level and between the EU and third states. The emergence of an EU anti-terrorism policy called for improved operational capacities within Europol, for instance, the establishing of a counter-terrorism task force within Europol responsible for collecting relevant information and intelligence and for producing periodic threat assessments. Moreover, Europol, as an international agency with legal personality,[70] has increasingly exercised its competence to enter into treaties with third states and bodies, as will be discussed in more detail in Chapter 5.[71] However, at the present time, Europol does not enjoy autonomous law enforcement powers and so it cannot carry out any operational activity in the territories of the Member States. Moreover, it would seem that there is not any widespread support to amend this current situation. Rather the commitment appears to be one of consolidating and stabilising its existing powers.

BOX 2.4

The Reform Treaty dedicates a provision to Europol: Article 69 G TFEU. This follows the same format as the provision dedicated to Eurojust, namely it lays down the 'mission' of the agency and calls for details on its structure, operation, field of action and tasks to be laid down in regulations adopted using the ordinary legislative procedure.

Europol's mission shall be 'to support and strengthen action by the Member States' police authorities and other law enforcement services and their mutual cooperation in preventing and combating serious crime affecting two or more Member States, terrorism and forms of crime which affect common interest covered by a Union policy'.

The Europol provision mentions two broad tasks which may be conferred upon Europol by means of regulations:

(a)   the collection, storage, processing, analysis and exchange of information forwarded particularly by the authorities of the Member States or third countries or bodies;
(b)   the coordination, organisation and implementation of investigative and operational action carried out jointly with the Member States' competent authorities or in the context of joint investigative teams, where appropriate in liaison with Eurojust.

In an effort to address concerns regarding the accountability of Europol, Article 69 G (2) TFEU calls for regulations to lay down procedures for 'scrutiny' of its activities by the European Parliament, together with national Parliaments. This is to be contrasted with the mere 'evaluation' role of parliaments *vis-à-vis* Eurojust. The provision of effective scrutiny possibilities will act as an important check on the power of Europol and will have a much needed legitimating effect.

European Police College

The European Police College (CEPOL) was established by a Council decision in 2000.[72] It has no legal basis in the EU Treaty, but was rather called for by the 1999 Tampere European Council in a drive to encourage improved *operational* approaches to transnational crime. The aim of CEPOL is to help cross-border training of senior police officers by developing and reinforcing cooperation and personal links between relevant national institutes and organisations. It is also obliged to develop links with third countries.

Some practical difficulties with the framework of CEPOL were revealed in a report on the first three years' operation of the College: it did not have a permanent seat, it was underfunded and lacked a legal personality. A series of Council decisions have since overhauled CEPOL and indeed the 2000 decision establishing it. It is now funded from the EU budget and has a permanent seat in Bramshill, UK. All indications suggest that this body is providing more and better training programmes.

European Police Chiefs Taskforce

The European Police Chiefs Taskforce (ECPT), established in 2000, is another body that has no formal legal basis in the EU Treaty. It, like CEPOL, was established at the behest of the 1999 Tampere European Council summit. However, in contrast to CEPOL, it has never been formalised by any EU legal or non-legal measure. This has led to criticisms of the body, not least because of the absence of transparency of its proceedings.[73] As its name suggests, the ECPT consists of the most senior police officers in the Member States. It is a high-level coordination body whose focus lies in planning joint operations and making policy recommendations to Council, although Monar argues that its weak structure means that it has been relegated to little more than a discussion forum with little operational input.[74]

ADDITIONAL BODIES

European Crime Prevention Network

The European Crime Prevention Network (EUCPN)[75] was established in 2001 on the basis of a Council decision.[76] It consists of a network of contact points designated by Member States and supported by a Secretariat provided by the Commission. Each Member State can appoint up to three contact points, one of which must be a representative from the national authorities responsible for crime prevention. The Commission also appoints a contact point. With its focus on crime prevention, this network cannot be classified easily under the headings of police cooperation or judicial cooperation.

The aims of the EUCPN are to develop various aspects of crime prevention at the EU level and support crime prevention activities at local and national level. It is to achieve these aims by way of a multidisciplinary approach, including identifying good practices in crime prevention and sharing knowledge and experience gained between Member States, accumulating and evaluating information on crime prevention activities, improving the exchange of ideas and information within the network, providing expertise and knowledge to the Commission and Council upon request, developing contacts and facilitating cooperation between Member States, contributing to developing local and national strategies on crime prevention, promoting crime prevention activities and by organising meetings, seminars and conferences.

Although covering all types of criminality, the EUCPN is to pay particular attention to the fields of juvenile, urban and drug-related crime (Article 3 of the EUCPN decision). In terms of its relations to other bodies and institutions the EUCPN decision provides that Europol and the European Monitoring Centre for Drugs are associated with the work of the network in matters with which they are concerned and that other relevant bodies may be associated with the work. The Secretariat must forward an annual report on its activities to the Council, which is required to endorse it and forward it to the European Parliament. The work of the EUCPN was to be evaluated by the Council for the first three years of its existence only.

How does the EUCPN fit into the broader EU approach to tackling crime? Although Article 29 EU refers specifically to 'preventing' crime, organised and otherwise, in order to achieve the objective of creating an area of freedom, security and justice, it is probably fair to say that the vast majority of effort at the EU level has gone into the other mentioned task of 'combating' crime.[77] This arguably lays the EU open to accusations that it is privileging a repressive approach over a preventative approach to crime. However, as the establishment of the EUCPN testifies, crime prevention is an acknowledged policy goal. Moreover, paragraph 2.6 of the Hague Programme called for the EUCPN to be 'professionalised and strengthened' with crime prevention being described as an 'indispensable part of the work to create an area of freedom, security and justice'. The Commission also published a communication on crime prevention in 2004.[78] De Kerchove suggests that the development of crime prevention policies by the EU would assist in the progression of the European Union from a judicial space in criminal matters to a veritable European space of criminal justice.[79]

NOTES

1. For instance, we do not discuss the common border management agency, FRONTEX, which although a first pillar agency has some impact on police activities. See Council Regulation (EC) 2007/2004 establishing a European Agency for the Management of Operational Cooperation at the External Borders of the Member States of the European Union of 26.10.2004 (OJ L 349 5.11.2004, pp. 1–11.).
2. S. Lavanex and W. Wallace (2005), 'Justice and home affairs: towards a "European public order"?' in H. Wallace, W. Wallace and M.A. Pollack, *Policy-Making in the European Union*, (15th ed.) Oxford: Oxford University Press, 457–80 at p. 470.
3. In Brussels it often goes by the name of CATS after the French *Comité de l'Article Trente-Six*. Traditionally, at the last CATS meeting of a presidency, the outgoing presidency hands over two porcelain cats, one white and one black, representing the police and the judiciary (it has not been decided which is which) to the incoming presidency. Always a source of much merriment.
4. See further J. Monar (2002), 'Institutionalizing freedom, security and justice', in J. Peterson and M. Shackleton (eds), *The Institutions of the European Union*, Oxford: Oxford University Press, pp. 186–209.
5. J. Monar (2006), 'Cooperation in JHA domain: characteristics, constraints and progress', *European Integration*, **28**(5), 495–509 at p. 499.
6. See Council document 6626/05, Brussels 21 February 2005. Also see *Statewatch bulletin*, **15**(1) (2005).
7. For instance see the discussion on the procedural safeguards framework decision and the Green Paper on criminal jurisdiction and *ne bis in idem* in Chapter 4.
8. See, for example, the Action Plan on the Hague Programme. Commission Communication on The Hague Programme: Ten priorities for the next five years. The Partnership for European renewal in the field of Freedom, Security and Justice. (COM(2005) 184 final, 10.5.2005).
9. Communication on the mutual recognition of judicial decisions in criminal matters and the strengthening of mutual trust between Member States (COM(2005) 195 final, 19.5.2005).
10. Communication on the implications of the Court's judgment of 13 September 2005 (Case C-176/03 Commission v Council). COM(2005) 583 final, 24.11.2005.
11. Communication on Evaluation of EU Policies on Freedom, Security and Justice: Evaluation of EU Policies on Freedom, Security and Justice. COM(2006) 332 final, 28.6.2006.
12. S. Lavanex and W. Wallace; above n. 2, at p. 469.
13. Peers refers to the 'rubber-stamping' role of EU leaders in respect of The Hague Programmes. S. Peers (2007) *EU Justice and Home Affairs Law*, Oxford: Oxford University Press, at p. 22.
14. For instance, in the field of discrimination law, see C-249/96 *Grant v South West Trains*, judgment of 17.2.98. For a comprehensive account of how the ECJ uses comparative law as a method of interpretation, see K. Lenaerts (2003), 'Interlocking legal orders in the European Union and comparative law', *International Comparative Law Quarterly*, **52**(4), 873–906.
15. G. Conway (2005), 'Judicial interpretation and the Third Pillar: Ireland's acceptance of the European arrest warrant and the *Gözütok and Brügge* Case', *European Journal of Crime, Criminal Law and Criminal Justice*, **13**(2), 255–83, at p. 278. Conway argues that, where possible, judicial weight should be given to the expressed intentions of the legislative drafters when interpreting third pillar measures and their implementation in national law.
16. C-440/05 *Commission v. Council ('Environmental crimes')*, judgment of 13 September 2005.
17. For a full list of cases and further discussion, see Chapter 4.
18. See also C-303/05 *Advocaten voor de Wereld*, judgment of 3 May 2007.

19. Further discussion on the actual interventions of the national courts and the ECJ in this field can be found spread throughout the various chapters of the book.
20. It has been argued that extending the jurisdiction of the ECJ through the activation of the so-called 'passarelle clause' in Article 35 EU is unlikely since the activation procedure is effectively as onerous as the formal treaty amendment procedure. See, for instance, E. Guild and S. Carrera (2005), 'No Constitutional Treaty? Implications for the Area of Freedom, Security and Justice', *CEPS Working Document, No.231*. It should be noted that discussions have already begun within the ECJ on how to adapt internally to the expansion of its jurisdiction over AFSJ matters.
21. Council Decision 2002/187/JHA of 28 February 2002 setting up Eurojust with a view to reinforcing the fight against serious crime (OJ L 63 6.3.2002. pp. 1–13), later amended in respect of budget issues only by Council Decision 2003/659/JHA of 18 June 2003 (OJ L 245 29.9.2003. pp. 44–5). See also Rules of procedure of Eurojust (OJ C 286, 22.11.2002. pp. 1–7).
22. Powers of direct action on a national territory may arise from national law where a Eurojust national member is empowered to act on his/her national territory. Similarly, Eurojust members may also have operational powers when acting within a Joint Investigation Team (see Chapter 3 for more). However, Eurojust members do not have Union-wide powers.
23. Although such roles have been officially envisaged at the EU level by the Commission. See below.
24. C. van den Wyngaert (2005), 'Eurojust and the European Public Prosecutor in the *Corpus Juris* model: water and fire?', in N. Walker (ed.), *Europe's Area of Freedom, Security and Justice*, Oxford: Oxford University Press, 201–39, at p. 210.
25. The Hague Programme: strengthening freedom, security and justice in the European Union, 4–5 November 2004 (OJ C 53, 3.3.2005, pp. 1–14) at para. 3.3.3.
26. Eurojust's contribution for the European Commission Communication concerning the future of Eurojust and the European Judicial Network, Council Document 13079/07, Brussels, 20 September 2007, at p. 6.
27. Article III-274.
28. It would also raise the question about more structured and formal lines of accountability of Eurojust. Currently there is no formal mechanism for regular parliamentary scrutiny of the work of Eurojust by either the European Parliament or the national parliaments, which inevitably raises legitimacy concerns.
29. Green Paper on conflicts of jurisdiction and the principle of *ne bis in idem* in criminal proceedings COM(2005) 696, final. 23.12.2005. See also Annexed Commission Staff Working Document SEC(2005)1767.
30. The Commission is to be 'fully associated' with the work of Eurojust and regular meetings ensure that Commission may offer its expertise to the unit. Eurojust also owes a duty to provide information concerning its work to the European Parliament and the Council.
31. Eurojust Decision 2002/187/JHA, above n. 21, at Article 26.
32. Eurojust Decision 2002/187/JHA, above n. 21, at Article 27.
33. Eurojust's contribution for the European Commission Communication concerning the future of Eurojust and the European Judicial Network, Council Document 13079/07, Brussels, 20 September 2007.
34. For further detail about JITs, see Chapter 3.
35. Eurojust's contribution for the European Commission Communication, see above, n. 26, at pp. 14–16.
36. On this point see C. Fijnaut (2006), 'Police Co-operation and the Area of Freedom, Security and Justice' in N. Walker (ed.), *Europe's Area of Freedom, Security and Justice*, Oxford: Oxford University Press, 253–58, at p. 253.
37. Proposal for a Council Decision establishing the European Police Office (Europol), COM (2006) 817 final, 20.12.2006.
38. See, for example, C. van den Wyngaert, above n. 24, at p. 235.
39. Eurojust's contribution for the European Commission Communication; above n. 26, at p. 13.

40. On 13 July 2004 the Eurojust College adopted a Decision on the implementation of the OLAF Regulation 1073/1999 which provides for various duties to cooperate with OLAF in the event that Eurojust or any of its members is subject to an OLAF internal investigation. This Decision does not affect cooperation efforts between the two bodies as called for in Article 26(3) and (4) of the Eurojust Decision; see above, n. 21.
41. Terms used in the UK House of Lords Select Committee on European Union report 'Judicial Co-operation in the EU: The Role of Eurojust', Session 2003-04, HL 138, 21.7.2004, at para. 68.
42. Eurojust's contribution for the European Commission Communication, above n. 26, at p. 17.
43. As a body with legal personality, Eurojust may conclude agreements with third parties.
44. Eurojust's contribution for the European Commission Communication, above n. 26, at p. 19.
45. The number of cases referred in 2003 was 300, while in 2004 it was 381. The majority of cases referred continue to be bilateral in nature although a marked increase in the number of multilateral cases as a proportion of the total was noted in 2004 (109 of the 381 cases were multilateral).
46. UK House of Lords report, above n. 41, at para. 20.
47. Council and Commission Action Plan implementing the Hague Programme on strengthening. freedom, security and justice in the European Union (OJ C 198, 12.8.05, pp. 1–12). At para. 2.3 under point (9).
48. Existing rules on data protection are enshrined in Eurojust's Rules of Procedure on the Processing and Protection of Personal Data (OJ C 68, 19.3.2005, p. 1).
49. Discussed in more detail in Chapter 4.
50. For a fuller account of this thesis, see A. Weyemberg (2005), 'Approximation of criminal laws, the Constitutional Treaty and the Hague Programme', *Common Market Law Review*, **42**, 1567–97.
51. Joint Action on the creation of a European Judicial Network of 29 June 1998 (OJ L 19, 7.6.1998, p. 4).
52. UK House of Lords report, above n. 41, at para. 80.
53. Cited in G. Corstens and J. Pradel (2002), *European Criminal Law*, Kluwer Law International, at p. 54.
54. Joint Action of 22 April 1996 adopted by the Council on the basis of Article K.3 of the Treaty on European Union, concerning a framework for the exchange of liaison magistrates to improve judicial cooperation between the Member States of the European Union 96/277/JHA (OJ L 105 27.4.1996, p. 1).
55. Joint Action 98/428/JHA of 29 June 1998 adopted by the Council on the basis of Article K.3 of the Treaty on European Union, on the creation of a European Judicial Network (OJ L 191, 7.7.1998, pp. 4–7) at Article 2(4).
56. http://www.ejtn.net.
57. Catalogue of the European Judicial Training Network 2006, at p. 5. Available via http://www.ejtn.net.
58. See for instance Communication on the mutual recognition of judicial decisions in criminal matters and the strengthening of mutual trust between Member States in May 2005. COM(2005) 195 final, Brussels, 19.5.2005. Staff Working Paper SEC (2005) 641.
59. http://www.eurojustice.org.
60. Convention based on Article K.3 of the Treaty on European Union, on the establishment of a European Police Office, (OJ C 316, 27.11.1995, p. 2) at Article 2.1.
61. Ibid.
62. Proposal for a Council Decision establishing the European Police Office (Europol); above n. 37.
63. See document 13887/07 EUROPOL 102, Brussels 16.10.07 and document 14363/07 EUROPOL 110. Brussels, 9.10.07.
64. Article 29 EU.
65. Issue of data protection will be discussed in more detail in Chapter 3.
66. Europol Convention: above n. 60, at Article 2(2).

67. See for instance Council Presidency Document 7868/06 and Statewatch (August 2006), 'The future of Europol' available via www.statewatch.org.
68. C. Fijnaut, above n. 36, at p. 255.
69. Europol Convention, above n. 60, at Articles 23(10) and 34.
70. Europol Convention, above n. 60, at Article 26.
71. Certain constraints are placed upon Europol's external powers by a Council decision of 2000, for instance rules with regard to the exchange of personal data and with precisely whom Europol is authorized to negotiate (OJ C 106, 13.4.2001, pp. 1–2).
72. Council Decision of 22 December 2000 establishing a European Police College (CEPOL) (OJ L 336, 30.12.2000, p. 1).
73. T. Bunyan, 'The EU's Police Chief Task Force (PCTF) and Police Chiefs Committee', available at http://www.statewatchorg/news/2006/mar/pctf.pdf.
74. J. Monar, above n. 5 at p. 504.
75. http://www.eucpn.org/.
76. Council Decision 2001/427 of 28 May 2001. OJ L 153/1, 8.6.2001. See also Rules of Procedure of 25.6.2001.
77. Although, prior to the entry into force of the Amsterdam Treaty, see the Council resolution on crime prevention in which the Commission was invited to reassess Community policies (e.g. social and economic) in the light of crime prevention. Council Resolution of 21 December 1998 on the prevention of organised crime with reference to the establishment of a comprehensive strategy for combating it, (OJ C 408, 29.12.98, pp. 1–4).
78. COM(2004) 165 final, 12.3.2004.
79. G. De Kerchove (2002), 'Améliorations institutionelles à apporter au titre VI du traité sur l'Union européenne dans le domaine de la sécurité intérieure', in G. De Kerchove and A. Weyembergh (eds), *Quelles Réformes pour l'Espace Pénal Européen?*, Brussels: Editions de L'Université de Bruxelles, 19–39, at p. 37.

3. Police cooperation in criminal matters

The EU-wide fight against crime is to be achieved in part by securing closer cooperation between national law enforcement organisations, including 'police forces, customs authorities and other competent authorities in the Member States'.[1] Much of the ideological and practical groundwork for police cooperation had been laid prior to the 1999 Amsterdam settlement, during the Maastricht and even pre-Maastricht era and to a great extent within the Schengen system. The Amsterdam Treaty built squarely upon these foundations.[2] It continued the historical trend in international police cooperation by emphasising *operational* cooperation between competent authorities.[3] It also highlighted the centrality of *information exchange* to cross-border cooperation and the effective fight against crime.[4] In order to facilitate these and other forms of cooperation the Treaty of Amsterdam enhanced the role of the pre-existing European police agency, Europol. This agency, and indeed the variety of European level bodies that have emerged to facilitate particular aspects of cooperation between national policing agencies in tackling cross-border crime (CEPOL and the European Police Chiefs Task Force), were discussed in full in Chapter 2.

It should be recorded at the outset that, although police and judicial cooperation are dealt with discretely for the purposes of this book, neither can be seen in complete isolation. From an institutional perspective, law enforcement agencies and judicial authorities differ in their set-up and roles across the jurisdictions of the EU and, of course, these differences are reflected in how they interact with each other. This state of affairs must be taken into account and dealt with at the EU level if cooperation between the various authorities involved in law enforcement is to be promoted and improved. This is why we see, for instance, measures to establish formal links and cooperation between agencies such as Europol and Eurojust.[5] Moroever, aspects of both police and judicial cooperation have been emphasised with respect to some overarching themed priorities of the EU in recent years, namely the fight against terrorism and organised crime. The post-9-11 EU anti-terrorism strategy has for instance been described as the Council's first serious attempt, since the Maastricht Treaty, to reconstruct police cooperation in a specific area and to do so directly on all points using *a more operational model.*[6]

Today, a whole range of EU measures are aimed at enhancing police cooperation, making this area of law and policy difficult to negotiate or fully grasp, but in many ways it is a much less secretive affair than it has ever been. At the heart of police cooperation lies the coordination efforts of Europol, but another key strand of activity lies in improving the flow of data between national agencies engaged in the function of law enforcement. This task necessarily raises complex operational and technical issues and, from a more legal perspective, it raises the matter of securing the privacy rights of those to whom the data relate. Interestingly, in order to enhance the goal of information exchange, and indeed achieve joint operational capacities more generally, a group of EU Member States have worked together to reach agreement, *outside* the framework of the European Union, but with the full intention of later incorporating the contents of that agreement into the EU legal order. This example of 'extra-EU' activity will be considered in more detail later in the chapter.

As will become clear from what follows, the objective of EU police cooperation, as reflected in the current Treaty settlement and in implementation measures to date, is not to secure an EU police force or even to create integrated EU capabilities. Rather it is to increase the effectiveness of law enforcement by national authorities.[7] It would seem crucial, then, that EU intervention is geared towards achieving this objective. Where it is not, because for instance the support framework provided is overly complex or cumbersome, national agencies would surely deem it more appropriate to cooperate amongst themselves on an ad hoc or more formal basis, acting bilaterally or multilaterally. Content to bolster their own national law enforcement capabilities in whatever ways possible, there appears, therefore, to be no appetite to transfer law enforcement powers *per se* to the EU. Rather, with a raft of cooperation measures and relevant EU-level actors and EU information databases now in place, attention has turned to streamlining and improving what already exists and attempting to instil greater understanding and trust as between national law enforcement systems so that better use can be made of existing EU-level coordination mechanisms. Europe's leaders seemed committed to this approach when they declared in the The Hague Programme in 2004 that the effective combating of cross-border organised and other serious crime and terrorism 'requires *intensified practical cooperation* between police and customs authorities of Member States and with Europol and *better use of existing instruments in this field*'.[8]

This chapter will begin by clarifying the extent of EU competences in the field of third pillar police cooperation. It will then highlight some of the main ways in which these powers have been exercised. The bulk of the chapter will then focus upon information exchange/data protection matters and 'extra–EU' police cooperation initiatives.

COMPETENCES

For the first time in EU history, the Treaty of Amsterdam included clear objectives and a detailed description of actions to be taken in the field of police and customs cooperation. It also strengthened the institutional framework and further developed the decision-making process in this area. The EU's objective of providing citizens with a high level of safety within an area of freedom, security and justice was henceforth to be achieved in part by developing 'common action among Member States in the field of police cooperation'. This, in turn, was to be achieved through 'closer cooperation between police forces, customs authorities and other competent authorities in the Member States, both directly and through the European Police Ofiice (Europol), in accordance with the provision of Articles 30 and 32'.[9]

Article 30 EU provides a non-exhaustive list of the types of common action to be pursued in the field of police cooperation and details how that cooperation should be promoted through Europol by 1 May 2004. The full text of Article 30 is repeated here.

1. Common action in the field of police cooperation shall include
    (a) operational cooperation between the competent authorities, including the police, customs and other specialised law enforcement services of the Member States in relation to the prevention, detection and investigation of criminal offences;
    (b) the collection, storage, processing, analysis and exchange of relevant information, including information held by law enforcement services on reports on suspicious financial transactions, in particular through Europol, subject to appropriate provisions on the protection of personal data;
    (c) cooperation and joint initiatives in training, the exchange of liaison officers, secondments, the use of equipment, and forensic research;
    (d) the common evaluation of particular investigative techniques in relation to the detection of serious forms of organised crime.
2. The Council shall promote cooperation through Europol and shall in particular, within a period of five years after the date of entry into force of the Treaty of Amsterdam:
    (a) enable Europol to facilitate and support the preparation, and to encourage the coordination and carrying out, of specific investigative actions by the competent authorities of the Member States, including operational actions of joint teams comprising representatives of Europol in a support capacity;

(b) adopt measures allowing Europol to ask the competent authorities of the Member States to conduct and coordinate their investigations in specific cases and to develop specific expertise which may be put at the disposal of Member States to assist them in investigating cases of organised crime;

(c) promote liaison arrangements between prosecuting/investigating officials specialising in the fight against organised crime in close cooperation with Europol;

(d) establish a research, documentation and statistical network on cross-border crime.

Article 32 EU mandates the Council to stipulate the conditions under which the competent authorities referred to in Articles 30 and 31 EU may operate in the territory of another Member State in liaison and in agreement with the authorities of that state while Article 33 EU clarifies that the exercise of responsibilities incumbent upon Member States with regard to the maintenance of law and order and the safeguarding of internal security shall not be affected by any EU provisions and actions in the field of police or judicial cooperation in criminal matters.

Of course, following the Treaty of Amsterdam, various policing obligations resulting from the Schengen *acquis* became matters of EU law. The Schengen rules provide for the abolition of border controls among Member States, while at the same time reinforcing control measures at common external borders. Police cooperation obligations on, for instance, cross-border surveillance and exchange of information between police authorities, were introduced so as to counteract any security deficit caused by the abolition of the checks at the internal borders.

Alongside this clear legal mandate for action provided by the EU Treaty, the Tampere and Hague European Council documents have emphasised, clarified and influenced the police cooperation agenda. One prominent example of influencing the agenda is the decision taken in the Hague Programme to adopt the principle of availability in respect of data sharing by national law enforcement agencies. This will be discussed in more detail below. The Commission has also played a useful role in outlining the state of play and identifying priorities in what it describes as a broad and complex area which is particularly difficult to keep track of.[10]

IMPLEMENTING COMPETENCES ON POLICE COOPERATION

Implementing police cooperation has been achieved by a variety of hard and soft law measures and through a variety of institutional actors. As we saw in Chapter 2, the trend for operationalising EU cross-border police cooperation can be facilitated by Europol. This coordinating agency can provide logistical support to national authorities (in the form of expertise or technical support) but it cannot itself carry out operations. Where Europol does become involved in assisting national police authorities it does so under the supervision and legal responsibility of the (lead) Member State concerned. An additional important function of Europol is to generate strategic reports (e.g. risk analysis, threat assessments) on the basis of information and intelligence supplied, for the most part, by national authorities. There has been some concern, however, that this function is to some degree being undermined by an uneven supply of data from national authorities – an indication of continuing reluctance among national police forces to share their data in this way. Encouraging a full and systematic flow of data upwards to Europol's databases will help to assist national law enforcement agencies to tackle cross-border crime. Of course, ensuring the integrity of this and other EU information systems is a distinct but related matter that will be considered below, but, first, our attention turns briefly to another particular strategy of EU police cooperation, namely that of promoting joint operations.

Joint Operations

One of the most practical and perhaps useful ways in which the EU can facilitate the fight against crime is by providing the framework for cross-border operations and joint operations between national police forces. Article 33 EU provides the legal basis for authorising the law enforcement authorities of one Member State to carry out operations on the territory of another 'in liaison and in agreement with the authorities of that state'. Even prior to the Amsterdam Treaty the Schengen Convention provided for the possibility of one Member State's police forces to operate on the territory of another Member State, notably when in 'hot pursuit' of a suspect where there is no time to inform the local authorities and in order to carry out surveillance.[11] With respect to joint operations, a novel and *sui generis* form of international operational cooperation has been provided for in the form of joint investigation teams (JITs).[12] The EU's 2000 convention on mutual legal assistance[13] first provided for the possibility of setting up a JIT by mutual agreement of the competent authorities of two or more Member States, for a specific purpose and a limited, extendable period of time, to carry out criminal investigations in one or more Member States. The convention also laid down rules governing the operation of JITs. Notably, teams will be subject to the laws of the Member State in which the team operates and bodies such as Europol and Eurojust can be involved. In the absence of the entry into force of the convention and in recognition of the potential value of managed joint investigations as a tool of operational cooperation, a framework decision on joint investigation teams was adopted in June 2002.[14] This instrument, which essentially repeated much of the text of the Convention, would allow for the setting up of JITs in advance of the ratification of the Convention. It is perhaps still too early to draw any conclusions as to the success or otherwise of JITs, but one cannot help but suspect that the relatively small number of JITs established to date[15] is an indication that there is some reluctance to establish them. This is perhaps not so surprising given the range of practical and cultural differences that are likely to exist. Recently, several awareness-raising initiatives have been launched to disseminate information about and to encourage the use of JITs. A support website was launched by Eurojust and Europol in late 2007[16] and a practice-based handbook on joint investigation is being drafted to assist those authorities who might consider setting up a JIT.[17]

Information Exchange

Member States have increasingly become advocates of data control and exchange to combat illegal migration, organised crime and international terrorism.[18] Advances in technology and the increase of cross-border and even so-called 'global threats' to security have led to a proliferation of surveillance systems and transnational information sharing between national law enforcement agencies throughout the world. The EU is by no means an exception in this regard. Indeed, the 2004 Hague Programme called for the setting up and implementation of a methodology for 'intelligence-led law enforcement at EU level'. In fact, the EU has adopted a whole raft of hard as well as soft law measures concerning the retention of certain types of data[19] and the sharing of information between national authorities in relation to specific matters.[20]

In order to enable the storage and processing of data, various databases have been set up. The main EU information systems currently in operation are a newly structured Schengen Information System known as SIS II, largely concerned with border control,[21] the SIRENE[22] system, responsible for the administration of SIS in each participating country and which may hold additional information about individuals registered on SIS, and the Europol computer systems (TECS) comprising an indexing system, a central information system with data on suspects and sentenced persons within its areas of competence, and a whole series of special, temporary analysis files which may contain extensive personal data on those entered into the central information system and also on individuals believed to be associates, informants, victims, contacts or witnesses.[23]

Mathieson has identified two common trends that have emerged in respect of the various information systems.[24] The first is the shift towards the *integration* and compatibility of systems which in effect allows more and more agencies to share, tap into and process increasing amounts of personal data for their own ends. This broad integration or 'interoperability' objective was emphasised by the Hague Programme in the context of combating terrorism, although its effects clearly extend well beyond this:

> The European Council calls on the Commission to submit proposals for enhanced interoperability between European databases and to explore the creation of synergies between existing and future information systems (SIS II, VIS and EURODAC) in order to exploit their added value within their respective legal and technical frameworks in the prevention and fight against terrorism.[25]

Following up on this mandate the Commission published a Communication on improved effectiveness, enhanced interoperability and synergies among European databases in the area of Justice and Home Affairs in late 2005.[26] This Communication, unusually, neither proposes a concrete legal measure nor formally defends a specific strategy for future legislation. Rather, it is an open-ended presentation of a wide spectrum of scenarios for the future of JHA databases, which, according to Hobbing, 'is clearly motivated by the unusually complicated subject matter concerned: if individual large-scale IT-systems already defy any easy comprehension, due to their technical and legal complexity, this is all the more true for a combination of such databases and their mutually interwoven links and dependencies'.[27] With that in mind there is clearly some merit in attempting to subject the increasing number of information systems to some form of common management.[28] But particular challenges and concerns remain and not least the extent to which non-crime-related databases can be accessed by internal security and intelligence services. The Commission suggests that the principle of proportionality should apply here so that access to information contained in the non-crime-related databases of VIS, EURODAC[29] and SIS II immigration data by law enforcement authorities, should only be permitted in the case of overriding public security concerns. Such concern could be assumed only where terrorist offences, as defined in the Council framework decision on the definition of terrorism,[30] or crimes falling under the competence of Europol are imminent.

Second, as the trend for more and interoperable information systems continues, so the degree of control at the level of the state decreases. Mathieson argues that national parliaments are no longer able effectively to scrutinise the ever-changing developments in this field: documents, to the extent that they are available, are detailed and complex and 'parliamentary debates become superficial and short, accepting the premises of ministries

and even police agencies'.[31] Moreover, as more and more systems inter-
lock – often driven by internal social forces and logic – it becomes more
difficult for states to question the need for such systems and their own participation in them.[32] Indeed, in Western society, where fear of crime and
insecurity are prevalent, political debate on new powers of surveillance
usually focuses on the citizens' security and the public, by and large,
support the extension of such powers.[33]

Both of the trends identified thus far (interoperability and decreased
state control) support the argument for systems of accountability and
control to be addressed at the EU level. Additional support can be found if
one considers the methodological principle underpinning the exchange of
law enforcement data in the EU – the principle of availability.

Endorsed by the European Council in the Hague Programme, this principle is to be operational from 1 January 2008. The EU's leaders affirmed
that they remained 'convinced that strengthening freedom, security and
justice requires an innovative approach to the cross-border exchange of
law-enforcement information. The mere fact that information crosses
borders should no longer be relevant.' Consequently, the principle of availability is defined as follows:

> throughout the Union, a law enforcement officer in one Member State who
> needs information in order to perform his duties can obtain this from another
> Member State and [that] the law enforcement agency in the other Member State
> which holds this information will make it available for the stated purpose, taking
> into account the requirement of ongoing investigations in that State.[34]

The principle of availability has characteristics in common with the
methodological approach of mutual recognition which underpins judicial
cooperation in criminal matters; this is so because it is based on the idea
that information needed to fight crime should be able to cross intra-EU
borders *without obstacles*.[35] Moreover, it raises the same need for *mutual
trust*, which in this context relates to the need for national police and security agencies to have some faith and confidence in the integrity of the law
enforcement system to which it is required to hand over what may well be
highly sensitive data concerning their own nationals. Securing a common
framework of rights at the EU level, for instance with regard to data protection, might be one way of securing such trust. Efforts to reach agreement
on a horizontal data protection framework decision in the third pillar will
be discussed below. Other non-legal and practical approaches to achieving
the same end already exist in the form, for instance, of common police
training initiatives. In short, the principle of availability marks a fundamental shift away from traditional forms of information exchange between
national agencies which have often been organized through bilateral or

multilateral agreements and on the basis of formal request procedures. Its successful implementation will almost certainly require a concerted effort to enhance confidence and trust between national law enforcement agencies.

In October 2005, the Commission adopted a proposal for a framework decision on the exchange of information under the principle of availability, the contents of which reveal the potentially far-reaching implications of the principle. The draft framework decision extends the principle to a wide range of data fields and there is an obligation to collect and store information 'for the sole purpose of making it available to the competent authorities of other Member States'.[36] This proposal has yet to be adopted and it is thought that a more limited version of the principle (in both scope and content) as contained in the Prüm Treaty (to be discussed below) is more likely to be adopted.[37] In any case, given the potential for this principle vastly to expedite and increase the flows of data between law enforcement agencies, it becomes vital to ensure that rigorous safeguards are in place, in particular in the form of robust data-protection arrangements, in order to guard against 'fishing expeditions' on the part of national security and police agencies and misuse of sensitive personal information.

So, while most of us would (reluctantly) agree that increased surveillance and information exchange between law enforcement agencies is a necessary component of modern crime control, we would probably also agree that limits to these powers must exist to prevent the infringement of civil liberties, such as the right to a private life as enshrined in Article 8 ECHR. The challenge for the EU is considerable in this regard as Peers succinctly summarises:

> But, as in other areas of Justice and Home Affairs law, the legal and political system of the European Union, with much more limited parliamentary and judicial control or supervision of the executive, and no developed framework for the accountability of operations, offers an escape from these national constraints, with the consequent risk that the delicate balance between liberty and security will tip dramatically in favour of the latter as the EU develops rules on the 'free movement of investigations'.[38]

Indeed, it would appear that exceptions to normal levels of scrutiny, accountability and constraints have been tolerated by the EU on matters concerning retention and sharing of information – often under the auspices of the 'fight against terrorism'. One clear example of the lack of control over the exchange and use of information was highlighted in the landmark judgment in *Organisation des Modjahedin du peuple d'Iran*.[39] This case concerned the validity of the Council's 'terror lists' which form a crucial part of the EU's financial sanctions system directed against certain persons and entities with a view to combating terrorism. Neither the Council nor the UK government was able to provide an answer to the question of which national decision was the basis for the placing of an alleged terror group in the 'terror list'. As a result the Court of First Instance (CFI) ruled that the Council had infringed the right to a fair hearing, the obligation to state reasons and the right to effective judicial protection. Given that the vast majority of EU counter-terrorism initiatives depend on information received from Member States (or bodies such as, for example, the UN Security Council), it seems necessary to have control systems in place to ensure that such information is not 'tainted' by torture or other inhuman or degrading treatment. And yet, as Geyer[40] points out, there is no common framework in place to regulate how such information enters the AFSJ. He suggests that this issue should be urgently addressed in order to ensure respect for international obligations and human rights law and in order to avoid further inevitable judicial challenges.

Much of the discussion about securing a common framework of rights as a corollary to the heavily security-focused criminal law enforcement agenda has centred upon the issue of data protection. Article 8 ECHR, the jurisprudence of the Strasbourg court and the Council of Europe's 1981 convention on data protection[41] provide the starting points on issues of privacy and data protection. In the EC, data protection legislation has existed since the mid-1990s,[42] but its focus was to protect against possible abuses by market actors or government agencies as service providers and explicitly excluded security and criminal law enforcement agencies from its ambit.[43] Today, the challenge is to safeguard privacy and to ensure robust data protection when governments are exercising their powers in the realms of security and policing.[44]

There is currently no horizontal data protection regime in relation to law enforcement matters at the EU level. Specific data protection measures are built into some, but not all, individual instruments that concern data exchange, e.g. the Schengen Convention, the Europol convention and the Prüm Treaty (see below), thus making the landscape incredibly complex and difficult to navigate. The case for a comprehensive EU data protection regime has been clearly and forcefully made, particularly in light of the proliferation of information systems and the principle of availability. In October 2005, the Commission submitted a proposal for a framework decision on the protection of personal data processed in the framework of police and judicial cooperation in criminal matters.[45] Over two years on, and at the time of writing, the framework decision has yet to be formally adopted, although a general approach was agreed at the JHA Council in November 2007. Sticking points have concerned whether the remit of the proposal should be extended to cover Europol and Eurojust, whether the proposal should cover cross-border and internal exchanges of information and how best to ensure an adequate level of protection when transferring data to third countries and international bodies.[46] Moreover, the European Data Protection Supervisor has drafted three critical opinions on the various incarnations of the proposed framework to date.[47] Ultimately the JHA council managed to secure a general agreement that the measure would only apply to cross-border exchange of personal data and that data may be transferred to third states only if a number of conditions, including prior consent, are met.

'EXTRA-EU' ACTIVITIES

The emergence of certain cooperation initiatives amongst groups of Member States outside the formal framework of the EU, but with direct links to the EU's objectives in the field of policing and security, has prompted much discussion in recent years. For some this activity is highly suspicious, it being perceived as a manifestation of distrust or at least lack of confidence in the ability of the EU system to deliver effectively upon desired policy outcomes, thereby considerably weakening that very system. Yet, on another view, these activities are highly pragmatic ways of pushing the EU agenda forward. As we have seen elsewhere in this book, the existing governance structures of the EU's third pillar are comparatively prohibitive and complex, making resort to other solutions more likely and ultimately more efficient. A brief account of two forms of extra-EU governance will be considered here, namely the G6 group and the 'Prüm Treaty'.

G6

The interior ministers of the six largest EU Members States have formed the so-called 'G6 laboratory' in order to provide an additional impetus to strengthening the EU's AFSJ by drawing up concrete proposals. This high-level political discussion group, which meets three or four times a year, was originally founded in 2003 by France, Germany, Italy, Spain and the UK. In March 2006, Poland became the sixth member. Although the meetings of the group cannot produce any binding measures as such, they appear to have achieved some success in influencing EU policy. For instance, the conclusions of the G6 meeting held in Heiligendamm, Germany, on 22 and 23 March 2006 record an instance of their direct impact upon EU police cooperation: 'The decision of the Council of Ministers for Justice and Home Affairs of 12 July 2005 designated Europol as the central agency for

euro counterfeiting, laying the groundwork for an even more efficient
fight against euro counterfeiting and successfully implementing the initiative launched at the meeting of interior ministers in Garmisch-
Partenkirchen.'[48] However, while their influence may indeed be positive,
this is not necessarily always the case. In the same conclusions they
recorded that 'the rapid implementation of the availability principle must
not depend on the adoption of a framework decision on data protection in
the third pillar'. Interestingly, the G6 group makes no effort to act in secret,
quite the contrary in fact, although documents under discussion are not
easy to come by. It also makes clear that other EU Member States can participate in the implementation of their proposals. However, despite the
openness and pragmatism of their efforts, this grouping of large states is
likely to be regarded with disdain by many of the other 21 smaller Member
States of the EU.

The Prüm Treaty

Another example of cooperation established outside of the EU framework
is the Prüm Treaty signed on 27 May 2005 by Belgium, Germany, Spain,
France, Luxembourg, the Netherlands and Austria, on the stepping up
of cross-border cooperation, particularly in combating terrorism, cross-
border crime and illegal migration.[49] The preamble to the Treaty identifies
its objective as the 'further development of cooperation, to play a pioneer-
ing role in establishing the highest possible standard of cooperation especially by means of exchange of information, . . . while leaving participation
in such cooperation open to all other Member States of the European
Union'. Immediately it is clear that the Prüm Treaty focuses predominantly
upon enhancing information exchange and that its objectives are directly
linked, in fact synonymous with, those of the EU.

In terms of content, in general it can be said that many of the provisions
in the Treaty represent significant advances in the extent to which States are
willing to cooperate in order to combat cross-border crime. The main provisions of the Treaty concern the exchange of DNA files and fingerprinting
data held in national databases and the exchange of other personal data
and non-personal data for major events with a cross-border dimension, in
particular sporting events; access to and exchange of vehicle registration
data; various measures to prevent terrorist offences, including the
exchange of data and the use of air marshals on aircraft; measures to
combat illegal immigration; measures to facilitate joint police operations
including in border areas; measures on requesting and providing mutual
assistance in connection with major events, disasters and serious accidents;
and measures formalising routine checks including registered vehicle

keepers, licences, addresses and telephone subscribers. A particularly notable provision of the Prüm Treaty is Article 25 which allows for a police officer from one State to act on the territory of another in urgent situations and in order to 'avert imminent danger to the physical integrity of individuals'.[50]

The Prüm Treaty, although adopted outside the legal framework of the EU, is now in the process of being incorporated into it. It will be recalled that a precedent for such behaviour was set in the EU by the experience of the Schengen agreement, which was also an extra-EU project later incorporated into the EC and EU legal framework by the Amsterdam Treaty. In early 2007, the Council agreed to work towards implementing the contents of the Prüm Treaty in EU law. At that meeting it was reported that there was very broad support for the proposal, even though there were also some concerns about the costs of implementation and reservations about Article 25 (measures in the event of imminent danger). The Council acknowledged that the contents of Prüm offered substantially improved and efficiently organised procedures for the exchange of information, in fact describing them as a 'quantum leap' in the cross-border sharing of information. A draft Prüm EU decision was published in June 2007 and at the time of writing the Council had agreed a general approach.

By choosing to negotiate the Prüm Treaty as they did, the signatory States did not only express a political desire to expedite information exchange between themselves in order to enhance security, they also chose to shun the institutional procedures provided in the EU Treaty altogether, including those which specifically allow for a 'differentiated' or 'twin-track approach' to be developed.[51] It has been argued that the implications of this for the credibility and the solidarity of the EU as an actor in criminal and security matters are potentially very damaging.[52] It has also been suggested that the Prüm experience significantly undermines the EU by allowing competitive and exclusive measures to emerge on issues that affect the EU as a whole.[53] Of course, as a matter of public international law, States are completely free to negotiate and make agreements in this way. What is perhaps curious about this particular situation is that the parties involved did this in order to pursue specific EU law objectives and with the intention, or at least the hope, that the fruits of their agreement would later be integrated into the EU legal order. Of course it remains to be seen to what extent this practice will continue in the future. Indications suggest that the group of states which took the initiative to the Prüm Treaty wish to continue to work together and to deepen their cooperation. There will be many hoping that the institutional reforms introduced by the Reform Treaty (RT), namely the adoption of the 'ordinary legislative procedure' combined with the emergency brake and enhanced cooperation procedure, will prevent future resort to intergovernmental negotiations outside the framework of EU law on criminal and policing matters.

NOTES

1. Article 29 EU. Note that this chapter will focus almost exclusively on police cooperation pursuant to the third pillar and make only passing reference to customs cooperation. On the links between police cooperation and EC law, and the issue of customs cooperation, see generally, S. Peers (2007) *EU Justice and Home Affairs Law*, Oxford: Oxford University Press, pp. 510–14.
2. In terms of territorial scope, the policing rules in the Schengen *acquis* (with the exception of the Schengen Information System (SIS) provisions) now apply to the UK, Ireland and Denmark. A number of non-EU states participate fully in the Schengen *acquis* by virtue of agreements with the EU. Iceland and Norway participate fully and Switzerland is in the process of doing so.
3. Article 30(1)(a) EU.
4. Article 30(1)(b) EU.
5. For more on the relationship between Europol and Eurojust, see Chapter 2. For more on the relationship between police cooperation and judicial cooperation generally, see C. Fijnaut (2006), 'Police co-operation and the area of freedom, security and justice', in N. Walker (ed.), *Europe's Area of Freedom, Security and Justice*, Oxford: Oxford University Press, pp. 253–8.
6. Ibid., at p. 246. Emphasis added.
7. However, some small inroads have been made into this underpinning ideology, as evidenced by the on going attempts to confer some limited operational powers on Europol.
8. The Hague Programme: strengthening freedom, security and justice in the European Union (OJ C 53, 3.3.2005, pp. 1–14) at para. 3.1.
9. Article 29 EU.
10. Communication from the Commission to the European Parliament and the Council: enhancing police and customs cooperation in the European Union. COM (2004) 376 final, 18.5.2004.
11. Note that the UK is a signatory of those parts of the Schengen *acquis* that relate to police operations except 'hot pursuit'.
12. See, generally, M. Plachta (2005), 'Joint investigation teams: a new form of international cooperation in criminal matters', *European Journal of Crime, Criminal Law and Criminal Justice*, **13**(2), 284–302.
13. Convention on Mutual Assistance in Criminal Matters between the Member States of the European Union, adopted on 29 May 2000 (OJ C 197, 12.7.2000, p. 1).
14. Council Framework Decision of 13 June 2002 on joint investigation teams 2002/465/JHA (OJ L 162, 20.6.02, p. 1).
15. By mid-2007, according to figures from Eurojust, only 16 JITs had been set up within the EU, of which only one involved the UK. This evidence was reported by the UK House of Commons Home Affairs Committee, 'Justice and Home Affairs Issues at the European Union Level', Session 2006-07, HC 76-I, 5.6.2007 at para. 92.
16. The web pages are available at www.eurojust.europa.eu/jits and www.europol.europa.eu/jits.
17. Note that a legal basis for the establishment of JITs is contained in the 2003 EU–US Agreement on mutual legal assistance between the European Union and the United States of America, signed on 25 June 2003 (OJ L181, 19.7.2002, p. 34).
18. T. Balzacq, D. Bigo, S. Carrera and E. Guild (2006), 'Security and the two-level game: the Treaty of Prüm, the EU and the management of threats', *CEPS Working Document No. 234*, Centre for European Policy Studies, Brussels, at p. 13.

19. For instance a controversial 2006 directive *obliges* electronic communication operators to retain *all* traffic data (i.e. details of who was involved and when as opposed to the actual content of telecommunications) and not just the data of crime suspects. The purpose of retaining the data is to assist 'the investigation, prosecution and detection of serious crime': Directive 2006/24/EC of 15 March 2006 on the retention of data generated or processed in connection with the provision of publicly available electronic communications services or of public communications networks and amending Directive 2002/58/EC (OJ L 105, 13.4.2006, pp. 54–63). The proposal of this directive was heavily criticized by the European Data Protection Supervisor and the directive itself has been challenged by Ireland before the European Court of Justice on the grounds that it was not adopted using an appropriate legal basis. See C-301/06 *Ireland* v *Council of the European Union, European Parliament*, judgment pending at the time of writing. For analysis of the directive see for instance P. Breyer (2005), 'Telecommunications data retention and human rights: the compatibility of blanket traffic data retention with the ECHR', *European Law Journal*, **11**(3), 365–75 and F. Bignami (2007), 'Protecting privacy against the police in the European Union: the data retention directive', *Chicago Journal of International Law*, 663–86.
20. For instance there are measures concerning terrorism, customs, football security, public order and immigration.
21. The UK does not have access to the SIS database since it does not participate in Schengen border control measures. For an overview of this system and the impact of the UK position, see UK House of Lords European Union Committee, 'Schengen Information System II (SIS II)' Session 2006/07, HL 49, 2.3.2007.
22. Supplementary Information Request at the National Entries.
23. In general, on information exchange systems, readers are directed to the civil liberties organization Statewatch which does an excellent job of monitoring and critiquing developments. See http://www.statewatch.org.
24. T. Mathieson (2006), 'Lex Vigilatoria – towards a control system without a state?', in S. Armstrong and L. McAra, (eds), *Perspectives on Punishment: The Contours of Control*, Oxford: Oxford University Press, pp. 119–31.
25. European Council, *Declaration on combating terrorism* 25.3.2004.
26. COM(2005) 597 final, 24.11.2005. For a detailed comment on this Communication, see P. Hobbing (2006), 'An Analysis of the Commission Communication (COM(2005) 597 Final of 24.11.2005) on Improved Effectiveness, Enhanced Interoperability and Synergies among European Databases in the area of Justice and Home Affairs.' (Available via www.libertysecurity.org.)
27. Ibid.
28. The Commission specifically mentions the External Border Agency FRONTEX as a possible candidate to manage EURODAC, SIS II and VIS. FRONTEX was established by Council Regulation 2007/2004 of 26.10.2004 (OJ L 349 5.11.2004, p. 2).
29. Which contains fingerprints of all persons who submit a claim for asylum within the territory of the EU.
30. Discussed further in Chapter 6.
31. T. Mathieson, above n. 24, at p. 128.
32. Ibid., at p. 130.
33. P. Breyer, above n. 19, at p. 366.
34. The Hague Programme, above n. 8, at para 2.1.
35. Although note that the Hague Programme identifies a list of conditions that should be observed in the implementation of the availability principle. This includes 'supervision of respect for data must be ensured' and 'individuals must be protected from abuse of data and have the right to seek correction of incorrect data'. Ibid. at para. 2.1.
36. Proposal for a Council Framework Decision on the exchange of information under the principle of availability. COM(2005) 490 final, 12.10.2005.
37. As the UK House of Commons Home Affairs Committee notes, this raises the possibility that the original design of an instrument introducing radical change to EU data

sharing will have been carried out outside the democratic processes of the EU; at para. 144.

38. S. Peers, above n. 1, at 499.
39. T-228/02, *Organisation des Modjahedin du people d'Iran* v *Council of the European Union*, judgment of 12 December 2006.
40. F. Geyer (2007), 'Fruit of the Poisonous Tree: Member State's Indirect Use of Extraordinary Rendition and the EU Counter-Terrorism Strategy', *Working Document No. 263 Centre for European Policy Studies*, available via http://www.ceps.be.
41. Council of Europe Convention for the protection of individuals with regard to automatic processing of personal data. Council Convention 108 (1 January 1981).
42. Directive 95/46/EC of the European Parliament and of the Council of 24 October 1995 on the protection of individuals with regard to the processing of personal data and on the free movement of such data (OJ L 281, 23.11.1995, p. 31).
43. F. Bignami, above n. 19.
44. Note that Article 68 of the EU Charter on fundamental rights guarantees protection of personal data in *all* the EU's activities.
45. COM (2005) 475 final, 4.10.2005.
46. The data protection regime for transfer of data to third parties is particularly significant in light of the Passenger Name Record (PNR) agreements between the EU and US. For more on this, see Chapter 5.
47. Most recently, Third opinion of 27 April 2007 on the proposal for a Council Framework Decision on the protection of personal data processed in the framework of police and judicial co-operation in criminal matters (OJ C 139, 23.06.2007, pp. 1–14).
48. Conclusions available via http://www.statewatch.org. Also available there is the Declaration agreed after the most recent meeting of the group on 18 October 2007.
49. Council Secretariat, Brussels, 7 July 2005, 10900/05.
50. This so-called 'imminent danger' measure, contained in Article 25 of the Treaty is quite a novelty in international police cooperation. It is cited as one of the reasons why the UK decided it could not participate in the Prüm negotiations. On Prüm generally and the UK position, see UK House of Lords, EU Committee, 'Prüm: an effective weapon against terrorism and crime?', Session 2006-07, HL 90, 9.5.2007.
51. See Article 40 EU which established the 'enhanced cooperation' mechanism.
52. T. Balzacq, D. Bigo, S. Carrera and E. Guild (2006), 'Security and the two-level game: the Treaty of Prüm, the EU and the Management of Threats', *Centre for European Policy Studies*, E. Guild and F. Geyer (2006), 'Getting local: Schengen, Prüm and the dancing procession of Echternach', *Centre for European Policy Studies*.
53. See ibid.

4. Judicial cooperation in criminal matters

CONTEXT AND GENERAL OVERVIEW

Judicial cooperation forms the central plank of the EU's criminal justice agenda. It is precisely within this field that the boldest attempts have been made to move on from the vagaries of the past, when international cooperation in criminal matters was notoriously slow, inefficient and carried out in the interests of the states concerned.[1] And yet it is also within this field that the impacts of the basic theoretical lacuna in the project of developing the EU as an area of freedom, security and justice are most prominent, resulting in institutional tensions and, ultimately, a legal landscape that lacks coherence. Building upon the discussion contained in the introduction and Chapter 1 of this book, and in order to convey more clearly the somewhat schizophrenic nature of EU judicial cooperation in criminal matters, this chapter will be structured around the legislative and non-legislative strands of development.

The Treaty of Amsterdam did not mark the beginning of the EU's role in criminal matters, nor did it produce a completely revolutionary approach to dealing with matters of inter-state cooperation. However, it is fair to say that it embodied and precipitated a significant shift away from the traditional approach based upon intergovernmental conventions and the principle of request. The import of certain Communitarian (supranational) elements to the hitherto largely intergovernmental third pillar created a completely unique and more ambitious governance framework for policy development. Most prominently, the EU was given more effective legal instruments through which to pursue cooperation between national criminal justice systems. Interestingly, the framework decision with its similar characteristics to the EC directive has all but replaced the convention as the EU instrument of choice for pursuing international cooperation in criminal matters. Of course, the decision-making procedure (which allows for proposals from either the Commission or a Member State, mere consultation of the European Parliament and unanimous approval in Council) and the restrictions on judicial accountability in the third pillar, reveal that national executives were not willing to relinquish their power in the criminal justice sphere to the same extent as in traditional EC policy spheres. Nevertheless, the Amsterdam Treaty reflected and heralded a new appetite for *integration* in order to tackle internal security threats. Henceforth, judicial cooperation in criminal matters was to form a key component of a new cross-pillar EU objective: developing the EU as 'an area of freedom, security and justice'. By way of reminder, the first paragraph of Article 29 EU reads as follows:

> Without prejudice to the powers of the European Community, the Union's objective shall be to provide citizens with a high level of safety within an area of freedom, security and justice by developing common action among the Member States in the fields of police and judicial cooperation in criminal matters and by preventing and combating racism and xenophobia.

Following the entry into force of the Amsterdam Treaty, the heads of State and Government of the then 15 Member States convened an extraordinary European council meeting in Tampere, Finland to discuss how to achieve the aspiration that is the AFSJ and to agree upon some common guidelines and principles for carrying forward this agenda over a five-year period (i.e. up to May 2004). The published Conclusions from this European Council helped to put flesh on the bones of the EU Treaty provisions by describing the political vision of an area of (criminal) justice.

> The enjoyment of freedom requires a genuine area of justice, where people can approach courts and authorities in any Member State as easily as in their own. Criminals must find no ways of exploiting differences in the judicial systems of Member States. Judgements and decisions should be respected and enforced throughout the Union, while safeguarding the basic legal certainty of people and economic operators. Better compatibility and more convergence between the legal systems of Member States must be achieved.[2]

But the real significance of the Tampere conclusions lay in the articulation of an underpinning methodology to be applied in order to achieve judicial cooperation in criminal matters:

> Enhanced mutual recognition of judicial decisions and judgements and the necessary approximation of legislation would facilitate co-operation between authorities and the judicial protection of individual rights. The European Council therefore *endorses the principle of mutual recognition which, in its view, should become the cornerstone of judicial co-operation in both civil and criminal matters within the Union.* The principle should apply both to judgements and to other decisions of judicial authorities.[3]

It is difficult to exaggerate the influence that this political decision has had on the emerging EU criminal justice agenda and indeed the degree of controversy it has caused in some quarters. It was suggested in the introductory chapter of this book that the principle of mutual recognition had been adopted as the cornerstone of criminal justice cooperation without a clear theoretical basis and with no discussion of the full ramifications of this choice. Like it or loathe it, that political choice, we argue, has certain logical consequences at the level of application, which many national legislatures and some national courts appear to have ignored when transposing and interpreting the framework decision on the European arrest warrant (EAW)[4] – the first legal instrument adopted to give effect to the principle of mutual recognition. This chapter will try to distil some of the key issues and debates on mutual recognition, but for a more detailed analysis readers are referred to the wealth of literature on the subject.

Besides this politically endorsed methodology for achieving the Treaty goal of 'closer cooperation', the Treaty expressly endorsed two other approaches: closer institutional (operational) cooperation and a minimum level of approximation. Article 29 EU, having outlined the objective of providing citizens with a high level of safety within an area of freedom, security and justice, continues:

> That objective shall be achieved by preventing and combating crime, organised or otherwise, in particular terrorism, trafficking in persons and offences against children, illicit drug trafficking and illicit arms trafficking, corruption and fraud, through
> – ...
> – closer cooperation between judicial and other competent authorities of the Member States including cooperation through the European Judicial Cooperation Unit ('Eurojust'), in accordance with the provisions of Articles 31 and 32,
> – approximation, where necessary, of rules on criminal matters in the Member States, in accordance with the provisions of Article 31(1) (e).

Article 31(1)(e) EU reads:

> Common action on judicial cooperation in criminal matters shall include:
> [. . .]
> progressively adopting measures establishing minimum rules relating to the constituent elements of criminal acts and to penalties in the fields of organised crime, terrorism and illicit drug trafficking.

Therefore, on the face of the Treaty, there is only an explicit legal basis for approximation in respect of *substantive* criminal law, a topic that, although forming part of the 'common action on judicial cooperation in criminal matters', is sufficiently distinctive to be considered in a separate chapter.[5]

As for other specific competences to coordinate criminal justice systems, Article 31(1) EU provides for

(a) facilitating and accelerating cooperation between competent ministries and judicial or equivalent authorities of the Member States, including, where appropriate, cooperation through Eurojust, in relation to proceedings and the enforcement of decisions;
(b) facilitating extradition between Member States;
(c) ensuring compatibility in rules applicable in the Member States, as may be necessary to improve such cooperation;
(d) preventing conflicts of jurisdiction between Member States;
. . .

This provision envisages some EU action in respect of various aspects of criminal *procedure*, but it might be deemed to be unclear on two levels. First, in terms of content, the list is non-exhaustive and the broadly drafted terms leave the door open for various and contested interpretations; subparagraph (c) is especially notable in this regard. Second, the provision does not stipulate *how* the EU is to act to secure the objectives contained in the list; there is no indication as to precisely which legal instruments should be used for this purpose and the provision simply refers to pursuing 'common action'. However, it does not follow from this that the Treaty drafters intended the Council to have free rein to act in the field of criminal procedures whenever a unanimous agreement can be reached. On the contrary, the attempts to define the extent of EU powers in the Treaty, combined with the stipulated decision-making procedure involving all of the political institutions, a clear choice of legal instruments[6] and provision for judicial oversight, including on grounds of 'lack of competence'[7] strongly points to the third pillar as a system of conferred powers and therefore limited competences (akin to the Community pillar). As such, any EU action in the third pillar requires an appropriate legal basis in the EU Treaty and must be able to satisfy both the principle of subsidiarity and the principle of proportionality. To date, the ECJ has invalidated two framework decisions on the ground that they had been erroneously adopted using a third pillar legal basis; the appropriate legal basis was in fact deemed to lie in the first Community pillar. The *Environmental crimes* and *Ship-source pollution* cases concern matters of substantive criminal law and are therefore discussed in Chapter 6. The Court has yet to invalidate a Framework decision for the wrong '*intra*-third pillar' basis. In fact, in the course of *upholding* the validity of the EAW in May 2007, the Court offered some helpful clarification of the Treaty provisions; for instance it put beyond doubt that the tool of approximation of national laws may extend beyond the substantive aspects enshrined in Article 31(1)(e) to those other more procedural aspects of criminal justice mentioned in Article 31.[8] This particular issue had been one of the 'sticking points' in the political negotiations on the draft framework decision on common minimum procedural rights for suspects and defendants (FDPR),[9] which will be discussed in more detail below. Another useful clarification from the ECJ was that the Council, in deciding upon the precise modalities of common action, '*may have a choice between several instruments in order to regulate the same subject-matter, subject to the limits imposed by the nature of the instrument selected*'.[10] On the facts in the case in hand, this led the Court to confirm the choice of a framework decision as appropriate for the subject matter of the EAW. This case and others that have a direct bearing upon judicial cooperation in criminal matters will be considered at appropriate junctures throughout this chapter.

It is notable that, despite high-level political endorsement of an ambitious legislative programme,[11] the pace at which legal texts are agreed in these matters has slowed in recent years. Discussions around adopting a European evidence warrant along the same methodological lines as the EAW have proved exceedingly difficult and, while political agreement is tantalisingly close, the measure remains to be formally adopted. Neither could agreement be reached upon the draft FDPR despite years of shuttle diplomacy by the Commission, thereby exposing the EU to allegations of prosecutorial bias in its legislative approach to pursuing criminal justice cooperation. A long-awaited legislative proposal on criminal jurisdiction to address the issue of multiple prosecutions has been stalled following concerns that a stronger evidence base is required, first to justify, and then focus, any EU intervention.[12] To be sure, the precise circumstances surrounding each of these examples varies, but the general message conveyed is one of scepticism. Political will for more legislation may be waning as time has revealed that touchstone texts such as the EAW have thrown up widespread legal concerns and challenges at the national level.

In light of this, it comes as a welcome development that the Commission is committed to engaging in much more widespread and in-depth consultation prior to the publication of draft proposals. The systematic use of impact assessments in the third pillar can only add to the so-called 'input legitimacy' of EU legislative action in this particularly sensitive policy field. It will also necessarily slow down the rate of legislative output – in our view a price worth paying if the result is a more informed, evidenced and legitimated EU criminal law regime.

But as the legislative agenda struggles, the various non-legislative approaches to promoting judicial cooperation in criminal matters have come to the fore. Notably here, the jurisprudence of the ECJ has played an important and influential role in defining the parameters of this agenda.

Other initiatives such as common judicial training and exchange programmes have emerged as an important and necessary means of promoting knowledge and trust between national judicial authorities, meanwhile
the pursuit of closer operational cooperation between relevant national
authorities continues and, as we saw in Chapter 2, Eurojust plays an
increasingly important coordinating and problem-solving role in this
regard. These non-legislative governance approaches will be considered in
more detail towards the end of this chapter.

It will become clear from the unfolding discussion on both the legislative
and non-legislative dimensions of judicial cooperation that, while there is
no doubt that the EU's role and influence in the sphere of criminal law has
increased in recent years, the underpinning concept remains one of coordinating the various systems of criminal justice of the Member States
rather than the development of an autonomous EU system of criminal
justice *per se*.

BOX 4.1

This broad rationale persists in the Lisbon Reform Treaty which
enshrines the principle of mutual recognition in the formal legal
framework of the EU for the first time. Indeed the revisions to the
institutional and legal settlement contained in the Reform Treaty
will go some considerable way to resolving some of the legal competence concerns and accountability deficits that have pervaded
this field throughout its relatively short history.

LEGISLATIVE APPROACHES

Mutual Recognition

As we have seen, the heads of State and government of the 15 EU Member
States at Tampere in 1999 endorsed the principle of mutual recognition
(MR) as the 'cornerstone' of judicial cooperation in criminal matters. In
doing so they laid the methodological path for pursuing the Treaty's objective of achieving an area of freedom security and justice through 'closer
cooperation'. Consequently, traditional judicial cooperation, based on the
'request principle', said to be characterised by its slowness and unpre-
dictability, would be progressively replaced by cooperation based on the
concept of near automatic acceptance and enforcement of all judicial deci-

sions made during criminal proceedings taken in one Member State by the appropriate authorities in all others. This reflected what Wouters and Naert refer to as a 'genuine paradigm shift in legal cooperation between Member States'.[13] But, as we will see in more detail below, Member States have been reluctant to embrace the full implications of the principle of mutual recognition, thereby dampening its revolutionary impacts. An ambitious legislative programme was drawn up to give concrete expression and application of this principle listing no fewer than 24 measures covering aspects of all stages of the criminal procedure: recognition and enforcement of pre-trial orders, final criminal judgments, sentencing and post-sentencing follow-up judgments.[14] Some progress has been recorded in the form of the adoption of framework decisions on the EAW,[15] the mutual recognition of orders freezing assets,[16] the mutual recognition of financial penalties[17] and the execution of confiscation orders.[18] A framework decision on a European Evidence Warrant[19] (EEW) designed to facilitate the gathering and movement of pre-trial evidence in criminal cases throughout the Union has yet to be formally adopted (although a general approach was agreed in Council on 1–2 June 2006). The EEW, envisaged as a natural accompaniment to the EAW, has faced greater resistance from Member States throughout the negotiation process – due in part to concerns about the envisaged application and consequences of the principle of mutual recognition learned from the experience of the EAW[20] and in part to the current absence of a heightened security climate that might otherwise force Europe's leaders to transcend these concerns and reach unanimous agreement. There are currently draft framework decisions implementing mutual recognition in respect of convictions,[21] transfer of sentenced persons by way of a European Enforcement Order,[22] the recognition of non-custodial pre-trial supervision measures by way of a European Supervision Order[23] and the recognition and supervision of alternative sanctions and suspended sentences (i.e. probation).[24]

The principle of mutual recognition, with its fundamental emphasis upon non-interference with national systems of criminal justice, seemingly offered a useful and popular mechanism for proceeding in the highly sensitive field of criminal law cooperation. It would permit States, by and large, to retain their own national criminal justice systems and thereby reduce the need for more intrusive action on the part of the EU, namely, through the harmonisation of national laws. As Alegre points out, for many '[t]he principle of respecting and recognising the laws and legal systems of all of our European partners is somehow more palatable than the idea of some sort of Brussels-led harmonisation of the criminal law in Europe'.[25] However, contrary to the position sometimes expressed (by certain national governments[26]), it was never envisaged that endorsement of the principle of mutual recognition would wholly preclude instances of harmonisation. So, according to the conclusions of the Tampere European Council, 'enhanced mutual recognition of judicial decisions and judgments *and the necessary approximation of legislation* would facilitate cooperation between authorities and the judicial protection of individual rights'. Furthermore the Commission has said that 'the concept of mutual recognition goes hand-in-hand with a certain degree of standardisation of the way States do things' but also (somewhat confusingly) noting that '[o]n the other hand, mutual recognition can to some degree make standardisation unnecessary'.[27] In order to understand the nature of the relationship between mutual recognition and harmonisation more fully it is helpful to explore the non-legal concept that lies at the heart of mutual recognition – that of trust.

Mutual Trust

If, pursuant to the principle of mutual recognition the rule is that Member States *do* execute and enforce each others' decisions (unless they can invoke one of the limited exceptions laid down in the legal instrument) it follows that the principle is premised upon a sufficient degree of trust and confidence as between Member States vis-à-vis their criminal justice arrangements. Member States should have confidence in the rules of another legal system itself but also trust that these rules will be properly applied.[28] Such a prerequisite for mutual recognition was indeed acknowledged in the earliest policy documents from the European Council and the Commission in which it was said that trust is grounded, in particular, on Member States' 'shared commitment to the principles of freedom, democracy and respect for human rights, fundamental freedoms and the rule of law'.[29]

Notably, the ECJ formally endorsed the principle of mutual recognition and mutual trust in a series of cases concerning the interpretation of Article 54 of the 1990 Convention implementing the Schengen Agreement (CISA) which establishes a *ne bis in idem* or 'double jeopardy' principle.[30] In its *Gözütok and Brügge* ruling the Court held that the Article 54 CISA principle *implies* that the Member States have mutual trust in their criminal justice systems and that each of them recognises the criminal law in force in the other Member State even when the outcome would be different if its own national law were applied.[31] The ECJ is clear that the variations in practice and procedure of the Member States are irrelevant since nowhere in the legal texts governing this *ne bis in idem* principle is it made conditional upon harmonisation of the criminal laws of the Member States.[32] From this, it would appear that the ECJ has spelled out the logical consequences and practical implications of applying the principle of mutual recognition; not only does it rest upon an assumption of mutual trust, meaning that decisions of the issuing state are recognised and given effect within the legal system of the executing state, but also that an application of the principle does not strictly require any harmonisation of national criminal laws.

However, the assumption of a genuine mutual trust that lies at the heart of an effective mutual recognition principle has been questioned, which in turn has led to a debate around the need for a greater degree of harmonisation as a prerequisite to the principle in fact.[33] Some have expressed concerns that, particularly in light of the recent waves of enlargement which have brought many developing criminal justice systems into the EU fold, it is naïve and inadequate to pursue a cooperation agenda that assumes a high level of trust and confidence between the judges of these national systems. The main reason cited for a lack of mutual trust is a concern that fundamental rights and procedural safeguards for suspects in the criminal justice systems are not consistently and adequately protected throughout the Union, as evidenced, for example, by judgments against Member States in the ECtHR, some even arguing that the principle of mutual recognition can actively lead to a diminution of rights protection.[34]

These concerns have prompted a more direct strategy *actively* to *promote* mutual trust from the political institutions. The Hague Programme which was the follow-up European Council document from Tampere, reinforced the centrality of the principle of mutual recognition to the criminal justice agenda of the EU but also formally linked its development to the enhancement of mutual trust between the Member States. Giving effect to the Hague Programme, the 2005 Commission Communication on Mutual Recognition[35] stated explicitly that 'reinforcing mutual trust is the key to making mutual recognition operate smoothly'. It anticipated that this could be achieved through a combination of *legislative* and *non-legislative* means. Concentrating here on the legislative dimension, the Commission envisaged that mutual trust might be enhanced through the approximation of substantive *and* procedural law *where necessary*. This was to revolve around two axes: ensuring that mutually recognised judgments meet high standards in terms of securing personal rights and also ensuring that the courts giving the judgments really were the best placed to do so. Progress on each of these 'axes' is considered later in this chapter, but suffice to note that each of them is linked to creating the conditions for a smoother application of the principle of mutual recognition. So, while the principle of mutual recognition does not strictly require harmonisation of national law, as confirmed by the ECJ, it is argued that some harmonisation is desirable to create the conditions of trust and confidence that underpin an effective application of that principle.

Mutual Recognition Instruments

As we saw above, an ambitious legislative programme to activate the principle of mutual recognition at various stages of the criminal process has
been put forward.[36] However, it should be noted that the precise nature of
mutual recognition varies from one framework decision to the next, according to their specific scope and purpose. Therefore there may well be distinctions in the procedural mechanisms and stipulated deadlines set by the
individual instruments as well as, for instance, distinctions in the grounds
for refusing recognition. Fichera and Janssens explain that 'mutual recognition is not a "one size fits all" instrument but rather a flexible tool that
needs to adapt itself, case by case, to the concrete needs of each new instrument'.[37] Space does not permit us to recount the individual features of each
of the mutual recognition instruments adopted to date. We therefore intend
to focus upon the first instrument that implemented this new core principle
of criminal justice cooperation: the EAW.[38] While subsequent instruments
necessarily vary the precise scope of the mutual recognition principle, this
legal instrument broadly set out a blueprint that would be replicated later.
As the first mutual recognition instrument to be adopted, implemented and
indeed evaluated, it also makes sense to use this instrument as a kind of
case-study on the mutual recognition principle.

The European Arrest Warrant

Adopted hastily following the terrorist attacks of 11 September 2001, the
framework decision on the EAW was intended to replace traditional extradition procedures with a simplified and expedited procedure for 'surrender'
of persons convicted or accused of crimes between the EU Member States.
Article 1 of the EAW defines 'European arrest warrant' as any judicial decision issued by a Member State ('issuing State') with a view to the arrest or
surrender by another Member State ('executing State') of a requested
person, for the purposes of conducting a criminal prosecution or executing
a custodial sentence or detention order. It goes on, 'Member States shall
execute any EAW on the basis of the principle of mutual recognition and
in accordance with the provisions of the framework decision.' Therefore,
the request from the issuing state is effectively taken on trust by the executing state, which may only refuse to enforce the arrest warrant in limited circumstances (as will be outlined below.) In a standard case, the EAW is sent
directly from the *judicial* authority of the issuing State to its counterpart in
the executing State, without the involvement of any diplomatic or political
intermediaries.[39] The depoliticisation of the process is one of the notable
features of the EAW compared to the previous extradition procedures and,

combined with the imposition of strict time-limits[40] on the executing State, the framework decision ensures easier and speedier surrender of suspects and criminals between EU States. One high-profile example of the EAW in practice concerned the surrender of Hussain Osman, one of the suspects in the July 2004 London bombings, who was sent back from Italy to the UK in a matter of weeks following the issue of an arrest warrant by the UK authorities. This case concerned suspected involvement in terrorist offences and, while it is easy to associate the EAW with the fight against terrorism, (especially given its expedited adoption immediately following the 9-11 terrorist events in the US), the material scope of the framework decision is in fact much broader than that. An EAW can be issued in respect of any criminal offence punishable under the criminal laws of the issuing State by a period of imprisonment of at least 12 months or, where a sentence has already been passed, at least four months.[41]

One of the central and groundbreaking features of the EAW procedure is the extent to which it limits the grounds for refusal of surrender as compared with the traditional extradition procedure. There are just three mandatory grounds for non-execution contained in the framework decision at Article 3: the existence of an amnesty in the executing State, where *ne bis in idem* applies to a final judgment in a Member State and where the suspect is a minor and cannot be held criminally responsible in the executing State. In addition to the mandatory grounds for non-execution there are eight 'optional' (i.e. voluntary) grounds for non-execution listed in Article 4, for instance where there is a pending prosecution in the executing Member State for the same acts, where the requested person is a national or resident of the executing Member State and that state agrees to enforce the sentence already passed against them and in certain instances of extraterritoriality. It is worth noting that the voluntary and mandatory reasons for refusal are voluntary or mandatory from the point of view of EU law. However, it is entirely possible that constitutional rules implementing the EAW in the Member States will render the voluntary reasons mandatory in the national context.[42]

Next, surrender *may* be made subject to one of three conditions listed in Article 5. First, if the sentence had been passed against the individual *in absentia* and they had not been summoned to the trial or otherwise informed of the trial, she or he must have an opportunity to apply for retrial. Second, where a life sentence could be imposed for the crime in question, the issuing State may be requested to guarantee that the sentence must be reviewable after 20 years at the latest. And lastly, the surrender of nationals and residents of the executing Member State may be subject to the condition that the suspect is returned to the executing state after trial to serve there any custodial sentence imposed.

Articles 3, 4 and 5 EAW therefore attempt to define a limited set of exemptions from and conditions to the application of mutual recognition. The very existence of these bars to surrender in the legislation highlights that the application of the principle of mutual recognition, while quasi-automatic, is not completely unfettered. By analogy with the principle in the field of the internal market whence it originates, it is most accurately and usefully understood as a governance tool or a methodological device that requires certain prerequisites and whose application is made subject to certain limitations or stipulated conditions.[43] While the prerequisites, exceptions and conditions may differ in the context of criminal law (logic-ally necessitated by the fundamentally differing objects and purpose of mutual recognition in criminal law as compared to the internal market) the fact remains that mutual recognition in each context is 'managed'.[44] However, as we will see further below, there has been a reluctance on the part of certain national legislatures to remain within the agreed and stipulated confines of management of the mutual recognition principle. Many have gone beyond the contours of the permissible conditions and exceptions outlined above when implementing the framework decision.

Controversy at the national level has been fuelled to some considerable extent by two features of the EAW, both of which fundamentally tip the balance of power in favour of the issuing State and away from the execut-ing State in the revised system of handing over suspected or convicted persons to other EU jurisdictions: these are, the partial abolition of the principle of double criminality and the almost complete abolition of the nationality exception as grounds for refusal to surrender.

First, and perhaps most controversially, Article 2(2) of the Framework Decision abolishes the principle of double criminality[45] in respect of 32 listed offences. In respect of these offences, as long as they are punishable in the issuing State by at least a three-year custodial sentence, EAWs must be enforced by the executing state even if the latter does not consider the act in question a criminal offence. Double criminality may still be, and often is, required for non-listed offences and for listed offences that fall below the three-year threshold. At the conceptual level, the abolition of this double criminality check for certain serious offences is a logical application of the principle of mutual recognition within a single area of criminal justice. On the basis that Member States share a sufficiently common approach towards basic elements of criminality such that there is a 'high level of confidence between Member States',[46] any differences in approach that do exist vis-à-vis this list of more serious crimes should not be an obstacle to judicial cooperation. However, playing down the logic of mutual recognition, various objections have arisen in response to this development, prompting calls for a review of the double criminality list and even for it to be limited to offences that the EU has already harmonised (e.g. terrorism, trafficking in human beings) or is intending to harmonise.[47] Concerns largely stem from the inroads that this development makes to the state's sovereign right to decide upon what acts should be criminalised in national law. In respect of certain offences there are quite considerable differences of approach across national jurisdictions which are likely to be strongly justified and defended according to specific national traditions of criminal justice (e.g. abortion, euthanasia, blasphemy, possession of drugs). With respect to these acts in particular, the removal of the double criminality check is remarkably sensitive, since it may lead to a situation where a State is required to surrender an own national to another jurisdiction to face trial for an offence which it does not itself criminalise.[48] Criticisms have also been levelled at the Article 2(2) list for being overly generic and imprecise. While this is not the case in respect of some of the more serious offences listed – all Member States can be expected to recognise a crime of 'murder', 'grievous bodily injury', 'rape' and 'arson' (even if such crimes do not reflect an EU interest *per se*) – other listed offences are unclear in that they are simply not recognisable as offences under their current label (e.g. 'swindling') or vague in that they may encompass more than one criminal act ('computer-related offences').[49] Could it be, then, that Article 2(2) offends the principle of the legality of criminal offences and penalties (*nullum crimen, nulla poena sine lege*) because it deprives individuals of knowing precisely whether acts they have committed constitute a criminal offence and, if so, what penalties attach thereto? Such a claim was in fact one of several made before the ECJ challenging the validity of the EAW in the case of *Advocaten voor de Wereld*.[50] The ECJ, however, rejected such a claim on the basis that the EAW does not seek to harmonise the constituent elements of the criminal offences in question.[51] Rather, as stipulated in Article 2(2), it enables surrender for certain listed offences without verification of the double criminality of the act if they attract certain punishments in the issuing Member State '*and as they are defined by the law of the issuing State*'.[52] Since the definition of offences and applicable penalties continue to be matters determined by the law of the issuing State, compliance with the principle of legality falls to the Member States, who themselves are obliged to comply with fundamental rights as a matter of EU law (Article 6 EU and Article 1(3) EAW).[53]

The second key aspect of the EAW that merits attention concerns its treatment of the traditional right for states to refuse to extradite their own nationals. A prominent and long-time feature of European extradition law, favoured by civil law systems, the nationality exception has been all but abolished by the EAW.[54] The basic position advocated by the framework decision is that Member States cannot refuse to surrender to another Member State one of their own citizens who is suspected of having committed a serious crime, on grounds that they are own nationals. In a single area of criminal justice built upon shared values and hence mutual confidence and trust, all criminal suspects should be treated equally, regardless of geographical location and nationality. However, some 'remnants of this age-old privelege remain'.[55] Most notably, nationality can constitute an optional ground for refusal to execute an EAW in circumstances where the executing State undertakes to enforce a previously issued sentence itself and an executing State may make surrender of an own national conditional upon return of that individual so that any sentence may be served locally.[56] Deen-Racsmàny and Blekxtoon show how the retention of these nationality rules, when combined with the simultaneous waiver of the double criminality requirement, could lead to serious 'loopholes' in practice.[57] For instance, a State could be in a position where it has agreed to enforce a sentence that has been imposed upon one of its nationals by another State, but the acts that served as a basis of the conviction do not constitute a criminal offence there. In such a situation, would or could the Member State release the individual immediately? Perhaps unsurprisingly, many States, in transposing the EAW have taken full advantage of the 'remnants' of the nationality exception contained in it. More seriously, some have even retained the exception in full defiance of the framework decision and some have been faced with litigation on this issue in their national constitutional courts, as will be discussed in more detail below. Suffice to say here that the nationality exception in modern EU 'extradition' remains conspicuously prominent.

Implementation and Evaluation of the EAW

It perhaps comes as no surprise, given the controversies surrounding some of the features of the EAW, that there would be problems with its implementation and application in national legal systems. Just in terms of *timeliness*, Italy became the last of the then 25 Member States to adopt implementing legislation, some 16 months after the expiry of the stipulated deadline (31 December 2003).[58] It will be recalled that, in the event of an analogous situation under the Community pillar, Italy could have been the subject of infringement proceedings brought by the Commission. However, since there is no such legal and judicial enforcement mechanism in the third pillar, this was/is not possible. Indeed, Article 35(7) EU is also unlikely as a route of judicial enforcement as it entails a formal complaint by one Member State against another, something which happens rarely in practice. Instead, national compliance of this (and other third pillar) legal measure(s) is encouraged and monitored by political means. The Commission has, to date, undertaken an annual evaluation exercise at the initial behest of Article 34 EAW and then the JHA Council,[59] and the Member States are also committed to a process of mutual evaluation (peer review) with which the Commission is fully involved. Additionally, there is an ongoing project in the Council to collect and analyse EAW data based upon a standard questionnaire to be completed by Member States. So what have these monitoring and evaluation mechanisms revealed to date about the *effectiveness* of national implementation and practical application of the EAW?

The initial Commission EAW evaluation report was published in February 2005,[60] but a revised version was produced in January 2006,[61] following Italy's belated implementation of the framework decision. These 'early' and 'provisional' reports conclude that the EAW has been an 'overall success' despite the delay in implementation. Thanks to the entirely judicial procedure, the single form and strict time limits, the Commission suggested that the average time to execute a warrant had fallen from more than nine months to 43 days.[62] From the period January to September 2004, 2603 warrants were issued, 653 persons arrested and 104 persons surrendered. It concluded that 'its impact is positive, since available indicators as regards judicial control, effectiveness and speed are favourable, while fundamental rights are observed'. These general and positive findings were also confirmed in the 2007 Commission report,[63] which confirmed that the EAW is used as a matter of course in all 27 Member States. The report indicates that the use of the EAW has grown year by year: 'For the whole of 2005, nearly 6900 warrants were issued by the 23 Member States that sent in figures (excluding Belgium and Germany), twice as many as in 2004. In over 1770 cases, the person wanted was traced and arrested. Unofficial figures for 2006 confirm this upward trend from year to year.'

However, while one cannot deny the positive impact of the EAW in terms of improved efficiency of judicial enforcement, ensuring that more suspects and criminals are quickly surrendered across borders to face justice, the Commission reports have also highlighted significant gaps in effective and full compliance of the framework decision by the Member States. The list of the types of measures that do not comply with the framework decision is long: the reintroduction of double criminality checks in respect of some or all of the 32 categories of offence, restrictions on the surrender of nationals, the designation of an executive rather than judicial authority as competent to deal with EAWs, restriction on the transitional application of the EAW, the alteration and even the addition of grounds for mandatory non-execution, the imposition of additional conditions and administrative requirements for the transmission of EAWs and the failure to apply the stipulated time limits for judicial decisions and appeals. And, to make matters worse, this kind of behaviour is widespread. The Commission listed 12 Member States, including the UK, as the worst offenders in terms of compliance with the EAW. One particularly prominent practice has been the insertion of a human rights exemption/bar to surrender clause in national legislation despite the absence of any explicit provision in the framework decision sanctioning such behaviour. This practice and the debates surrounding mutual recognition and human rights will be examined in more detail below.

Much of this evidence points to the conclusion that many national legislatures have acted in a manner that is incompatible with the terms of the framework decision. Moreover, their behaviour is incompatible with the *spirit* of the framework decision in that it evidences and perpetuates a degree of mutual *distrust* among the Member States. This in turn undermines the very *raison d'être* of the EAW, namely, to secure cooperation on the basis of mutual recognition.[64] National legislatures appear reluctant to embrace fully the principle of mutual recognition in practice and therefore have resorted to behaviour reminiscent of the traditional approach to international cooperation in criminal matters, namely, the protection of national control and interests.

A further example of unhelpful political meddling in the application of the EAW occurred recently, when the Portuguese presidency responded to concerns that the EAW procedure was being used for crimes perceived as minor, such as the theft of a piglet or possession of three ecstasy tablets. Although these offences fall squarely within the legal scope of the framework decision, it had been questioned whether surrender pursuant to an EAW was really proportionate to the objectives of the framework decision. In short, the significant costs involved in surrendering a suspect to a foreign jurisdiction for such 'minor' offences should be weighed in the balance by the national authorities when deciding whether to issue a EAW. The Portuguese presidency therefore suggested that the principle of proportionality, as a general principle of EU law, should be applied by the authorities of the issuing state in determining whether an EAW would be an appropriate course of action.[65] This suggestion should be buried, for several reasons. Although one can see that the deployment of significant resources by the authorities of one State for the purposes of handing over a suspect to another State to face trial for the theft of a piglet might raise some eyebrows, the effect of inserting a proportionality test could very well mean that a person could escape arrest and therefore prosecution *altogether*, simply because she or he has exercised their right to move to another Member State. This would completely undermine the objective of the EAW which is precisely to facilitate the prosecution of crime across national borders on the basis of mutual recognition of judicial decisions, as if the EU constituted a single judicial area, so that a wanted person is treated in the same way irrespective of her or his location in the EU territory. Moreover, there is an important point of principle at stake here. If it is agreed that theft is a crime for which an accused should be tried and, if guilty, punished, it should not affect the decision to prosecute the fact that the thing stolen was of low monetary value.[66] Likewise, if it has been agreed that surrender for the purposes of prosecution should apply to all crimes that meet a particular punishment threshold in the issuing State and that threshold is met, perceptions of triviality or the estimated administrative costs involved in the executing state should not interfere with the initial decision to issue a warrant.

Judicial Challenges

What then of the response of national judiciaries to the EAW, the very institutions which were entrusted to effect the principle of mutual recognition? In fact, the response appears to have been mixed. To be sure, in certain Member States implementation of the framework decision has raised real constitutional concerns. Resistance to the EAW, or at least to obligations arising from the framework decision on the grounds that they are incompatible with certain constitutionally protected rights, have resulted in various clashes in the national constitutional courts. To date, three national courts have declared the implementation of the EAW unconstitutional for not respecting the limitation or prohibition of the extradition of nationals.[67]

On 27 April 2005, the Polish Constitutional Court annulled the provision of national law (adopted specifically to implement the EAW) authorising surrender of Polish nationals on the grounds that it conflicted with the Constitution.[68] As a result, the Polish Constitution was revised to bring it into line with European obligations pursuant to the EAW, and the Polish Code of Criminal Procedure was amended. The Constitutional Court had suspended the application of the ruling to allow these amendments to take place without disturbing the system of surrender. Several months after this ruling the German *Bundesverfassungsgericht* annulled the entire German law implementing the EAW because it did not adequately protect German citizens' fundamental rights as enshrined in the national Constitution.[69] More precisely, it ruled that the German legislator had not exercised its competences within the margin of appreciation left by the EAW in a manner congruent with the German *Grundgesetz*. The national legislation was annulled with immediate effect, with no account being taken of the legal and practical consequences of such an action at the EU level.[70] So, from 18 July 2005 until 2 August 2006, the date on which the new German implementing measure was adopted, Germany was technically in breach of its EU law obligations and surrender to and from Germany of suspects and criminals pursuant to the EAW was not possible. A confusing situation arose whereby requests for the surrender of non-German nationals would be treated as requests for extradition pursuant to the pre-existing Conventions and yet Germany continued to issue EAWs for other Member States. Moreover, in response to Germany's position, the Spanish and Hungarian authorities, on the grounds that Germany was no longer acting on the basis of mutual trust, invoked the principle of reciprocity and rejected any EAW requests from Germany. Later, in 2005, the supreme court of a third state, Cyprus, also annulled the national implementing law on the ground that the surrender of nationals was unconstitutional.[71]

A challenge to the EAW itself came before the ECJ in the form of a preliminary reference from the Belgian Cour d'Arbitrage. In *Advocaten voor de Wereld*,[72] the Court had been asked to rule upon the compatibility of the EAW with the EU Treaty on both procedural and substantive grounds. Procedurally, the appropriateness of the legal basis of the framework decision (Article 34(2)(b) EU) was called into question. In particular the referring court questioned whether a framework decision was the appropriate instrument bearing in mind the fact that framework decisions were to be adopted 'only for the purpose of the approximation of the laws and regulations of the Member States'. Advocaten voor de Wereld argued that, since the EAW was not adopted for this purpose, the appropriate instrument was a convention. In terms of the substance, the Belgian court asked whether the abolition of the double criminality requirement for certain offences contained in Article 2(2) was compatible with Article 6(2) EU, and more specifically with the principles of legality in criminal proceedings and the principle of equality and non-discrimination. The Grand Chamber of the ECJ in its judgment of 3 May 2007 upheld the validity of the EAW on all counts and in doing so validated one of the most controversial pieces of EU or EC legislation ever adopted. The ECJ was able to do this by reading and interpreting the framework decision through the prism of its underpinning methodology – mutual recognition.

Addressing the first question, the Court confirmed that the Council is empowered to choose which instrument to adopt in order to regulate a particular subject matter, subject to the limits imposed by the nature of the instrument and where the conditions governing the adoption of such a measure are satisfied. It also clarified that approximation of national laws as a methodological approach to securing common action as defined in Article 31 EU could not be restricted to defining the substantive elements of certain crimes as a literal reading of the Treaty would suggest. At paragraph 29 the Court was explicit about the relationship between mutual recognition and approximation:

> *The mutual recognition of the arrest warrants issued in the different Member States in accordance with the laws of the issuing State concerned requires the approximation of the laws and regulations of the Member States with regard to the cooperation in criminal matters and, more sepcifically, of the rules relating to the conditions, procedures and effects of surrender as between national authorities.*

The ECJ then listed numerous provisions of the framework decision that were precisely intended to have an approximating effect, including Article 2(2) on double criminality and Articles 3 and 4 on the grounds of non-execution. In those circumstances, a framework decision is an appropriate instrument to regulate the EAW field, a conclusion not invalidated by the fact that such a field had previously been governed by international conventions.

Concerning the question of whether the abolition of double criminality breaches the the principle of legality in criminal matters, the Court confirmed that both this principle and the principle of equality and non-discrimination constitute general principles of Community law binding upon EU institutions and Member States alike in accordance with Article 6 EU and, notably, '*reaffirmed in . . . the Charter of Fundamental Rights of the European Union*'.[73] As we saw above, the ECJ argued that Article 2(2) of the framework decision cannot be found to infringe the principle of legality since the duty of compliance with this principle necessarily falls to the Member States who remain responsible for defining the offences and the applicable penalties based on the categories of offence set out in Article 2(2).

Finally, on the question of equality and non-discrimination, the Court rejected the argument advanced by Advocaaten Voor De Wereld that the removal of verification of double criminality for 32 categories of offence in Article 2(2) EAW gives rise to an unjustified difference in treatment as between individuals depending on whether the facts alleged to constitute the offence are or are not on the list.[74] Those individuals, it argued, would thus be judged differently with regard to the deprivation of their liberty.[75] Without deciding whether the situation of such persons is comparable, thereby necessiting similar treatment, the ECJ claims that the 'distinction is, in any event, objectively justified'.[76] With regard to the 32 listed categories of offence

> *. . . the Council was able to form the view, on the basis of the principle of mutual recognition and in the light of the high degree of trust and solidarity between Member States, that, whether by reason of their inherent nature or by reason of the*

punishment incurred of a maximum of at least three years, the categories of offence in question feature among those the seriousness of which in terms of adversely affecting public order and safety justifies dispensing with the verification of double criminality.[77]

The Court makes short shrift of the argument that the lack of precision in the definition of the categories of offence in Article 2(2) gives rise to a risk of disparate implementation, thereby compounding the equality and discrimination problem. It points out that it is not the objective of the Treaty to harmonise the substantive criminal law of the Member States and that '*nothing in Title VI of the EU Treaty . . . makes the application of the European arrest warant conditional on harmonisation of the criminal laws of the Member States within the area of the offences in question*'.[78]

Accordingly, the ECJ held that Article 2(2) EAW is not invalid as it does not breach Article 6(2) EU.

Of course, in some Member States, the EAW does not raise major constitutional concerns at all; that is the case for the UK, for example. Interestingly, only two EAW cases have thus far reached the House of Lords and in both cases the UK court adopted a purposive reading of provisions of the Extradition Act 2003 (which concerned procedural conditionalities over and above those strictly provided for in the EAW) in order to implement the spirit and requirements of the framework decision.[79] In neither case did the court refuse to execute the arrest warrants. These cases hold out some hope that the erroneous provisions of the Extradition Act and other implementing acts will be 'corrected' by national judges through the principle of conform interpretation, which the ECJ explicitly extended to the EU's third pillar in its *Pupino* judgment.[80] By way of conclusion to this section, it can be said that the judicial responses to the EAW and implementing legislation vary from state to state. Even where similar questions are raised as to the compatibility of the EAW implementing laws with constitutional guarantees, different courts have adopted different approaches to cooperating with the EAW approach.[81]

EAW: Mutual Recognition and the Protection of Human Rights

Attention now shifts squarely to the relationship between human rights and mutual recognition. Why and how should rights be secured in an EU criminal justice system based upon the mutual recognition of criminal decisions? In addressing these questions, we will highlight the situation as regards the EAW once again, although much of what follows concerns rights and the third pillar in general.

Few would deny the central importance of safeguarding procedural guarantees in any system of criminal justice. 'Criminal proceedings are an area where vital interests of society and of the individual collide.'[82] In order to ensure a balance between the two, and to ensure that a just outcome is achieved, the law has recognised certain procedural guarantees that must be afforded to the individual suspect by the State as long as he or she is formally suspected of having committed a criminal act. Most fundamental of the rights afforded to suspects are perhaps the right to be presumed innocent and the right to a fair trial, both of which have a long history and are enshrined in international human rights treaties such as the International Covenant on Civil and Political Rights, the American Convention on Human Rights and, most pertinently for our purposes, Article 6 ECHR.

Of course, the EU, though not a signatory to the ECHR, is committed to respecting its contents since human rights protection constitutes a general principle of EC and EU law.[83] The EU Charter of Fundamental Rights[84] also contains guarantees pertaining to criminal proceedings,[85] and, while it is not at present a legally binding document,[86] the ECJ has explicitly referred to it in its *Advocaten* judgment.[87] At the political level, EU leaders have consistently expressed the central baseline of individual rights protection in pursuing greater judicial cooperation in criminal matters: 'If serious criminal conduct receives an equivalent response and procedural guarantees are comparable throughout the Union, the possibilities of improving coordination of prosecution, whenever greater efficiency can be reconciled with respect for individual rights, must be examined.'[88]

With this political and legal framework in mind, the pertinent question becomes, within the confines of an emerging transnational EU criminal justice system, *how best* to secure such rights. When and how are rights to be secured in the context of a cooperation based upon the principle of mutual recognition? At what level and stage of proceedings should rights be identified and enforced?

According to the logic of mutual recognition, the strict answer to this question is that rights should be protected and defended *in the first state*; i.e. the state that has issued a warrant or other judicial decision. This is because mutual recognition demands that national judicial authorities incorporate and apply decisions delivered in another jurisdiction with the minimum of fuss and questioning, taking on trust that the procedures applied or to be applied in the issuing state are human rights-compliant. As we saw above, such trust between national authorities is said to be based upon the common values and shared commitment to human right protection across the entire EU, as demonstrated by the state's formal commitments pursuant to the ECHR. Where a Member State does breach its human rights obligations, it is for the violating State to remedy the situation, with the ultimate possibility that an individual can bring the State before the ECtHR. It is on the basis of this reasoning that there is no specific reference to human rights as a ground for refusal to execute an EAW in the framework decision.

However, this logic has been questioned. Leaf and van Ballegooij argue that '[t]he European Commission's interpretation of mutual recognition in terms of "issuing state control" is flawed to the extent that it requires executing judicial authorities to relinquish their responsibility to ensure that fundamental rights are protected'.[89] In the context of the EAW, it is argued that, despite the absence of any provision for refusing or conditioning surrender of an individual on human rights grounds in the text of the framework decision, a broad reading of other provisions that refer to rights protection (Article 1(3) and the 12th and 13th recitals of the preamble to the framework decision) empowers national legislatures and national judicial authorities to do just that.[90] Consequently, in the UK, as in almost all Member States, the legislation implementing the EAW includes a human rights safeguard. Section 21 of the UK Extradition Act 2003, for example, obliges national judges to consider 'whether the person's extradition would be compatible with the Convention rights within the meaning of the Human Rights Act 1998'. Where it is deemed incompatible the person must be discharged.

A handful of national extradition cases, heard prior to the entry into force of the EAW, have been widely cited in support of retaining a human rights check in the executing Member State under the EAW regime.[91] In *ex parte Ramda*[92] the English High Court held that extradition of Ramda, who was wanted for trial in France, accused of involvement in the Paris Metro bombings in 1995, would be incompatible with the right to a fair trial as contained in Article 6 ECHR. There was deemed to be a real risk that a fair trial would be denied to Ramda if extradited to France since allegations that incriminating evidence against him had been obtained through torture would not be considered in the substantive trial against him. To the extent that this case evidences the continued occurrence or risk of serious human rights violations within the territory of the EU, it is of course, worrying. And there is no doubt that it reflects and perpetuates a lack of trust and confidence as between national criminal justice systems, which in turn makes cooperation on the basis of mutual recognition, as described above, difficult to swallow in practice.[93] However, we would argue that reading a human rights exception into the EAW is not an *appropriate* or in fact an *effective* response: a more appropriate response would be to secure common rights standards at the EU level, which will be discussed below.

In support of reading a human rights exception into the EAW, the limited extradition jurisprudence of the ECtHR has been relied on. In the *Soering* case,[94] the Strasbourg court established for the first time that extradition proceedings *per se* constitute a risk of violation of the Convention and, consequently, that the ECHR applied to them. Although *Soering* concerned a breach of Article 3 ECHR, the Court also said that it could 'not *exclude that an issue might exceptionally be raised under Article 6 [. . .] by an extradition decision in circumstances where the fugitive has suffered or risks suffering a* flagrant *denial of a fair trial in the requesting country'*.[95] The applicability of the *Soering* principle to Article 6 ECHR was confirmed in *Mamatkulov*.[96] So, the argument goes, if Article 6 ECHR is capable of being engaged in extradition proceedings, albeit in limited circumstances, it must also be capable of being engaged in EAW proceedings within the EU. However, a closer analysis of the ECtHR caselaw on extradition reveals that, with respect to the situation of the EU and the development of the AFSJ, it would be extremely difficult, nigh on impossible, for an EU Member State to be found in violation of its ECHR obligations by a decision to surrender an individual to another Member State. Both *Soering* and *Mamatkulov* concerned extradition to non-parties to the Convention (USA and Uzbekistan, respectively) and the former case concerned risk of the death penalty being imposed, something which could clearly not happen in the EU, where capital punishment is absolutely prohibited. In the case of *Chamaïev*,[97] which did concern extradition to a state party, Russia, and in particular to the federal state of Chechnya, the Court ruled that execution of the decision to extradite would be in violation of Article 3. The Court found that, since the decision had been made, so many facts had come to light regarding the situation in that part of Russia that the execution of the decision, without a substantial reconsideration of the circumstances, would put Georgia in violation of its Convention obligations.[98] Here, a massive amount of information was relied on by the ECtHR (international reporting from organisations such as the Council of Europe, Amnesty International, the Helsinki Committee, etc.) to enable it to find that Georgia, if it executed the extradition decision, could be said objectively to know that the applicant faces a real risk of treatment contrary to Article 3. This is to be compared with the decisions regarding the other applicants in this case in respect of whom the extradition decisions had already been executed and where the Court found that it could not be said that Georgia should have been aware of any risks such as to put it in violation of its Convention obligations.

Now, it is difficult to imagine one or several EU Member States descending into a situation comparable to Chechnya without the EU either collapsing or suspending the concerned Member States in accordance with the Article 7 EU sanctioning procedure for human rights violations by EU Member States. With the exception of capital punishment, the level of violation known to the requested State required for there to be a violation of

Article 3 ECHR by virtue of an extradition decision seems more severe than the 'serious and persistent breach' required for the activation of the suspension procedure in Article 7(2) TEU. This is emphasized by the fact that the ECtHR would seem to require a 'flagrant'[99] violation of fair trial rights in order for an extradition decision to be in violation of Article 6 ECHR, whereas the Article 7 TEU standard of 'serious and persistent' applies equally with respect to all the principles mentioned in Article 6 TEU. It appears obvious from the very high threshold imposed by the ECtHR that it does not want the states party to the ECHR to use extradition proceedings as an excuse to pass judgment on the systems of criminal justice in requesting states. Although the violation of the Convention resulting from the extradition decision is completely independent from an eventual substantive violation in the requesting state resulting from the consequent criminal proceedings,[100] violations in general must be rampant and well documented so as to make it unlikely, appreciated from the objective and reasonable position of the executing state, that the suspect will *not* suffer similar treatment upon surrender. In the absence of such compelling objective evidence in the EU, any refusal to surrender on human rights grounds in the EU is likely to constitute little more than a value judgment about the national procedures of other Member States, with little deference to the fact that foreign procedures may contain different but equivalent procedural safeguards. Moreover, asserting rights at the level of exception may be carried out disparately across Member States with the genuine possibility that more diligence will be paid when a case involves the surrender of an own national. One might deduce from this that the inclusion of a human rights exception in national legislation implementing the EAW is less about the protection of individual rights stemming from a genuine and real concern about the procedural standards of other Member States and more about asserting some kind of national 'moral highground' or at least preserving national autonomy to decide where and where not to surrender suspected persons.

Harmonising Criminal Procedures: the Procedural Safeguards Framework Decision (RIP)

So, if mutual recognition instruments never intended rights to be protected and enforced at the level of exception by the executing state, and if our argument concerning the ECHR extradition cases above is correct, how else might the procedural rights of individuals caught up in the cross-border criminal disputes be secured by the EU? Should the EU do more than confer certain basic procedural rights and a provision expressing broad commitment to respecting fundamental rights in each mutual recognition instrument, as it did in the EAW?[101] The answer to this latter question is probably 'yes' and the reason is linked directly to the choice to secure judicial cooperation in criminal matters in the EU through the mechanism of mutual recognition. Indeed, following the endorsement of the principle of mutual recognition the Commission made the case for common EU action to protect the procedural rights of suspects and defendants as 'the logical counterbalance to other mutual recognition measures'.[102] In the spring of 2004 a Proposal for a Framework Decision on certain procedural rights applying in proceedings in criminal matters throughout the European Union (FDPR) was published.[103] The Commission argues convincingly that common procedural safeguards are a necessary corollary to a criminal justice system that largely operates on the basis of mutual recognition. If the EAW is directed towards ensuring more effective action against national and transnational offending (i.e. the repressive elements of criminal justice), the FDPR is directed towards ensuring that the rights of those affected by this greater efficiency are properly secured.[104] Common standards would help to secure greater trust between authorities of different criminal jurisdictions within the EU and thereby secure a more effective application of the principle of mutual recognition. As Peers succinctly summarises, 'in the absence of harmonized procedural rights . . . the "free movement of prosecutions and sentences" could arguably lead to the violation of the right to a fair trial'.[105] At a general level, the protection of human rights in the context of criminal proceedings is an important 'measure of a society's civilisation'.[106] Criminal procedures can therefore both reflect and influence the *identity* of the emerging EU system of criminal justice – giving it a more human and legitimate face.[107] Moreover, the approach of securing a *common* set of rights for all suspects and defendants upholds the principle that 'all are equal before the law', something which cannot be said of the approach of securing rights at the level of exception as discussed above.

However, despite all of this justification, substantial political backing by the EU's leaders in the Hague Programme and the Commission's best efforts, a framework decision addressing these issues has not been adopted, prompting continued concern that the criminal justice of the EU is currently too heavily biased towards securing efficiency of prosecution. But if it was broadly agreed that the harmonisation of minimal procedural rights is desirable, why then the delay in progress, the convoluted, protracted negotiations and the ultimate abandoning of the proposal?

In fact, the problem was largely one of feasibility, not desirability. In the language of EU law, it was a problem of legal competence and acting within the confines of limited powers conferred. In the absence of any obvious legal basis in the Treaty for EU action in the field of procedural rights, the Commission, in its 2003 Green Paper, appealed to the logic of implied competences. With reference to the broad commitments to securing defence rights and fair proceedings in the high-level political 'scoping documents' of the AFSJ agenda, and with reference to securing the effective operation of the mutual recognition principle, the Commission put forward Article 31(1)(c) EU as an appropriate legal basis for the adoption of the FDPR. This provision, as will be recalled, empowers the EU to take 'common action' in the realm of judicial cooperation in criminal matters to ensure the compatibility of rules applicable in the Member States 'as may be *necessary* to improve such cooperation'.[108] It is not therefore a *carte blanche* for the EU to legislate in the field of national criminal procedures but a broad reading of this provision could, according to the Commission, provide a legal basis for some limited approximation of procedural law. Indeed, the Council Secretariat and most Member States were willing so to construe Article 31(1)(c) EU. However, certain Member States – Ireland, Austria, Czech Republic, Slovak Republic, Denmark and Malta – remained unconvinced.[109] The extent to which legal basis concerns may have been a convenient 'cover', masking a deeper reticence on the part of Member States to allow the EU to interfere in their national criminal procedural regimes and hence limit their sovereignty over such matters, remains a matter for speculation. The fact remained that not all national governments were willing to accept Article 31(1)(c) EU as an appropriate legal basis and therefore a unanimous vote in favour of the FDPR was always out of reach.

As to the rights selected by the Commission to be contained in the FDPR, the original proposal submitted on 3 May 2004 contained the following: access to legal advice, free access to interpretation and translation, special protection for particularly vulnerable suspects, the right to communicate (including consular assistance for foreign suspects) and the duty of the state to provide a written notification of rights (the 'Letter of Rights'). However, methodological concerns have been raised concerning the Commission's selection of rights, bearing in mind its justifications for staking a competence claim for the measure which, in essence, was to secure mutual trust as a prerequisite for the implementation of the principle of mutual recognition.[110] If, as the Commission argues, harmonisation of criminal procedural law is a *necessary* component of achieving mutual recognition (to the extent that it can realise and legitimise the underpinning basis of mutual trust), it must ensure that its proposals are both guided and limited by this position. The challenge therefore becomes one of identifying clearly, ideally on the basis of solid empirical evidence, those disparate national procedural rules which are actively hindering judicial cooperation and the operation of the principle of mutual recognition.[111] Only

where this can be done should there be interference with national procedural laws and the introduction of European minimum standards. Sadly,
despite its strength of conviction on this matter, the Commission failed to
do this.

Other concerns dogged the proposal too. Perhaps inevitably, as negotiations continued in the quest for unanimous political approval, so the rights
and standards in the draft were watered down. This in turn raised concerns
as to whether the FDPR could add any value to the existing protection
scheme offered by the European Convention on Human Rights. To be sure,
securing a floor of rights *below* the level enshrined in the ECHR would
amount to a breach of EU law,[112] but, securing a set of rights *identical* to
those contained in Article 6 ECHR in the FDPR would be advantageous,
in that the distinctive features of the EU legal regime, namely the binding
nature of legislation, the requirement of effective implementing measures
and the oversight of the ECJ, would ensure more efficient protection and
more effective compliance of those rights.[113] Identical wording also has the
advantage of removing uncertainty and potential ambiguities that would
inevitably emerge from a multiplication of differently worded relevant
texts,[114] and yet this was *not* the route that the Commission chose. As for
the FDPR *adding value* in terms of the scope and substance of the fundamental rights – for instance through more explicit information rights – it
became an up-hill struggle to convince certain Member States that this was
even desirable or that such minor advances really justified EU legal intervention at all.

A group of six disgruntled Member States put forward a counter-
proposal to the FDPR in April 2006. Cyprus, the Czech Republic, Ireland,
Malta, Slovakia and the UK presented a non-binding Political Resolution
to the Council which, according to a UK Home Office official, 'sets out a
range of practical measures based on recognized good practice Member
States could take, mainly related to legal assistance and to interpreters'.[115]
Nonetheless, efforts continued to secure approval of the FDPR. The
Austrian Presidency at the JHA Council Meeting of 1–2 June 2006 suggested further limiting common minimum standards to the right to information, the right to legal assistance, the right to interpretation and the
right to translation of procedural documents for any person subject to
criminal proceedings only, with an emphasis upon general standards rather
than specific details. The German Presidency worked hard to resolve ongoing concerns and ambiguities and produced what appeared to be a work-
able text in December 2006. However, even this failed to convince all
Member States and the Commission formally withdrew the draft framework decision.

BOX 4.2

The text of the new TFEU would remove many of the obstacles which have hindered the adoption of the framework decision on procedural safeguards. Having formalised the status of mutual recognition in Article 61(3) TFEU, Article 69 A(2)(b) goes on to mandate the approximation of the 'rights of individuals in criminal procedure [. . .] to the extent necessary to facilitate mutual recognition of judgments and judicial decisions and police and judicial cooperation in criminal matters having a cross-border dimension'.

In addition to providing this express legal competence to adopt, presumably, a *directive* on procedural safeguards, the TFEU also provides for the application of the 'ordinary legislative procedure', i.e. 'the joint adoption by the European Parliament and the Council of a regulation, directive or decision on a proposal from the Commission' (Article 249 A TFEU) although Member States also share a right of initiative with the Commission (Article 61 I TFEU). This procedure, similar to the current co-decision procedure, removes the right of veto from national governments and is likely substantially to facilitate the passage of legislation.

It should be noted that, despite the previously rehearsed difficulties in respect of adopting measures that harmonise procedural aspects of criminal law, some progress has been recorded. A framework decision on confiscation of crime-related proceeds, instrumentalities and property[116] seeks to extend and secure effective powers of confiscation for Member States where persons are convicted of an offence defined by EU law and committed within the framework of a criminal organisation. This piece of legislation does not seek to harmonise the substance of a specific crime as such, rather it has a harmonising impact by introducing similar provisions into the different internal procedural systems concerning the proceeds of crime. The underlying aim is to prevent and combat money laundering, which has consistently been heralded as lying at the very heart of organised crime.[117]

Another cross-cutting piece of legislation that seeks to harmonise criminal procedures has been adopted on the standing of victims in criminal proceedings.[118] This framework decision introduces a number of specific and minimum rights, safeguards and principles that must be secured by Member States for all victims in its criminal legal system, including the right to be heard and provide evidence, the right to receive information and protection and communication safeguards. This framework decision is notable for several reasons. First, it is one of the few pieces of legislation adopted or proposed under the third pillar that is concerned specifically with the rights and protection of individuals who find themselves caught up in the criminal justice system.[119] Second, it was in response to a question referred by a national court concerning the interpretation of this framework decision that the ECJ handed down its *Pupino*[120] judgment, perhaps its most significant ruling to date under the third pillar.

Interestingly, the Commission remains determined to pursue this procedural approximation agenda. In its Action Plan implementing The Hague Programme,[121] it provided an extensive list of proposed future approximating legislation, the overwhelming majority of which concerns criminal procedures. The issues mentioned are criminal jurisdiction, presumption of innocence, in absentia trials, evidence and witnesses, sentencing harmonisation and analysis of detention procedures and reviews.

NON-LEGISLATIVE APPROACHES

Attention now shifts from the legal instruments to the non-legislative governance environment of achieving judicial cooperation in criminal matters. By 'non-legislative' we mean all those policy initiatives or 'out-puts' that are not framework decisions, conventions or decisions, even if they might have a legal content or impact. Included under this heading is *the case law of the ECJ, the establishment of closer institutional cooperation* and so-called practical *'confidence-building measures'*.

Case Law of the ECJ: Mutual Recognition and the Principle of *ne bis in idem*

We have referred to the role and case law of the ECJ throughout this and other chapters of the book. This section will focus exclusively upon the use by the ECJ of the principle of mutual recognition as a tool to interpret Article 54 of the pre-Amsterdam Convention Implementing the Schengen Agreement (CISA).[122] It has been in response to questions referred from national courts about the precise scope of this provision that the Court has endorsed the principle of mutual recognition as the methodological and conceptual centre of gravity for EU judicial cooperation in criminal matters and, importantly, has expounded on the legal consequences of such a reality. The Court's rulings are therefore highly instructive as to how it conceives of the AFSJ more generally. Moreover, this set of cases has produced a broadly consistent and welcome interpretation of the Article 54

CISA principle of *ne bis in idem*, a principle which in essence maintains that an individual should not have to run the risk of prosecution in respect of the same acts more than once in a single EU area of criminal justice. Before examining the case law it is worth highlighting the significance of the *ne bis in idem* rule both generally and as enshrined in the CISA and the ongoing political efforts to introduce a legislative instrument on this principle and the related issue of criminal jurisdiction.

Generally speaking, and as traditionally understood, the *ne bis in idem* rule offers an important principle of judicial protection for the individual in the context of a fair trial.[123] Additionally, it seeks to safeguard the legitimacy and integrity of the legal system and of the state by safeguarding decisions which intend definitively to end criminal proceedings. In this sense it plays an important role in upholding the principles of legal certainty and *res judicata* (finality) of criminal decisions.[124] The *ne bis in idem* rule has long since formed an integral aspect of most domestic systems of criminal justice, and is even reinforced as such by certain international human rights instruments.[125] The CISA definition of *ne bis in idem* was to expand the geographical reach of the principle beyond the domestic arena for the first time. The text of Article 54 CISA reads as follows:

> A person whose trial has been finally disposed of in one Contracting Party may not be prosecuted in another Contracting Party for the same acts provided that, if a penalty has been imposed, it has been enforced, is actually in the process of being enforced or can no longer be enforced under the laws of the sentencing Contracting Party.

The CISA definition of the *ne bis in idem* principle was adopted precisely to transcend the purely national context with which it is traditionally and historically associated. As such the principle would apply in relations *between* EU Member States, i.e. it covers final judgments rendered in *other* Member States within the EU.

The significance of this principle within the EU criminal legal order is further evidenced by its appearance in the EU Charter of Fundamental Rights[126] and in various framework decisions establishing the mutual recognition of national criminal law decisions as a ground (either mandatory or voluntary) for refusal to recognise/enforce foreign decisions.[127]

Following the integration of CISA into the EU third pillar *acquis* by the Treaty of Amsterdam (in force May 1999) there were calls for EU legislation to strengthen and clarify the *ne bis in idem* principle in the new context of developing the EU as a single 'area of freedom, security and justice'.[128] These calls were eventually addressed in part with the publication of a Green Paper on *ne bis in idem* and the related issue of criminal jurisdiction in December 2005.[129] In this Green Paper the Commission outlined the possibilities for the creation of a common procedural mechanism which would facilitate the choice of the most appropriate jurisdiction within which to bring criminal proceedings. With the establishment of a balanced mechanism for choice of jurisdiction in place, it was thought that the *ne bis in idem* principle could then be reconsidered, in particular as regards the clarification of key aspects of the principle, the conditions for its application and the applicable derogations.[130]

It was hoped that agreement on a procedure for allocating criminal jurisdiction would mean that the principle of *ne bis in idem* would no longer act, as it currently does, as a limited and arbitrary mechanism for the allocation of jurisdiction. At present, in the absence of common rules at the international level (UN, Council of Europe or the European Union) to determine which state has jurisdiction over a crime,[131] there is an increased likelihood of the initiation of parallel prosecutions for the same facts in different Member States. National prosecution authorities may of course ask for assistance from the EU judicial cooperation body, Eurojust, in deciding upon the appropriate forum for prosecution since it is empowered to facilitate the settlement of disputes on positive and negative jurisdiction conflicts.[132] Indeed, some success has been recorded here but Eurojust itself acknowledges that its facilitation capacity in this regard is not being fully exploited by national authorities. In the combined absence of any duty on national authorities to refer a case to Eurojust and any authority for Eurojust to issue binding decisions, parallel prosecutions within the EU may still persist.[133] It can be seen how in these circumstances the CISA principle of *ne bis in idem* might work in a somewhat arbitrary way to determine jurisdiction by simply pre-empting it elsewhere once a final decision barring further prosecution has been taken in one State. The Commission states that 'by giving preference to whichever jurisdiction can first take a final decision, its effects amount to a "first come first served" principle'.[134] It had been hoped that the proposals put forward in the Green Paper would put an end to this.

Responses to the Green Paper, however, revealed concerns about the true extent of the problem of conflicts of criminal jurisdiction in practice, the role and rights of the defendant in any procedure to determine jurisdiction and also the extent to which the Green Paper proposals might interfere with national procedures relating to investigation and prosecution. Consequently, the Commission put to tender the carrying out of a further impact assessment exercise. At the time of writing it is unclear if and when a legislative proposal will appear. What is clear is that any emergent legislative text dealing with the Article 54 CISA principle of *ne bis in idem* as it operates between the EU Member States will have to take account of a now relatively significant body of ECJ case law on this issue.

Following its incorporation into the EU legal framework and consequently, the new AFSJ context, Article 54 CISA has been the subject of a whole raft of questions referred to the ECJ by national courts.[135] Most of the cases have called for an interpretation of the concepts of *bis* ('finally disposed of') and *idem* ('same acts'), although more recently the Court has been asked to consider the 'enforcement condition' enshrined in the second part of Article 54 CISA. In general it can be said that the Court has offered a consistent and useful clarification of the scope of Article 54 CISA.

According to the ECJ the notion of '*bis*', or more precisely the definition of a trial 'finally disposed of' in Article 54 CISA, is to be understood as any decision which has the effect in principle of precluding further proceedings in the jurisdiction in which it was handed down. Consequently Article 54 CISA precludes further criminal proceedings in a different Member State following an out-of-court financial settlement by a public prosecutor,[136] a decision of a court by which the accused was acquitted finally because prosecution of the offence was time-barred,[137] and a final decision acquitting the accused for lack of evidence.[138] In each of these cases the important thing for the ECJ was whether a final decision acquitting the applicant had the effect that she or he is to be treated as innocent in the jurisdiction in which the decision was handed down. If so, the effect of 54 CISA is the *ipso facto* extension of that effect throughout the EU, thereby pre-empting criminal jurisdiction in any other State over the facts at issue in those proceedings.

As for the definition of *idem* or the 'same acts' within the meaning of Article 54 CISA, the ECJ rejected any consideration other than the material facts making up the offence.[139] Thus, neither legal classification of the offence nor the interests protected were to be taken into account in determining whether a person had been tried twice *in idem*. In *Van Esbroeck* the Court held that '*the only relevant criterion for the application of Article 54 of the CISA is identity of the material acts, understood in the sense of the existence of a set of concrete circumstances which are inextricably linked together . . . in time, in space and by their subject matter*'.[140] Applying that definition to the facts, the Court said that the import and export of the same drugs constituted the 'same acts' within the meaning of Article 54 CISA in principle, but acknowledged that this was for the national court to determine in practice. The *Van Esbroeck* definition of the 'same acts' has been confirmed in later case law.[141]

Let us now turn to the reasoning of the ECJ. How was it able to reach these broad interpretations of Article 54 CISA? First and foremost, this has been made possible by conceiving of Article 54 CISA as imposing mutual recognition of final decisions in criminal proceedings. In its first case on Article 54 CISA, *Gözütok and Brügge*, the Court began by acknowledging that neither Title VI EU, nor the Schengen Agreement, nor CISA, require, for the application of Article 54 CISA, any '*harmonisation, or at least the approximation, of the criminal laws of the Member States relating to procedures whereby further prosecution is barred*'.[142] '*In those circumstances*', there is a '*necessary implication that the Member States have mutual trust in their criminal justice systems and that each of them recognises the criminal law in force in the other Member States even when the outcome would be different if its own national law were applied.*'[143] Accordingly, the provisions of CISA are to be interpreted on the basis of an assumption that Member States have mutual trust and confidence in each other's legal systems. The Court, adopting its familiar interpretive technique of invoking the principle of *effet utile* of provisions then suggests that its own wide interpretation of the *ne bis in idem* principle is the only interpretation which gives useful effect to the 'object and purpose of Article 54 CISA' rather than to procedural or purely formal matters, which, after all, vary as between Member States.

Crucially, then, what did the Court consider the 'object and purpose of Article 54 CISA' to be? At paragraph 38 of its judgment the Court held that the object '*is to ensure that no-one is prosecuted on the same facts in several Member States on account of his having exercised his right to freedom of movement*'. It reached this understanding of the CISA principle by considering it within the broader legal context of the EU's third pillar. The ECJ makes clear that since the Treaty of Amsterdam and the integration of the Schengen *acquis* into the framework of the EU, Article 54 CISA had become part of a new, broader integration objective of maintaining and developing the EU as an area of freedom, security and justice in which the free movement of persons is guaranteed and protected.[144] In fact, the ECJ has consistently and ostensibly couched its Article 54 CISA judgments in terms of the protection of the freedom of movement, although on occasion other factors, pertinent to the conception of the AFSJ as a whole, have also been weighed in the balance, such as the objective of 'preventing and combating crime'[145] and the fact that the *ne bis in idem* principle constitutes a general principle of EU law, and as such incorporates other principles, such as the legal certainty and legitimate expectations.[146] Indeed, it has been argued that the reference to the freedom of movement in the ECJ's case law on the principle of *ne bis in idem* is *only* convincing if read as an expression of a more fundamental conception of the AFSJ as a whole.[147] This is because, first, there is no necessary material link between the risk of multiple prosecutions and the freedom of movement and, second, conceptually the question of whether an individual should be tried or not is always logically prior to the question of whether she or he should enjoy freedom of movement. Therefore, duplicitous criminal proceedings in different jurisdictions within the AFSJ are intolerable *not* because they potentially affect an individual's willingness to exercise her or his freedom of movement, but because they risk exposing the individual to divergent outcomes which must be avoided in a *single* area of freedom, security and justice.[148]

The case law discussed thus far deals with the first part of Article 54 CISA which perhaps lends itself to be interpreted through the prism of mutual recognition, with the effect that the interests of the individual are served over and above those of the state. But how would the Court deal with those aspects of Article 54 CISA which sit less comfortably with the principle of mutual recognition and the 'new' legal environment of the AFSJ, the so-called 'enforcement condition' which qualifies the principle contained in Article 54 and the exceptions to the Article 54 contained in Article 55 CISA? Thus far, the Court has only been asked to rule on the scope of the enforcement condition. According to this, the prohibition on criminal prosecutions for the same acts applies only if the penalty 'has been enforced, is actually in the process of being enforced or can no longer be enforced under the laws of the sentencing Contracting Party'. This opens the door to the possibility of a second prosecution with a different outcome on the same facts in another Member State for an individual who has already had a sentence passed against them but who are simply awaiting execution of that sentence. It is certainly arguable that the enforcement condition is superfluous within an area of EU criminal justice, where cross-border enforcement is facilitated by EU instruments such as the EAW. Put simply, the rationale of the enforcement condition – to avoid impunity for absconding convicts in cases where a conviction is not (fully) enforced – becomes obsolete in the AFSJ legal environment, making it difficult to avoid the conclusion that the only interest this provision serves is some national interest of a Member State retaining as much power as possible over individuals on its territory. Of course the removal of this enforcement condition can only be effected by the EU's legislator, and indeed this has been mooted in the context of the Green Paper on criminal jurisdiction discussed earlier.

The ECJ has now ruled on the notion of 'enforcement' of criminal penalties[149] within the meaning of Article 54 CISA and a further request for a preliminary ruling is pending.[150] In *Kretzinger*,[151] the Court confirmed that a suspended custodial sentence constitutes a penalty 'actually in the process of being enforced' within the meaning of Article 54 CISA.[152] This finding was based upon the fact that suspended custodial sentences are still intended to penalise the unlawful conduct of a convicted person. As Advocate General Sharpston points out, '*a suspended custodial sentence incorporates within it a penalty which is being enforced*', since suspension of a custodial sentence is always made dependent on the offender respecting certain conditions over a probation period.[153] As soon as the sentence is enforceable and during that probation period the penalty must be regarded as 'actually in the process of being enforced'. Activation of the custodial sentence is possible if the probation conditions are not met. If the offender respects the conditions applicable during the probation period, he is then (depending on the Member State) either recorded as having duly served his sentence or regarded as though the offence and the conviction had never taken place.[154] At this point, the penalty must be regarded as 'having been enforced' within the meaning of Article 54 CISA. However, a penalty imposed by a national court is not to be regarded as 'having been enforced' or 'actually in the process of being enforced' where the defendant was for a short time taken into police custody or detained on remand pending trial within the meaning of Article 54 CISA, since that provision only applies once the 'trial has been disposed of'. Both of these forms of deprivation of liberty precede the final judgment and therefore cannot fall within the meaning of Article 54 CISA, even if they are, by virtue of national law, to be taken into account in the subsequent enforcement of any custodial sentence.[155] The Court further justifies this interpretation with reference to the different underpinning objectives of pre-trial detention on the one hand and the enforcement condition on the other. The former is 'of a preventative nature' while the latter seeks to avoid a situation in which a person whose trial has been finally disposed of in the first State can no longer be prosecuted for the same acts and therefore ultimately remains unpunished if the State in which sentence was first passed did not enforce the sentence imposed.[156]

A third question asked of the ECJ was whether, and to what extent, the provisions of the EAW have an effect on the interpretation of the notion of 'enforcement' within the meaning of Article 54 CISA. As will be recalled, a Member State may issue an arrest warrant to another Member State for the surrender of a requested person for the purposes of 'conducting a criminal prosecution or *executing a custodial sentence or detention order*'.[157] However, both the Advocate General and the ECJ made short shrift of the claim by Mr Kretzinger that the mere option open to the sentencing state to issue a EAW for this purpose is sufficient to satisfy the Article 54 CISA enforcement condition. Such an interpretation would run counter to the actual wording of that provision, which expressly requires the enforcement condition to be satisfied, i.e. that the penalties must actually be enforced.[158] There cannot, by definition, have been any enforcement of a sentence when an EAW is issued precisely for that purpose.[159] Moreover, the Court supports its finding that the interpretation of Article 54 of the CISA cannot depend on the provisions of the EAW with reference to the legal uncertainty that would otherwise ensue as a result of the differing scopes of the instruments.[160] The Court therefore confirmed that the option open to a

Member State to issue an EAW has no effect on the interpretation of the notion of 'enforcement' within the meaning of Article 54 CISA – a finding not undermined in any way by the fact that the judgment relied on in support of a European arrest warrant is given *in absentia*.[161]

If one were to criticise the ECJ's ruling in *Kretzinger* it would be to express disappointment that it did not call into question the continued validity of the enforcement condition enshrined in Article 54 CISA. A 'reading down' of certain parts of the *ne bis in idem* provisions of the CISA seems, to us, justified by the fact that the text of those provisions antedates by some ten years the creation of the AFSJ. The AFSJ must be held drastically to have altered the legal context under which they are interpreted. The ECJ has already proved itself willing to incorporate the principle of mutual recognition as an interpretative principle in dealing with Article 54 CISA, leading to results which would no doubt be considered surprising by the drafters of the text. The suggested reading down would, again according to us, be no less called for in the novel context of the AFSJ. Undoubtedly, it is just a matter of time before the Court is asked to rule upon the scope of the exceptions to the Article 54 principles contained in Article 55 CISA. But even the narrowest of interpretations of these by the Court could not negate the fact that their very existence, like that of the enforcement condition, conflicts with the very logic of the principle of mutual recognition.

Institutional Cooperation

As you might expect in a policy field which is expressly about ensuring 'cooperation' between relevant national authorities, securing closer institutional cooperation forms a key non-legislative aspect of combating cross-border criminal activity. This has been pursued, in accordance with the wording of Article 31 EU,[162] largely through the auspices of European level coordination bodies such as Eurojust and through the formal establishment of specialised cooperation such as with the Joint Investigation Teams.[163] As we have already seen, there is an ongoing debate about the extent to which the EU should confer operational or decisional powers upon organs such as Eurojust in the criminal field. This is highly controversial because it would mark a significant conceptual shift away from the EU as a broker of cooperation between relevant national agencies (which essentially leaves national criminal justice systems intact) to the EU as a body with autonomous, enforceable and direct powers of investigation and prosecution (which directly 'interferes' with national criminal justice systems). However, it may be that this prospect is not as unpalatable as it once was. With a raft of EU legislative instruments in place (or forthcoming) to secure immediate recognition and enforcement of national criminal judgments and, in some areas of serious cross-border crime, common definitions of offences and penalties, at least the prospect of a European 'body' with direct powers to decide upon whether or not to prosecute certain 'euro-crimes' (in a national court) is more conceivable. In addition to the issue of legal competence, the development of existing bodies or the creation of new bodies with operational powers raises important queries about necessary safeguards for individuals and lines of both political and judicial accountability.

Leaving aside these unresolved questions of principle, it is clear that the facilitation of practical coordination through bodies such as Eurojust remains a key component of EU efforts to secure judicial cooperation in criminal law matters. Readers are referred to Chapter 2 for a full discussion of institutional roles and practices.

Confidence-building Measures

Finally, a range of other non-legislative mechanisms that contribute to the attainment of achieving judicial cooperation in criminal matters can be said to come under the broad heading of 'confidence-building' measures. With mutual recognition firmly entrenched at the heart of the criminal justice policy, problems with its application and enforcement have tended to relate in some way to an absence of mutual trust between relevant national authorities. Consequently, as legislation emerges securing cooperation either through mutual recognition or harmonisation, so it has become more urgent to develop complementary and mutually reinforcing measures to strengthen mutual understanding and trust among judicial authorities and different legal systems. The 2004 Hague Programme called for an explicit effort in this regard. In response the Commission published a Communication on mutual recognition and the strengthening of mutual trust between Member States,[164] in which it identified the principle of mutual recognition as the lynchpin of all other forms of policy action in this field. According to this Communication, the success of the principle of mutual recognition depends upon mutual trust between Member States, which in turn should be reinforced by adopting the harmonisation of certain procedural and substantive criminal laws and by pursuing non-legislative *practical flanking measures*.[165] Three flanking measures were identified.

First was the need for improved evaluation mechanisms that would seek, not only to evaluate the implementation of policies in the field of justice, but also to provide a stronger and more informed basis from which to propose new instruments. The Hague Programme states that 'evaluation of the implementing as well as the effects of all measures is, in the European Council's opinion, essential to the effectiveness of Union action'. This 'tool' would be particularly significant in respect of third pillar matters considering the absence of formal infringement procedures to ensure proper transposition and implementation by Member States, yet successful evaluation requires a united and concerted effort from Member States to be open and 'up-front' about their acts of transposition. They must supply sufficient information to the Commission in the implementation reports, something which cannot be taken for granted (e.g. there were substantial problems in this regard with the second implementation report of the framework decision on the status of victims in criminal proceedings). Of course, implementation reports are particularly important in the context of the third pillar since they constitute the only public record of the quality of national transposition measures. Evaluating the implementation of other third pillar instruments such as conventions and protocols (most commonly used in connection with the fight against crime and for police and customs cooperation) is even more problematic because, unlike framework decisions, these instruments make no provision either for a formal duty for Member States to notify compliance or for reports monitoring national implementation.[166] Following the mandate given to the Commission by the Hague Programme and its own Action Plan, the Commission has published a Communication on the 'Evaluation of EU Policies on Freedom, Security and Justice'.[167] The purpose of this Communication is to set up a mechanism for a thorough evaluation of AFSJ policies, in a spirit of 'partnership' with Member States and EU Institutions.

A second flanking measure concerns the building of a 'common legal culture' by improving networking among relevant national practitioners and by developing mutual knowledge of the different judicial systems. To this end, the Commission has published a Communication on judicial training in the EU,[168] which advocates a role for the EU in reinforcing and strengthening existing training of judges, prosecutors and lawyers. Its primary aim is to offer increased financial assistance for judicial training in Union and Community law to existing national and European organisations such as the European Judicial Training Network, the Judicial Network in criminal matters, the European Institute of Public Administration and the European Law Academy. It advocates, through increased cooperation of these actors, the development of a European strategy of multiannual judicial training. It further intends to build on the pilot project for the exchange of magistrates and organise EU workshops to promote cooperation between Member States of the legal profession with a view to establishing best practices.

Lastly, the Commission also called for an increased level of financial support from the EU to enhance judicial cooperation in criminal matters. Under the Financial Perspectives 2007–2013,[169] the EU has devoted considerable resources to matters of criminal justice. For instance, the framework programme on fundamental rights and justice[170] will play an important role in supporting and improving judicial training of professionals in matters of EC/EU law as mentioned above. While the EU has funded and supported numerous projects that promote judicial cooperation in the past, the agreement on Financial Perspectives 2007–2013 demonstrates a recognition that financial capacity and distribution constitutes an important governance mechanism for achieving policy objectives in the area of freedom, security and justice.

NOTES

1. The limits of the traditional approach to inter-state judicial cooperation were highlighted in the introduction to the book, along with the changing circumstances that rendered such an approach unsatisfactory. You are advised to read the introduction and Chapter 1 prior to reading this chapter.
2. Tampere European Council Conclusions, 15–16 October 1999, at para. 5.
3. Ibid., at para. 33; emphasis added.
4. Council Framework Decision on the European arrest warrant and the surrender procedures between Member States 2002/584/JHA (OJ L 190, 18.7.2002, pp. 1–20).
5. Chapter 6.
6. Article 34 EU.
7. Article 35 EU.
8. C-303/05 *Advocaten voor de Wereld*, judgment of 3 May 2007, at para. 32.
9. Proposal for a Framework Decision on certain procedural rights applying in proceedings in criminal matters throughout the European Union, COM(2004) 328 final, 28.4.2004.
10. Ibid., at para. 37.
11. See the Commission's 'Hague action plan' – Commission Communication on the Hague Programme: Ten Priorities for the next five years; The partnership for European renewal in the field of Freedom, Security and Justice, COM(2005) 184 final,10.5.2005.
12. See Green Paper on Conflicts of Jurisdiction and the Principle of *ne bis in idem* in Criminal Proceedings COM(2005) 696, final, 23.12.2005 and the responses thereto. See also the Annex to the Green Paper SEC(2005) 1767, Brussels, 23.12.2005. For a comment see M. Fletcher (2007), 'The problem of multiple criminal prosecutions: building an effective EU response', *Yearbook of European Law*, vol 26, 33–56.
13. J. Wouters and F. Naert (2004), 'Of arrest warrants, terrorist offences and extradition deals: an appraisal of the EU's main criminal law measures against terrorism after "11 September"', *Common Market Law Review*, **41**, 909–35, at p. 919.
14. Programme of measures to implement the principle of mutual recognition of decisions in criminal matters (OJ C 12, 15.1.2001, p. 10). For more on mutual recognition at the *pre-trial* phase, see Commission green paper on mutual recognition of non-custodial pre-trial supervision measures, COM (2004) 562 final, 17.8.2004. On mutual recognition *post-trial* see Commission green paper on the approximation, mutual recognition and enforcement of criminal sanctions in the European Union COM(2004) 334 final, 30.4.2004.
15. EAW, above n. 4.
16. OJ L 196, 2.8.2003, pp. 45–55.
17. OJ L 76, 22.3.2005, pp. 16–22.
18. OJ L 328, 24.11.2006, pp. 59–78.
19. COM(2003) 688 final, 14.11.2003.

20. For instance concerns about the proposed abolition of the dual criminality along the same lines as the EAW has led Germany to negotiate an exemption in respect of six types of serious crime, including terrorism.

21. COM(2005) 91 final, 17.3.2005.

22. In particular, Austria, Sweden and Finland have presented an ambitious draft framework decision on the mutual recognition and enforcement of sentences of imprisonment in the EU (OJ C 150 21.6.2005 pp. 1–16).

23. COM(2006) 468 final, 29.8.2006.

24. France and Germany have presented a draft framework decision on the recognition and supervision of suspended sentences, alternative sanctions and conditional sentences (OJ C 147, 30.6.2007, pp. 1–16).

25. S. Alegre (2002), 'The myth and the reality of a modern European judicial space', *New Law Journal*, 986.

26. For instance the UK government, who in fact were responsible for the planting of the seed of mutual recognition as the mechanism for enhancing the ability of national legal systems to work more closely in both civil and criminal matters, at the Cardiff European Council in June 1998.

27. Communication on mutual recognition; above n. 14.

28. Ibid.

29. Programme of measures to implement the principle of mutual recognition; above n. 14.

30. 19 June 1990. OJ L 239, 22.9.2000, pp. 19–62.

31. Joined Cases C-187/01 and C-385/01, *Gözütok and Brügge*, judgment of 11 February 2003.

32. Ibid., at para. 32. Later confirmed in C-436/04 *Van Esbroeck*, judgment of 9 March 2006, at para. 29 and C-467/04 *Gasparini*, judgment of 28 September 2006, at para. 29. The ECJ also reaffirmed this point in respect of the European arrest warrant framework decision in C-303/05 *Advocaten voor de Wereld*, judgment of 3 May 2007, at para. 59.

33. See e.g. G. de Kerchove and A.Weyembergh (eds) (2005), *La Confiance Mutuelle au sein de l'Espace pénal Européen. Mutual Trust in the European Criminal Area*, Brussels: Éditions de L'Université de Bruxelles.

34. See for instance B. Schünemann (2007), *Criminal Law Forum*, 'Alternative-Project for a European criminal law and procedure', **18**(2), 227–51.

35. Communication on the mutual recognition of judicial decisions in criminal matters and the strengthening of mutual trust between Member States COM(2005) 195, Brussels, 19.5.2005. See also Annexed Staff Working Paper SEC(2005) 641, Brussels, 19.5.2005.

36. Programme of measures to implement the principle of mutual recognition; above n. 14.

37. M. Fichera and C. Janssens (2007), 'Mutual recognition of judicial decision in criminal matters and the role of the national judge', *ERA Forum*, **8**(2), 177–202, at p. 183.

38. EAW; above n. 4.

39. However, it has been noted that many EAWs are simply posted as 'alerts' on the SIS (Schengen Information System) or via Interpol and these options for transmitting EAW requests are not necessarily directed at one Member State. The UK House of Lords Select Committee on the EU reported that this was the reason why there is a large discrepancy between the number of requests received in the UK and the number of arrests made – very few turned out to have a connection with the UK. In the period 1 January 2004 to 22 February 2006, the UK received 5732 EAWs. Of these, 175 have resulted in an arrest in the UK, with 88 persons being surrendered. House of Lords Select Committee on the EU, 'European Arrest Warrant Recent Developments', session 2005–2006, HL 156, 4.4.2006, at para. 21.

40. There are three significant time limits: the first two relate to the adoption of a final decision on executing the request. First, in the event that the requested person consents to his/her surrender, the implementing state must take a final decision on the execution within 10 days of that consent (Article 17(2)). Second, in the absence of consent from the requested person that decision should be taken within a 60-day period, with the

possibility of an additional 30 days in 'specific cases' after the arrest of the requested person (Article 17(3) and (4)). The third time limit relates to the physical surrender of the requested to the requesting state. This should occur within 10 days of the final decision on the execution with the possibility for a commonly agreed later date by the two judicial authorities in limited stipulated circumstances (Article 23). The consequences for breach of this latter time limit are particularly serious – the person in question must be released from custody in the implementing State (Article 24(5)).

41. EAW; above n. 4, at Article 2(1).
42. See judgment of the *Bundesverfassungsgericht* of 18 July 2005, 2 BvR 2236/04. This is discussed further below.
43. On the limits of the internal market analogy, see S. Peers (2004), 'Mutual recognition and criminal law in the European Union: has the Council got it wrong?', *Common Market Law Review*, **41**, 5–36; V. Mitsilegas (2006), 'The Constitutional Implications of Mutual Recognition in Criminal Matters in the EU', *Common Market Law Review*, **42**, 1278; and S. Lavanex (2007), 'Mutual recognition and the monopoly of force: limits of the single market analogy', *Journal of European Public Policy*, **14**(5), 762–79.
44. A term coined by K. Nikolaïdis. For a recent exposition, see K. Nikolaïdis and S.K. Schmidt (2007), 'Mutual recognition on "trial": the long road to services liberalization', *Journal of European Public Policy*, **14**(5), 717–34.
45. Also referred to as 'dual criminality'.
46. EAW; above n. 4, at paragraph 10 of the Preamble.
47. Interestingly, in its report of 29 September 2004, the Committee on Civil Liberties, Justice and Home Affairs called for harmonisation measures to be adopted in respect of all 32 categories of serious offences listed in article 2 of the Framework Decision on the European Arrest Warrant (A6-0010/2004 final, p. 10).
48. In order to alleviate concerns about the abolition of double criminality, Article 4(7) of the framework decision confers a discretion on the executing Member State to refuse execution if there is some sort of connection with its territory (i.e. the offence has been committed in whole or in part in its territory).
49. The European Evidence Warrant also abolishes dual criminality for the same 32 categories of offence as the EAW. Concerns about the poor definition of certain of those offences have led Germany to secure an exemption for five years in respect of terrorism, computer-related crime, racism and xenophobia, sabotage, racketeering and extortion or swindling.
50. C-303/05, *Advocaten voor de Wereld*, judgment of 3 May 2007.
51. Ibid., at para. 52.
52. Ibid., at para. 51.
53. Ibid., at para. 53.
54. Previous attempts to move away from the nationality exception had been made (the Convention relating to extradition between the Member States of the European Union 1996) but were limited and received only reluctantly. For a full discussion of the nationality exception see Z. Deen-Racsmàny and R. Blekxtoon (2005), 'The decline of the nationality exception in European Extradition', *European Journal of Crime, Criminal Law and Criminal Justice*, **13**(3), 317–63.
55. Ibid., at p. 335.
56. EAW, above n. 4, at Article 4(6) and Article 5(3), respectively. See also Articles 32 and 33 for some additional, limited remnants of the nationality privilege.
57. Z. Deen-Racsmàny and R. Blekxtoon, above, at n. 54.
58. For detailed comment on the implementation of the EAW in Italy, see F. Impalà (2005), 'The European Arrest Warrant in the Italian legal system: between mutual recognition and mutual fear within the European area of Freedom, Security and Justice', *Utrecht Law Review*, **1**(2), 56–78.
59. The JHA Council asked the Commission to update its evaluation of the EAW to 1 June 2007 with the entry of Romania and Bulgaria into the Union on 1 January 2007. Council Press Release No 8849/05, 3.6.2005, p.10; document No 8842/1/05, 19.5.2005.
60. COM(2005) 63 final, 23.2.2005.

61. COM(2006) 8 final, 24.1.2006.
62. In the case of suspects consenting to be surrendered, the Commission reports that the average time has fallen to only 13 days.
63. COM(2007) 407 final, 11.7.2007.
64. F. Impalà, above n. 58.
65. Doc no. 10975/07 DG H 2B.
66. Where some discretion is allowed in determining whether to bring a formal prosecution in accordance with the opportunity principle, the choice is generally one of pursuing the case before the courts or applying some alternative courses of action, such as fixed penalties, warning schemes for minors or referral to measures designed to address the causes of offending, increasingly based upon principles of restorative justice. Public interest factors are often taken into account in deciding whether a formal prosecution is needed and, if not, what the alternative might be.
67. Similar challenges were heard in other national jurisdictions but failed, for instance in Greece and the Czech Republic, where the national courts held that the national constitutions should not form an obstacle to the effective transposition of EU law.
68. Judgment of 27 April 2005, P1/05.
69. Judgment of 18 July 2005, above, at n. 42.
70. The Polish Constitutional court had delayed the application of its judgment for 18 months to allow for new implementing legislation to be adopted and indeed urged the legislator to advance greater levels of cooperation in criminal matters to secure the realisation of the Union's aims. On the distinctive approaches adopted by national courts to the constitutional conflicts raised by the implementation of the EAW FD, see J. Komárek (2007), 'European Constitutionalism and the European Arrest Warrant: in search of the limits of "contrapunctual principles" ', *Common Market Law Review*, **44**, 9–40.
71. Judgment of 7 November 2005, Ap. No. 294/2005.
72. C-303/05 *Advocaten voor de Wereld*, judgment of 3 May 2007.
73. Ibid., para. 45.
74. Ibid., para. 55.
75. Ibid., para 55.
76. Ibid., para 58.
77. Ibid., para 57.
78. Ibid., para 59.
79. *Office of the King's Prosecutor (Brussels)* v. *Armas* [2005] UKHL 67, [2005] 3 WLR 1079 and *Dabas v High Court of Justice in Madrid, Spain* [2007] UKHL 6, [2007] 2 WLR 254. For a discussion of *Armas* and other cases on the EAW heard before UK courts, see N. Padfield (2007), 'The European Arrest Warrant: between trust, democracy and the rule of law – the implementation of the European Arrest Warrant in England and Wales', *EU Constitutional Law Review*, **3**, 253–68.
80. C-105/03 *Pupino*, judgment of 16 June 2005. For a discussion of this case, see Chapter 1.
81. E. Van Sliedregt (2007), 'The European Arrest Warrant: between trust, democracy and the rule of law – introduction', *EU Constitutional Law Review*, **3**, 244–52.
82. S. Trechsel (2005), *Human Rights in Criminal Proceedings*, Oxford: Oxford University Press, at p. 7.
83. Article 6 EU. See C-303/05 *Advocaten voor de Wereld*, judgment of 3 May 2007, at para. 45. As a matter of EC and EU law, the EU institutions when exercising their competences and EU Member States when implementing, applying and seeking to derogate from EU law are bound by the guarantees enshrined in the ECHR.
84. The Charter of Fundamental Rights of the European Union, proclaimed in Nice on 7 December 2000 (OJ C 364 18.12.2000, pp. 1–22).
85. Article 47 contains the right to an effective remedy and a fair trial; Article 48 refers to the presumption of innocence and rights of the defence; Article 49 to the principles of legality and proportionality of criminal proceedings and penalties; and Article 50 to the right not to be tried or punished twice in criminal proceedings for the same criminal offence.

86. Although note that the Reform Treaty provides a legal basis for the EU to accede to the ECHR. See Chapter 1.
87. C-303/05 *Advocaten voor de Wereld*, judgment of 3 May 2007, at para. 46. This was only the second time that the ECJ has explicitly referred to the Charter, the first time being in C-540/03, judgment 27 June 2006 *European Parliament* v *Council (Family Reunion case)*, judgment 27 June 2006. Prior to that only the CFI and the Advocates General had mentioned it.
88. Vienna Action Plan of the Council and the Commission on the implementation of the area of freedom, security and justice of 3 December 1998 (OJ C 19, 23.1.1999, pp. 1–15).
89. M. Leaf and W. van Ballegooij (2006), 'The future of EU criminal justice: making mutual recognition work', *European Arrest Warrant Project* article available via http://www.eurowarrant.net. Note, however, that certain rights are guaranteed to the requested person in Article 11(2) EAW.
90. See, for instance, P. Garlick (2005), 'The European Arrest Warrant and the ECHR', in R. Blekxtoon and W. van Ballegooij (eds) (2005), *Handbook on the European Arrest Warrant*, The Hague: T.M.C.Asser Press, 167–182 at p. 169.
91. S. Alegre and M. Leaf (2004), 'Mutual recognition in European Judicial Cooperation: a step too far too soon? Case Study – the European Arrest Warrant', *European Law Journal*, **10**(2), 200–217; S. Douglas-Scott (2004), 'The Rule of Law in the European Union – Putting the security into the Area of Freedom, Security and Justice', *European Law Review*, **29**(2), 219–42; P. Garlick, above n. 90; E. Guild (2004), 'Crime and the EU's Constitutional Future in the Area of Freedom, Security and Justice', **29**(2), *European Law Review*, 219–42.
92. [2002] EWHC 1278 (Admin).
93. The wider question is whether one should consider the English system of admission of evidence as paradigmatic of fair trial practices, and in particular section 78 Police and Criminal Evidence Act 1984. In most other European systems, the principle is that of 'free weighing of evidence' which means that everything is in principle admissible but a court can decide that its probative value is so low that it makes no difference either way. It is very likely that, if the torture allegations in *Ramda* had been substantiated, a French court would have taken anything said in association very lightly.
94. *Soering* v. *United Kingdom*, judgment of 7 July 1989.
95. Ibid., at para. 113. Similarly, assistance in criminal matters by way of execution of a sentence must only be refused '*in circumstances where the fugitive has suffered or risks suffering a flagrant denial of justice in the requesting country*': *Drozd and Janousek* v *France and Spain* (26 June 1992) at para. 110.
96. *Mamatkulov and Abdurasulovic* v. *Turkey*, judgment of 4 February 2005 (judgment of the First Section of 6 February 2003).
97. *Chamaïev et autres c. Géorgie et Russie*, judgment of 12 April 2005.
98. Ibid. ['*[L]a Cour juge avéré que, si la décision d'extrader, M. Guélogaïev, prise le 28 novembre 2002, était mise à exécution sur le fondement des évaluations faites à cette date, il y aurait violation de l'article 3 de la Convention*' (para. 368)]
99. As was pointed out in a dissenting opinion in *Mamatkulov*, '*[w]hat constitutes a 'flagrant' denial of justice has not been fully explained in the Court's jurisprudence*'. The dissenting judges were of the opinion that the use of the word 'flagrant' clearly '*intended to impose a stringent test of unfairness going beyond mere irregularities or lack of safeguards in the trial procedures such as might result in a breach of Article 6 if occurring within the Contracting State itself*'. See above, n. 97, dissenting opinion of Judges Rozakis, Bratza, Bonello and Hedigan.
100. See *Mamatkulov*, above n. 97.
101. Article 1(3) specifies that nothing in the framework decision has the effect of modifying the obligation to respect fundamental rights and principles under Article 6 EU. Article 11(2) provides that the requested person has the right to legal counsel and to an interpreter: EAW, above n. 4.

102. Commission Green Paper on Procedural Safeguards for Suspects and Defendants in Criminal Proceedings. COM(2003) 75, 19.2.2003, at p. 10.
103. COM(2004) 328 final, 28.4.2004.
104. The Commission's programme in respect of defence rights was being pursued as an integral part of the mutual recognition strategy and the wider AFSJ agenda and not merely in response to criticisms of the European Arrest Warrant. See Morgan, C. (2005), 'The European Arrest Warrant and Defendants' Rights: An Overview' in Blekxtoon, R, and van Ballegooij, W, see above n. 90, at 195–208.
105. Peers, S. (2007), *EU Justice and Home Affairs Law* (2nd ed.) Oxford: Oxford University Press, at p. 429.
106. On this, see J.A. Andrews (ed.) (1982), *Human Rights in Criminal Procedure – A comparative study*, London: Martinus Nijhoff Publishers, at p. 8. See also S. Trechsel above, n. 82.
107. Even if it cannot be described as an *autonomous* system of criminal justice.
108. Emphasis added.
109. The Commission regarded this position as an act of 'bad faith' on the part of these Member States, who had earlier informally agreed to be bound by the Council Legal Service opinion on this issue, which found that Article 31(1)(c) EU did provide an appropriate legal basis. See document 12902/04 JUR 399 COPEN 117. Note that arguments that suggest that a unanimity vote in Council could circumvent the need for a clear legal basis in the Treaty are not satisfactory. To argue that, whatever a unanimous Council decides, it had the competence to decide, is fundamentally to misunderstand the legal settlement of the EU as agreed by the Amsterdam Treaty.
110. Lööf, R. (2006), 'Shooting from the hip: proposed minimum rights in criminal proceedings throughout the EU', *European Law Journal*, **12**(3), 421–30.
111. Ibid.
112. Lööf, ibid., notes that recital 8 FDPR may be used to undermine the aim of promoting compliance with existing fair trial rights at a common, high standard. This recital reads '[t]he proposed provisions are not intended to affect specific measures in force in national legislations in the context of the fight against serious and complex forms of crime, in particular terrorism'.
113. Note that, for the Commission, the aim 'is not in any way to replace or even complement the EctHR' but 'rather to achieve better standards of compliance with the ECHR'.
114. See B. M. Zupančič and J. Callewaert (2007), 'Relationship of the EU framework to the ECHR', *ERA Forum*, **8**(2), 265–71.
115. Cited in House of Commons Home Affairs Committee, 'Justice and Home Affairs Issues at the European Union Level.' Session 2006–07, HC 76-I, 5.6.2007, at para. 220.
116. Framework Decision 2005/212/JHA of 24 February 2005 (OJ L 68, 15.3.2005, p. 49).
117. See para. 51 of the Tampere European Council Conclusions, 15–16 October 1999.
118. Framework Decision 2001/220/JHA of 15 March 2001 (OJ L 82, 22.3.2001, p. 1).
119. Note that reference is made to this framework decision in a number of framework decisions harmonising the definition and penalties of specific offences. See, for instance, Article 10 of Council Framework Decision 2002/475/JHA of 13 June 2002 on combating terrorism (OJ L 164, 22.6.2002, p. 3) and Article 7 of Council Framework Decision 2002/629/JHA of 19 July 2002 on combating trafficking in human beings (OJ L 203, 1.8.2002, p. 1).
120. C-105/03 *Pupino*, judgment of 16 June 2005. See Chapter 1 for further discussion of this ruling.
121. Council and Commission Action Plan implementing the Hague Programme on strengthening freedom, security and justice in the European Union of 10 June 2005, at point 4.2 (OJ C 198, 12.8.2005, pp. 1–22).
122. Convention Implementing the Schengen Agreement of 19 June 1990 (OJ L 239, 22.10.2000, pp. 19–62).
123. A common rationale of the *ne bis in idem* principles in all its various forms is to protect individuals against possible abuses by the State of its *ius puniendi*.

124. See, for instance, M. Friedland (1969), *Double Jeopardy*, Oxford: Oxford University Press; P. McDermott (1999), *Res Judicata and Double Jeopardy*, London: Butterworths. On the relationship between the principle of finality and the protection of the individual against the *ius puniendi* of the State see the Law Commission's Report, Double Jeopardy and Prosecution Appeals (March 2001) available at www.lawcom.gov.uk, at pp. 37–8.

125. For example, Article 4 of Protocol 7 of the ECHR (of 22 November 1984) and Article 14(7) of the UN International Covenant on Civil and Political Rights.

126. Article 50 reads, 'No one shall be liable to be tried or punished again in the criminal proceedings for an offence for which he or she has already been finally acquitted or convicted within the Union in accordance with the law.' In terms of scope, the principle enshrined in Article 50 appears to apply both within and between criminal jurisdictions in the EU. However, its terminology is more akin to the ECHR definition of the principle than that enshrined in 54 CISA. For a comparative analysis of the principle of *ne bis in idem* as interpreted in the EU and ECHR contexts and a normative explanation for the differences in approach, see R. Lööf (2007), '54 CISA and the principles of *ne bis in idem*' *European Journal of Crime, Criminal Law and Criminal Justice*, **15**(3), 309–34.

127. For instance in the EAW the principle acts as a *mandatory* ground for refusal to execute an arrest warrant whereas the framework decision on the execution in the EU of orders freezing property or evidence only names the principle of *ne bis in idem* as an *optional* ground for non-execution (OJ L 196 2.8.2203, pp. 45–55).

128. Vienna Action Plan; above n. 88. See also the Commission Programme of measures to implement the principle of mutual recognition; above n. 14.

129. Green Paper on Conflicts of Jurisdiction; above n. 12. A Greek proposal for a Framework Decision on *ne bis in idem* in 2003 was not seriously pursued largely owing to its limited scope and the retention of numerous exceptions to the principle (OJ C 100 2003, p. 4).

130. Note that these two stages are broadly similar to the framework suggested by the Freiburg Proposal. However, unlike the Commission's suggested approach, the Freiburg Proposal also included the 'safety-net' accounting principle as a third stage. 'Freiburg Proposal on concurrent jurisdictions and the prohibition of multiple prosecutions in the European Union', November 2003, Max Planck Institute, Freiburg.

131. Rather each Member State recognises some of the multiplicity of jurisdictional principles recognized by international law – the territoriality principle, the universality principle, the active and passive personality principles, the effects doctrine, the protective principle and the representational principle. All Member States agree on the territoriality principle – crimes committed wholly or partly within their territory fall within their jurisdiction – but there is no formal hierarchy of jurisdictional claims. See G. Conway (2003), 'Ne Bis in Idem in International Law', *International Criminal Law Review*, **3**, 217–44, at p. 225.

132. According to Article 4 of the Eurojust Decision it is competent to act in relation to the same types of crime and offences for which Europol is competent to act (in accordance with art. 2 of the Europol Convention of 26 July 1995). Moreover, at the request of a competent authority of a Member State, and in accordance with its objectives, Eurojust may assist in investigations and prosecutions relating to 'any other offence'. See Council Decision 2002/187/JHA of 28 February 2002 setting up Eurojust with a view to reinforcing the fight against serious crime (OJ L 63 6.3.2002. pp. 1–13). Also see its 'Guidelines for deciding "Which Jurisdiction Should Prosecute?"' included in the Annex of the Eurojust Annual Report 2005.

133. It has also been acknowledged that the variable status of national Eurojust members (whose powers are determined by national rather than EU law) may, in practice, have an impact upon the determination of an appropriate jurisdiction for prosecution. Finally, it is acknowledged in the Green Paper that Eurojust's powers apply in respect of certain offences (albeit a long list which includes at least those crimes for which Europol is competent) and therefore it could not suggest a solution to every conflict of

jurisdiction that arises. Of course, an 'EU solution' to positive conflicts of jurisdiction relating to non-harmonised offences may be vigorously resisted by Member States for important national policy reasons. After all, it is arguable that a single criminal area only exists in respect of those crimes that have been positively harmonised by the EU. See Green Paper on Conflicts of Jurisdiction; above n. 12.

134. Ibid., at p. 3.
135. See Joined Cases C-187/01 and C-385/01 *Gözütok and Brügge*, judgment of 11 February 2003; C-469/03 *Miraglia*, judgment of 10 March 2005; C-436/04 *Van Esbroeck*, judgment of 9 March 2006; C-467/04 *Gasparini*, judgment of 28 September 2006; C-150/05 *Van Straaten*, judgment of 28 September 2006; C-288/05 *Kretzinger*, judgment of 18 July 2007 and C-367/05 *Kraijenbrink*, judgment of 18 July 2007. C-297/07 *Klaus Bourquain* is pending before the ECJ. It concerns the issue of enforcement of criminal penalties. C-272/05 *Bouwens* was removed from the Court's Register by the President by an Order of 7 June 2006 following an indication by the referring Belgian court that a preliminary reference was no longer necessary in light of the judgment made in *Van Esbroeck*.
136. Joined Cases C-187/01 and C-385/01 *Gözütok and Brügge*, judgment of 11 February 2003.
137. C-467/04 *Gasparini*, judgment of 28 September 2006. This case confirmed that a ruling on the substantive merits of the case was not a necessary component of the *ne bis in idem* rule enshrined in Article 54 CISA. The Court rejected the Advocate General's preference for a substance-based approach and instead opted for a procedure-based approach which amounted to holding that any bar to further proceedings in the first jurisdiction, procedural or otherwise, barred proceedings in all the others. This case also put paid to any suggestion that the earlier case of C-469/03 *Miraglia* could be interpreted as a general rule that a trial cannot be considered 'disposed of' until there is a ruling on the merits of the case. In *Miraglia*, Dutch prosecutors had finally closed proceedings prior to any adjudication on the merits of the case with reference to 54 CISA because duplicitous proceedings were going on in Italy only then to rely on 54 CISA again to refuse judicial cooperation to the Italian authorities. It must be considered that the ECJ limited itself to holding that 54 CISA *itself* could not be used to prevent criminal proceedings from being brought *anywhere*.
138. C-150/05 *Van Straaten*, judgment of 28 September 2006.
139. This factual approach to the concept of *idem* is in stark contrast to the legal approach of classification of offences embodied in the ECHR principle of *ne bis in idem*. On the implications of this distinction see Lööf, R., above n. 126.
140. C-436/04 *Van Esbroeck*, judgment of 9 March 2006, at paras 36–38.
141. See Case C-150/05 *Van Straaten*, judgment of 28 September 2006, Case C-467/04 *Gasparini*, judgment of 28 September 2006 and Case C-288/05 *Kretzinger*, judgment of 18 July 2007.
142. C-385/01 *Gözütok and Brügge*, judgment of 11 February 2003 at para. 32.
143. Ibid., at para. 33.
144. Ibid., at para. 36.
145. Article 2 EU. See, also, C-469/03 *Miraglia*, judgment of 10 March 2005.
146. See C-150/05 *Van Straaten*, judgment of 28 September 2006, at para. 59.
147. See R. Lööf, above n. 126.
148. Lööf suggests that the ECJ conceives of the AFSJ as a single social contractual unit within which there can be no divergences in the normative status of individuals vis-à-vis the collective. Ibid.
149. C-288/05 *Kretzinger*, judgment of 18 July 2007.
150. C-297/07 *Klaus Bourquain*.
151. Case C-288/05 *Kretzinger*, judgment of 18 July 2007.
152. Ibid., at para. 42.
153. AG Opinion delivered on 5 December 2006, at paras 46 and 49.
154. Ibid., at para. 48.
155. *Kretzinger*, at para. 50.

156. Ibid., at para. 51.
157. EAW, above n. 4, at Article 1. Emphasis added.
158. *Kretzinger*, judgment of 18 July 2007, at para. 59.
159. Ibid., at para. 61.
160. Ibid., at para. 62.
161. Ibid., at para. 66.
162. Article 31(1)(a) states that common action on judicial cooperation in criminal matters shall include 'facilitating and accelerating cooperation between competent ministries and judicial or equivalent authorities of the Member States, including, where appropriate, cooperation through Eurojust, in relation to proceedings and the enforcement of decisions'. Furthermore, it adds that cooperation of national authorities through Eurojust is to be encouraged by promoting support and cooperation between Eurojust and other European-level bodies such as Europol and the European Judicial Network. Article 32 EU provides that the Council can adopt measures allowing for the competent authorities in the field of police and judicial cooperation to operate in the territory of other Member States.
163. Council Framework Decision of 13 June 2002 on joint investigation teams (OJ L 162 20.6.2002, p. 1).
164. Communication on the mutual recognition and mutual trust; above n. 35.
165. Ibid., at p. 8.
166. A first evaluation of the monitoring of the national implementation of AFSJ policies identifies particular deficiencies in respect of the third pillar while acknowledging that the evaluation process is still often premature given the infancy of many policies. Commission Communication: Report on the Implementation of the Hague Programme for 2005, COM (2006) 333, final, 28.6.2006.
167. COM(2006) 332, final, 28.6.2006. The Communication includes a series of fact sheets on each policy area to facilitate the assessment of the implementation of EU instruments in that area. It lists 'objectives' of each policy sub-area and then provides a series of 'indicators' that may form useful benchmarks for evaluation.
168. COM(2006) 356, final, 29.06.2006.
169. Commission Communication of 14 July 2004 to the Council and the European Parliament 'Financial Perspectives 2007–2013' COM(2004) 101 final, 14.7.2004.
170. Commission Communication establishing for the period 2007–2013 a framework programme on fundamental rights and justice (OJ C 211, 30.8.2005, p. 6).

5. The external dimension of EU action in criminal matters

In 1997, McGoldrick, in his *International Relations Law of the European Union*,[1] illuminated the manner in which the EU had emerged as a significant actor on the international stage. However, then as now, this development was less mature and cohesive in the area of criminal justice than in other spheres of activity. For instance, it was not until late 2005 that the first overall strategy was elaborated in an effort to bring a much needed element of coherence to the external dimensions of this important policy area. This was brought about in direct response to the political demands made in the November 2004 Hague Programme. The 'Strategy for the External Dimension of JHA: Global Freedom, Security and Justice' endorsed by Europe's leaders is examined in the final section of this chapter.

The reasons for the limited onus upon the external dimension of EU activity in this field are in some measure formal. As Monar reminds us, 'When justice and home affairs (JHA) were for the first time introduced by the Treaty of Maastricht (1993) as a policy-making domain of the EU, no provision was made for cooperation of the Union with third countries.'[2] As we noted earlier in the book,[3] it was only with the conclusion and entry into force of the Treaty of Amsterdam that the first steps were taken to address this fundamental constraint. Even then the perspective of the Union remained – perhaps unsurprisingly – primarily inward looking. It is, for example, instructive to note that there are no references in the existing treaties to the external objectives of the area of freedom, security and justice.[4]

Even in the pre-Maastricht era, however, the area of external relations in the criminal justice sphere was not a complete wasteland. By way of illustration, the possession of EC legislative competence gave rise, even at that time, to a parallel competence over international treaties. Thus, in 1988, negotiations were conducted in Vienna on the UN Convention against Illicit Traffic in Narcotic Drugs and Psychotropic Substances, the first of the modern era of global instruments addressing crimes of international concern.[5] Article 26(c) of that text made provision for its signature by 'regional economic integration organizations which have competence in respect of the negotiation, conclusion and application of international agreements in matters covered by this Convention . . . .' Article 27(2) authorised the deposit of instruments of formal confirmation by the same which were required to contain a declaration of the extent of the competence in question. In June 1989, the Community signed this UN multilateral treaty. Subsequently a Council Decision authorised the deposit of the instrument of confirmation. The associated declaration of competence is revealing: 'the European Economic Community is at present competent for questions of commercial policy relating to the substances frequently used in the illicit manufacture of narcotic drugs and psychotropic substances, questions which are dealt with in Article 12 of the Convention'.

Given this involvement it is perhaps unsurprising that the Commission was to become engaged in the subsequent informal policy discussions initiated by the G-7 Summit meeting in Houston, Texas in July 1990. These were designed to address what were perceived to be the insufficiencies in the approach of the Convention to the problem of chemical diversion.[6]

The 1988 UN Convention was also the first international treaty instrument to require the domestic criminalisation of money-laundering, an obligation binding only on the individual Member States. Notwithstanding this fact, the then EEC was to have a voice in the informal process of standard setting in this field which was to follow and which continues to the present.

At the July 1989 Paris Summit Meeting of the Heads of State or Government of the seven major industrialised nations, joined by the President of the Commission, it was concluded that there was an urgent need for action on various aspects of the international drugs problem, including the laundering of its proceeds. In that context a decision was taken to create the Financial Action Task Force on Money Laundering (FATF).[7] This is an informal and ad hoc grouping with an agenda which is focused on countering the laundering of the proceeds of crime and (since October 2001) the financing of terrorism. Though located within the OECD in Paris it is not formally part of that or any other international organisation. It consists of a number of industrialised or otherwise strategically important countries. Interestingly for present purposes, the European Commission and 15 of the 27 EU Member States are members of the FATF.[8] The remaining 12 participate in MONEYVAL – a FATF-style regional body which operates under the auspices of the Council of Europe in Strasbourg.[9] The FATF is perhaps best known for its package of 40 Recommendations. These were first formulated in 1990 and have since been revised and extended in 1996 and 2003.[10] Shortly after the 9-11 terrorist attacks on the United States, its mandate was extended to countering the financing of terrorism and a range of Special Recommendations were adopted in this sphere.[11]

There are several points worthy of mention in this context. First, and from the outset, its package of Recommendations has focused on three central areas: (i) improvements to national criminal justice systems; (ii) the strengthening of international criminal and administrative cooperation; and (iii) enhancing the role of the financial system and other relevant private sector actors in the prevention of these forms of criminal conduct.[12] Second, the Task Force has put in place a highly intrusive process of peer review through which it seeks to evaluate the formal compliance with and effective implementation of its standards by its member countries (though not the Commission).[13] Third, it has a capacity to sanction members and (controversially) non-members for serious non-compliance.[14] Such procedures have been utilised against an EU Member State (Austria)[15] and a (then) candidate country for admission (Hungary).[16] Finally, it is not without interest that 'thus far the Community has adopted three directives on money laundering (and a series of other measures including those on confiscation and cash movements) which have been justified on the basis of the need to comply with FATF requirements and incorporate FATF-produced standards in Community law'.[17] The first of those Directives was of course a pre-Maastricht text.[18]

In more recent times, and especially since the amendments brought about by the Treaty of Amsterdam and the Treaty of Nice, the prospects for the EU to become a formal actor on the international stage and thus to require less emphasis on informal mechanisms and strategies of influence have increased. It is to that subject that this chapter now turns.

COOPERATION WITH THIRD STATES AND BODIES: GENERAL

Since, as a matter of public international law, the capacity of a non-state body to engage in international relations (and in particular to conclude treaties) is seen as the key to determining the possession and extent of the separate international legal personality which it enjoys, it is understandable that much of the recent EU literature has come to focus on this issue. Certainly, the treaties do not endow the EU with express legal personality. However, an examination of the practice of the EU institutional actors arguably reveals its implied legal personality.[19] In what follows we sketch developments in three areas: the limited practice of the EU in the conclusion of international agreements within the scope of Title VI EU, the coordination of EU negotiations in multilateral fora and subsequent ratification, and the competence and practice of specialised bodies within the institutional architecture of the third pillar, especially Europol and Eurojust, to conclude agreements with third parties. This will be followed by a more detailed exposition of the extensive and by no means uncontroversial practice with regard to the United States of America.

EU Competence to Conclude International Agreements

The basis for the conclusion of international agreements under the third pillar flows from the interaction of Articles 24 and 38 EU. Article 38 EU stipulates that agreements referred to in Article 24 EU, a second pillar provison, may cover matters falling under the third pillar. Article 24 EU reads:

1. When it is necessary to conclude an agreement with one or more States or international organisations in implementation of this title, the Council may authorise the Presidency, assisted by the Commission as appropriate, to open negotiations to that effect. Such agreements shall be concluded by the Council on a recommendation from the Presidency.
2. The Council shall act unanimously when the agreement covers an issue for which unanimity is required for the adoption of internal decisions.
3. When the agreement is envisaged in order to implement a joint action or common position, the Council shall act by a qualified majority in accordance with Article 23(2).
4. The provisions of this Article shall also apply to matters falling under Title VI. When the agreement covers an issue for which a qualified majority is required for the adoption of internal decisions or measures, the Council shall act by a qualified majority in accordance with Article 34(3).
5. No agreement shall be binding on a Member State whose representative in the Council states that it has to comply with the requirements of its own constitutional procedure; the other members of the Council may agree that the agreement shall nevertheless apply provisionally.
6. Agreements concluded under the conditions set out by this Article shall be binding on the institutions of the Union.

So, according to this distinctive procedure, 'the Council authorizes the Presidency to open negotiations with third countries or international organizations and concludes such negotiations on a recommendation by the Presidency'.[20] Here, the Presidency has the right of initiative, the general decision-making rule is that of unanimity, and there is no role afforded to the European Parliament. Furthermore Article 24(5) stipulates that 'No agreement shall be binding on a Member State whose representative in the Council states that it has to comply with the requirements of its own constitutional procedure . . .'.

Given these complexities it is perhaps not surprising that this treaty-making facility has been utilised only relatively infrequently. Indeed, its primary use thus far has been in the context of developing the post 9-11 relationship with the United States, a subject discussed in greater detail in the next section of this chapter. Examples of its use elsewhere include the 2003 agreement between the EU and Iceland and Norway on the application of certain provisions of the 2000 Convention on mutual assistance in criminal matters,[21] and that concluded between the same parties on surrender procedures.[22] Interestingly the earlier treaty associating these two Nordic States with the Schengen *acquis* was 'negotiated in accordance with the sui generis rules applicable to that issue set out in the Schengen Protocol'.[23]

BOX 5.1

Article 188 L TFEU empowers the EU to conclude international agreement with third countries or international organisations:

'where the Treaties so provide or where the conclusion of an agreement is necessary in order to achieve, within the framework of the Union's policies one of the objectives referred to in the treaties, or is provided for in a legally binding Union act or is likely to affect common rules or alter their scope.'

Under Article 188 N(8) TFEU, the voting arrangements in Council for the conclusion of such acts mirror those applicable in the substantive policy.

Coordination of EU Negotiations in Multilateral Fora

A second form of external activity relevant to criminal justice matters flows from the negotiation of multilateral agreements in other fora, and in particular within the United Nations and the Council of Europe. In this regard Article 37 EU 'provides for the coordination of EU action in international conferences and the defence of relevant common positions in conferences.[24] A number of such common or joint positions have been adopted in practice. Examples include, at the global level, the negotiations surrounding the UN Convention against Transnational Organised Crime and its Protocols[25] and those concerning the conclusion of the UN Corruption Convention.[26]

Given the modern emphasis on strategies of prevention, the engagement of the private sector and like matters in the development of international criminal justice measures, it is increasingly unusual for such negotiations to lack a cross-pillar dimension. In such instances the resulting process can be both complex and cumbersome. The negotiation of the 2005 Council of Europe Convention on Laundering, Search, Seizure and Confiscation of the Proceeds from Crime and on the Financing of Terrorism[27] (commonly known as the Warsaw Convention) well illustrates this reality.[28] In 1990, the Council of Europe adopted a multilateral convention on money laundering and the confiscation of criminal proceeds[29] which thereafter came to assume a central role in the facilitation of pan-European cooperation in this high-profile sphere. It was eventually ratified by, *inter alia*, all EU Member States and came to be considered to be part of the *acquis* of the Union. Its importance in the evolution of a coordinated EU response to money laundering is well illustrated by a Joint Action of 3 December 1998.[30] Building upon the fact of full Member State participation it sought to ensure, among other matters, that no reservations were made or upheld by EU countries in relation to two of the critical provisions of the 1990 Convention. This measure was, in turn, amended and strengthened by a Council Framework Decision of 26 June 2001.[31]

Following detailed consideration in Strasbourg, the European Committee on Crime Problems (CDPC) of the Council of Europe established a mechanism to review the 1990 text in the light of subsequent developments and to update it and complement it as necessary. The relevant committee of the experts (PC-RM) consisted of delegations from each state party, supplemented by a range of other representatives and observers. Both the European Commission and the Secretariat General of the Council were invited to send representatives, though without the right to vote.

Given the presence on the agenda of matters such as the *prevention* of money laundering (the focus of the money laundering Directives) it was clear that the negotiations would cover areas within the competence both of the Community and of the third pillar. Accordingly, in addition to obtaining a mandate for the Commission to take part in the negotiations, a Council Common Position was also proposed. Framed in general terms the primary purpose of this initiative was to ensure that 'the provisions drawn up in the framework of the Council of Europe shall be compatible with instruments drawn up on the basis of Title VI of the EU Treaty'.[32] To this end the acting Presidency of the Council, assisted by the Commission, was charged with coordinating the position of the Member States and seeking to arrive at a common standpoint on relevant Title VI issues.[33]

The negotiations took place in Strasbourg in seven separate sessions between December 2003 and February 2005. They were far from straightforward and were characterised by the necessity for the EU grouping to meet separately with considerable frequency, often on a daily basis, in advance of the commencement of the formal sessions and on occasion immediately after the same. The text of the new Warsaw Convention was approved by the CDPC in March and it was adopted by the Committee of Ministers of the Council of Europe in May 2005.[34]

Though a review of the resulting text is beyond the scope of this work, it would be fair to say that existing EU instruments had a significant impact. This is perhaps particularly evident in the provisions dealing with Financial Intelligence Units[35] and access to information on bank accounts and banking transactions.[36] In addition the emphasis in the Common Position that the Convention apply equally to the financing of terrorism was fully realised.[37] Two other factors are particularly worthy of note for present purposes. First, Article 49 makes express provision for the 'European Community' to participate in the treaty regime as established. Second, Article 52(4) was specifically inserted to save Community and Union rules in the mutual relations of EU Member States. Upon its adoption the Community and the Member States of the EU made the following declaration on this matter:

> The European Community/European Union and its Member States reaffirm that their objective in requesting the inclusion of a 'disconnection clause' is to take account of the institutional structure of the Union when acceding to international conventions, in particular in case of transfer of sovereign powers from the Member States to the Community.
>
> This clause is not aimed at reducing the rights or increasing the obligations of a non-European Union party vis-à-vis the European Community/European Union and its Member States, inasmuch as the latter are also parties to this Convention.
>
> The disconnection clause is necessary for those parts of the Convention which fall within the competence of the Community/Union, in order to indicate that European Union Member States cannot invoke and apply the rights and obligations deriving from the Convention directly among themselves (or between themselves and the European Community/Union). This does not detract from the fact that the Convention applies fully between the European Community/European Union and its Member States, on the one hand, and the other Parties to the Convention, on the other; the Community and the European Union Member States will be bound by the Convention and will apply it like any party to the Convention, if necessary, through Community/Union legislation. They will thus guarantee the full respect of the Convention's provisions vis-à-vis non-European Union parties.[38]

Subsequently, in June 2005, the Action Plan implementing the Hague Programme called for early attention to be given to the signature of the

Warsaw Convention on behalf of the EC.[39] However, as of June 2007, and notwithstanding the EU-sensitive nature of the text, action on this matter was still pending 'due to disagreements between Member States'.[40]

Agreements between Specialised EU Bodies and Third Parties

Turning now to a separate and third form of external action in criminal matters, namely, the extent to which the ever-increasing range of organs and bodies which have emerged within the institutional architecture of the third pillar are empowered to formalise relations with non-EU countries and institutions and have exercised such powers in practice. Here attention naturally turns to the position concerning Europol and Eurojust.[41]

In so far as Europol is concerned, it will be recalled that Article 26 of its constituent instrument endows it with legal personality and Article 42 directly addresses relations with third states and third bodies.[42] A Council Act of 3 November 1998 in turn establishes the procedures which must be followed.[43] These are somewhat complex. As Nilsson has remarked:

> . . . it is the Council that unanimously determines the third State or non-European Union body with which agreements are to be negotiated. In a second step, the Council gives its authorisation to Europol to begin the negotiations. Before the negotiations actually begin, the Director of Europol must consult with the Management Board of Europol. In a third step, the Council approves the agreement unanimously.[44]

In instances in which it is envisaged that the resulting agreement will permit the exchange of personal data, further strictures apply.[45]

Although the Europol Convention entered into force in October 1998, it was not until March 2000 that the Director was provided with the necessary authority to enter into negotiations. The relevant Council Decision provided this in respect of 23 named countries and three international bodies.[46] However, in an associated declaration, the Council expressed the view that priority should be afforded 'to the accession candidates, the Schengen cooperation partners (Iceland and Norway), Switzerland and Interpol'.[47] It is of some interest to note that the United States did not feature in this priority grouping. The March 2000 Decision has been amended on occasion since in order to extend the range of countries in question.[48]

In practice two broad categories of cooperation have emerged. In the words of the 2006 Europol Annual Report: 'Operational agreements allow for the exchange of personal data with a cooperation partner. Strategic agreements make it possible for the two involved parties to exchange strategic and technical information and provide training. They do not allow for the exchange of personal data.'[49] As of late 2007, Europol had concluded operational agreements with six non-EU countries (Canada, Croatia, Iceland, Norway, Switzerland, USA) and with Interpol. Several of these also make provision for Liaison Officers to be stationed at the Europol Headquarters in The Hague.[50] Strategic agreements had been finalised with seven non-EU members (Albania, Bosnia and Herzegovina, Colombia, FYROM, Moldova, Russia, Turkey) and with the World Customs Organization and the UN Office on Drugs and Crime (UNODC). Further negotiations with other potential partners were in train.

As with the Europol Convention, the Council Decision of 28 February 2002 setting up Eurojust stipulates expressly that it possesses legal person-ality.[51] In addition, it authorises the conclusion of agreements with inter-national organisations and bodies and with the 'authorities of third States which are competent for investigations and prosecutions'.[52] In common with Europol, special additional protections apply to the transmission of personal data.[53] All agreements with third states and bodies must be approved by the Council. That said, the external controls on this aspect of the work of Eurojust are, for reasons which are not entirely clear, less onerous than in the case of Europol. As Nilsson has noted: 'Neither the Council, nor any of its preparatory bodies, such as Coreper or the Article 36 Committee, has ever had the occasion to discuss, on a horizontal level, with whom Eurojust should begin or maintain external relations.'[54] Left, save in respect of the United States, to its own devices, the practice has emerged in a manner which no doubt reflects the operational realities and the practical opportunities which have arisen in practice. As of late 2007, agreements had been concluded only with three non-EU countries (Iceland, Norway, USA). However, as is clear from its 2006 Annual Report, further possibilities are under active negotiation or in contemplation.[55]

COOPERATION WITH THE UNITED STATES OF AMERICA

The subject of EU–US cooperation in the criminal justice sphere is by no means new. Indeed, it pre-dates the Maastricht Treaty and the creation of the third pillar. It will be recalled that, from the mid-1970s, the Trevi Group, created under the auspices of European Political Cooperation, acted as a forum to coordinate responses to, among other matters, international ter-rorism.[56] The structure included the so-called 'Friends of Trevi', among whom were counted both the US and Canada.[57] Similarly, in the post-Maastricht period, transnational criminal justice issues have continued to arise for consideration in several contexts and particularly at the various high-level meetings with the US which take place within the framework of regular consultation formalised by the new Transatlantic Agenda of 1995. That said, there is little indication that this relationship was afforded a particularly high priority in either Brussels or Washington prior to the attacks on the Twin Towers in September 2001. As was noted above, for example, the Europol Convention of 1995 paved the way for the creation of formalised relationships between that new body and non-Member States and relevant international organisations. Yet, in 2000, the United States was not placed within the priority group for early engagement. Even less emphasis was placed by Brussels on the possibility of taking advantage of the EU to negotiate agreements with non-Member States in the associated sphere of judicial cooperation in criminal matters. The US, for its part, seemed largely content to rely on existing bilateral relationships with the then 15 Member States in both the police and judicial cooperation areas.

Such attitudes were to be radically transformed by the terrorist outrage perpetrated against the US on 11 September 2001.[58] Acting with unprecedented speed, the European Council was able to meet in extraordinary session on 21 September and adopt a detailed and ambitious plan of action to combat terrorism. Characterised as a 'coordinated and interdisciplinary approach embracing all Union policies',[59] it laid particular emphasis on the following themes:

- Enhancing police and judicial cooperation;
- Developing international legal instruments;
- Putting an end to the funding of terrorism;
- Strengthening air security;
- Prioritising cooperation with the United States; and
- Coordinating the EU's global action.

In giving effect to this new 'priority objective' the Council would ensure that the 'approach is reconciled with respect for the fundamental freedoms which form the basis of our civilisation'.[60] On the following day, the Presidency convened a meeting with the Ambassadors of the candidate countries. They agreed unanimously to align themselves with the Action Plan.[61] On 4 October, the European Parliament adopted a highly supportive resolution.[62]

Prior to 9-11, there is no indication that the possibility of the EU concluding agreements with the US in the areas of extradition or mutual legal assistance was under serious contemplation. These sensitive issues had, in practice, been within the sole province of individual Member States when it came to contacts with third countries. Thus all 15 had bilateral extradition treaties with the US, while 11 had signed or ratified mutual assistance agreements.[63] Furthermore, there existed significant tensions in relationships. Some, such as opposite attitudes to the death penalty, were differences of long standing. Others, including detention of suspects at Guantanamo, trial by Military Commissions and approaches to the International Criminal Court, were of a more recent vintage.

Taking account of these factors, it was something of a surprise when, on 20 September 2001, the Justice and Home Affairs Council agreed 'on the principle of proposing to the US that an agreement be negotiated . . . in the field of penal cooperation on terrorism'.[64] On the same day a joint EU–US Ministerial Statement identified 'police and judicial cooperation, including extradition' as one of the areas in which they would 'vigorously pursue cooperation'.[65] It was not long, however, before this terrorism-specific focus was lost.[66] Similarly, it soon became clear that the discussions would extend beyond extradition, which was the area of greatest American interest, to embrace improvements in mutual assistance in the investigation and prosecution of crime. This was a subject area heavily favoured by the EU, but one which, at least initially, does not appear to have been a major US priority. At the informal JHA meeting in Santiago de Compostela in February 2002, this process was given the necessary political endorsement. This was followed by the adoption on 26 April of a negotiation mandate, thus paving the way for the first round of talks which took place at the end of June.[67] Two agreements were eventually concluded in the spring of 2003 and signed at the White House on 25 June.[68]

In discussing the nature, scope and value of the resulting texts, several points should be borne in mind. First, the discussions took place in the strictest of secrecy. Formal announcements during the process were infrequent and uninformative. The drafting history has not been made public. Second, these have not been the only developments within Europe relevant to these areas of concern with potential treaty implications for the US. One can point, for example, to the conclusion of an amending protocol to the European Convention on the Suppression of Terrorism.[69] Significantly – and unlike the text of the 1977 original – this has been drafted in such a way as to permit the US to become a Party.[70] In addition, the US participated in several of the sessions of negotiations in Strasbourg of the 2005 Warsaw Convention on money laundering and terrorist financing and is eligible to become a Party to it.[71] This has, among other matters, extended opportunities for international cooperation in these areas, including enhanced access to bank account information. Third, it is of importance to bear in mind that these EU–US agreements are *not* intended to be comprehensive in terms of their coverage. Finally, as stressed by the UK Home Office in its Explanatory Memorandum to the House of Lords European Committee, they do not preclude the negotiation of future bilateral treaties.[72] Indeed, a new UK–US Extradition treaty was negotiated in tandem with the EU process.[73]

The emphasis by the EU, from the outset, was placed on *adding value* to the existing treaty relationships of Member States. As the Danish Presidency put it in September 2002 in Copenhagen, for this reason the 'Presidency concentrates on the subjects contained in the negotiation mandate, including the new forms of legal assistance which modern technology has made possible . . . .'[74] It follows from the nature of this exercise that the 'value added' will differ significantly from one Member State to another: the more recent and more comprehensive the coverage in existing bilaterals the less the practical significance of what has been achieved in these 'package deal' negotiations.[75] Similarly, the need to interface with a large number of treaties of a bilateral nature necessitated an emphasis on flexibility rather than rigidity in the elaboration of these agreements.

For these reasons, among others, an evaluation of the significance of these texts is by no means straightforward. Notwithstanding its obvious limitations, some indications can be gleaned by examining the outcome against the known negotiating priorities of both sides. The results, on this basis, are particularly disappointing for the US, for whose benefit the initiative was launched. Perhaps the three most significant objectives of the US in the area of extradition were (1) to narrow down the political offence exception, (2) to address problems connected with the extradition of nationals, and (3) to modernise the definition of extraditable offences so as to utilise a penalty threshold approach rather than an archaic list of offences. Of these only the last finds reflection in the final text.[76]

The priorities of the EU in this sphere fared much better. These revolved primarily around building in adequate safeguards and guarantees concerning such sensitive matters as the death penalty and the protection of human rights and fundamental freedoms. The issue of capital punishment is treated in Article 13. This retains the traditional discretion to refuse extradition in capital cases. In the view of the Council Secretariat the final formulation constitutes an advance, though a modest one, in that it is no longer dependent upon assurances being provided on a case-by-case basis by the US authorities.

The outcome of the negotiations in the area of fundamental rights and freedoms is more complex and less transparent, but may well be of more significance. At first glance the extradition agreement appears to do little in this area. It contains no explicit human rights clause to regulate instances in which there may be an ECHR bar to extradition, nor is there a specific prohibition of surrender for trial before military tribunals or other special courts. Here coverage of an explicit nature is confined to the Preamble. This records that the parties are 'mindful of the guarantees under their respective legal systems which provide for the right to a fair trial to an extradited person, including the right to adjudication by an impartial tribunal established pursuant to law'. Given the obvious sensitivities of the US on this matter – and its domestic political importance – such treatment in the final text is encouraging.

Furthermore, immediately prior to scrutiny in the House of Lords, it became apparent, on the basis of 'leaked' internal documents from Brussels, that the inclusion of a non-derogation provision was regarded as 'a major achievement' in this context. It is embodied in Article 17 and reads as follows:

1.   This Agreement is without prejudice to the invocation by the requested State of grounds for refusal relating to a matter not governed by this Agreement that is available pursuant to a bilateral extradition treaty in force between a Member State and the United States of America.
2.   Where the constitutional principles of, or final judicial decisions binding upon, the requested State may pose an impediment to fulfilment of its obligations to extradite, and resolution of the matter is not provided for in this Agreement or the applicable bilateral treaty, consultations shall take place between the requested and requesting States.

In an internal memorandum of 24 February 2003, the impact of Article 17(2) is described thus:

> This provision may . . . be invoked by Member States which on the basis of their constitutional principles consider to refuse extradition in cases of special courts or where they have concerns about rights to a fair trial. The Presidency notes that this provision should be read also in the light of the preamble paragraph that makes reference to fair trials.[77]

Subsequently the text was revised, at the instance of the EU, to include reference to final judicial decisions binding on the requested state; terminology which can be read as covering the decisions of, *inter alia*, the European Court of Human Rights.

Interestingly there is no obvious basis for restricting or confining this form of reading of Article 17(2) to the fair trial issue alone. Consequently, the Select Committee of the European Union in the UK House of Lords explored the interpretation of this provision with Home Office representatives and at some length. The outcome was summarised by Lord Grenfell, the Chair of the Select Committee, in a letter of 12 June 2003 to the relevant Under Secretary of State at the Home Office, as follows: 'We . . . particularly welcome the clarification that the non-derogation provision . . . constitutes an implied ground for refusal of extradition on ECHR grounds . . . and that this interpretation is shared by other Member

States.'[78] To the extent that this is so it is a notable achievement and constitutes an important though imperfect precedent.

The mutual assistance negotiations when subject to the same form of examination reveal much the same outcome.[79] For instance, none of the priority issues identified by the US find reflection in the final text. By way of contrast, the goal of the EU of extending the scope of assistance to selected areas covered by the 2000 EU mutual assistance convention[80] and its 2001 protocol,[81] and securing associated improvements in the efficiency of the operation of this area of assistance, are extensively treated. Looked at in this light it can be argued that there is a significant 'valued added' to mutual assistance by virtue of the conclusion of the agreement. On the other hand, and as noted earlier, some of the same ground (and in particular that of access to bank account and related information) is covered in the 2005 Warsaw Convention which is open to participation by the United States. Furthermore the Second Additional Protocol to the European Convention on Mutual Assistance in Criminal Matters, concluded under the auspices of the Council of Europe in 2001,[82] was in large measure inspired by the EU Convention of 2000 and covers many of the same areas as the EU–US Agreement. This is an open instrument in that participation is not confined to Council of Europe states.[83] Consequently, the US could seek to become a party should it so wish. In short, several of the apparent advantages contained in the EU–US text are available to the US through other mechanisms, ones which have the potential to extend to a broader range of European countries.

It can of course be argued that the significance of these agreements with the US should be viewed more broadly. This would include the symbolic importance of Europe and America being seen to stand 'shoulder to shoulder' in the fight against terrorism. Such symbolic matters also have an EU-specific dimension. As Mitsilegas has noted, the agreements 'constitute an unprecedented step for the European Union towards becoming a global player in the area of criminal law and policy'.[84] In this context it is perhaps not without relevance that, though the agreements were negotiated within a time-frame so tight as to preclude meaningful scrutiny by the national parliaments of EU Member States,[85] and were signed in a welter of positive publicity, as of late 2007 a sense of urgency to bring them into force had yet to manifest itself. This may in part be due to the formal complexities inserted in the instruments themselves.[86] For instance, as has been noted elsewhere, Article 3(2)(a) requires 'the exchange of written instruments between Member States and the USA which acknowledge the application of their bilateral agreements in the light of the provisions of the EU–USA agreements'.[87] However, as of 17 October 2007, some 12 Member States 'still needed to finalise the constitutional procedures with regard to these bilateral instruments'.[88] For its part the administration of President Bush did not transmit the two agreements to the US Senate for its advice and consent until late September 2006 and, as of the time of writing, the relevant Senate hearings had yet to take place.[89]

These were not the only EU–US agreements to emerge as a consequence of the focus of transatlantic relations on terrorism. As has been pointed out elsewhere, '[in] a response to the nature of the September 11 attacks, US legislation adopted in November 2001 required all air carriers operating flights to, from or through the USA to provide US Customs with electronic access to data contained in their automatic reservation and departure control systems.'[90] Concerns over the possible impact of the measure on EU carriers and associated issues of compatibility with European data protection legislation prompted the Commission to initiate negotiations with Washington. These were long and difficult, but, in 2004, and following a Commission Decision on the adequate protection of personal data, the EC–USA PNR (passenger name record) agreement was concluded.[91]

The European Parliament, with the support of the European data protection supervisor, then sought the annulment by the European Court of Justice of the decision which had authorised its conclusion. The grounds for challenge were that the authorising decision breached fundamental rights, the principle of proportionality, the fundamental principle of the data protection directive, and that it had been adopted incorrectly on the basis of Articles 95 and 300(2) EU. In its judgment of 30 May 2006,[92] the Court upheld the challenge solely with reference to the legality issue. It 'found that both the adequacy decision and the agreement were adopted under the wrong legal basis and should be annulled'.[93] As a consequence, the original agreement had to be denounced by the Council.[94] Assisted by the Court, which had provided a limited window of opportunity in which the authorities could address the resulting practical difficulties, further discussion took place between Brussels and Washington, out of which a new (interim) agreement emerged in October 2006.[95] This so-called 'EU–US PNR' agreement, unlike its first pillar predecessor, finds its legal basis in Articles 38 and 24 EU. A long-term agreement was finally concluded in July of 2007.[96]

Data protection concerns have also loomed large in the building of formal relationships with the US in the sphere of police and prosecutorial cooperation. By way of context, it will be recalled that the two major themes of the post 9-11 action plan relevant to law enforcement cooperation were to enhance the effectiveness of anti-terrorism measures within the EU and to maximise collaboration with the US. In the former sphere the task was facilitated by, among other matters, the fact that Europol's subject matter mandate had embraced terrorism since 1 January 1999.[97] Consequently, it was possible to fit many of the initiatives which had been identified within already existing structures. This included, for example, the timely and systematic sharing with Europol of all useful data on terrorism, and the creation of a specialist anti-terrorism team within Europol itself.[98]

The measures in the terrorism action plan designed to improve police cooperation with the US were not quite so straightforward. One of the central themes was to improve and consolidate a framework of cooperation between Europol and the US. However, as we have seen, no formal agreement had yet been concluded between them. Consequently, Ministers urged that the maximum opportunities afforded by the Convention should be taken to establish *informal* cooperation pending the expedited conclusion of such an agreement.[99]

An interim agreement (excluding the transmission of personal data) was signed on 11 December 2001.[100] Its purpose is to enhance cooperation in the prevention, detection and investigation of crimes within the subject matter mandate of Europol including, but not limited to, terrorism.[101] This goal was to be achieved, in particular 'through the exchange of strategic and technical information'.[102] The text also provides for the exchange of Liaison Officers – an option since taken up by both parties.[103] This development has, in turn, assisted in meeting associated goals such as the establishment of close working relations between the Europol team of counter-terrorism specialists and their American counterparts. In December 2001, the Council also authorised the Director of Europol to open negotiations for a further agreement which would include exchange of personal data and related information. That second or supplemental agreement was finally adopted by the JHA Council on 19 December 2002 and signed the following day.[104] It was, in turn, the subject of an exchange of letters which contains amplifications or clarifications of the proper interpretation of several of its key provisions.[105]

Its purpose, as set out in Article 1, is to 'enhance cooperation in preventing, detecting, suppressing and investigating criminal offences within the respective jurisdiction of the parties, in particular by facilitating the reciprocal exchange of information, including personal data'. This must be read in conjunction with Article 3 entitled 'Scope of Assistance' and Article 5 on 'General Terms and Conditions'. Paragraph 1(a) of the latter has been the source of some debate. It is worded thus:

> 1. (a) Transmission of information under this agreement to, and its further processing by, the receiving Party shall be for the purposes set forth in the request, which shall be deemed to include the prevention, detection, suppression, investigation and prosecution of any specific criminal offences, and for any specific analytical purposes, to which such information relates. Where the receiving Party seeks the use of such information for other purposes, it shall ask for the prior consent of the Party that furnished the information.

It will be noted that this uses, in its first sentence, the terminology 'the prevention, detection, suppression, investigation and prosecution of any specific criminal offences'. It will be recalled that, under Article 2 of the Europol Convention, its competence is restricted in a number of ways. Of particular relevance for present purposes, it is permitted to operate only in relation to certain specified offences and not on an all-crimes basis. This remains the position with the amending protocol of 27 November 2003.[106] The question thus arises if, by virtue of Article 5(1)(a), the US will be in a position to use information transmitted by Europol for a wider range of purposes, i.e., in respect of matters which lie beyond its remit.

Unfortunately this issue is not clarified by the treatment of Article 5 in the Exchange of Letters. Indeed the reverse is the case. It is worded as follows:

> The Parties agree that the phrase 'prevention, detection, suppression, investigation and prosecution of any specific criminal offences and for any analytical purposes to which such information relates' as used in Article 5, paragraph 1 *sub* (a), includes, *inter alia*, exchange of information pertaining to immigration investigations and proceedings, and to those relating to *in rem* or *in personam* seizure or restraint and confiscation of assets that finance terrorism or form the instrumentalities or proceeds of crime, even where such seizure, restraint or confiscation is not based on a criminal conviction.

It will be recalled, in particular, that Europol does not possess a general mandate in respect of immigration; this is restricted to matters involving illegal smuggling of human beings.[107] Also of a somewhat problematic character is the extension of cooperation to civil forfeiture proceedings.[108] In the course of UK Parliamentary scrutiny the Government made it clear that, in its view, Article 5, properly constructed, restricts the use of information to matters within Europol's competence and that accordingly 'immigration matters not involving illegal smuggling of human beings would be outside the mandate'.[109] This is by no means the sole matter of controversy. Others include the issue of the adequacy of the treatment of data protection.[110]

Important though such issues are, it is appropriate to recall that even without the spur provided by 9-11 they would have arisen for consideration eventually in the course of the formalisation of the transatlantic relationship in this sphere. Nor should it be forgotten that these agreements do open up the possibility of adding real value in the efforts to combat terrorism. How far this is realised in practice will depend, in large measure, on how credible an actor Europol becomes in this sphere. In the wake of 9-11 significant steps were taken to make a reality of its formal mandate in the counter-terrorism sphere. This was further reinforced in the aftermath of the Madrid bombings. In its declaration on combating terrorism of 25 March 2004, the European Council announced the revision and strengthening of the September 2001 terrorism action plan. In this context it called on Member States to reinforce the counter-terrorism capacities of Europol and to ensure that it is provided with all relevant criminal intelligence related to terrorism as soon as it is available. It also announced its intention to further strengthen cooperation with the US, although no new formal agreements involving Europol appear to be in contemplation at present.

As noted at an earlier stage, the network of formal agreements with the US now extends to prosecutorial matters. Following detailed discussions, an agreement between Eurojust and the US was signed in November 2006 and entered into force in January 2007.[111] It is designed to improve cooperation between the US Department of Justice and Eurojust 'to facilitate the co-ordination of investigations and prosecutions involving the United States and one or more Member States, and to facilitate development of relevant best practices, and assessment of crime trends'.[112] The focus is explicitly on 'serious forms of transnational crime including terrorism'.[113] Interestingly it contains a provision which enables the scope of the agreement to evolve in tandem with future development in Eurojust's mandate and competences.[114] It also envisages the secondment of a US liaison prosecutor[115] and this opportunity was immediately activated. Reflecting the differences in philosophy and approach to data protection between Europe and the US, the operative parts of the text are dominated by detailed treatment of privacy and data protection issues.[116]

CONCLUDING REMARKS

From the above it is evident that the formal tools provided by the treaties to enable the EU to be an actor in its own right in the international criminal justice sphere are limited, complex and cumbersome. It is no doubt in part for these reasons that the use of such powers in practice has been characterised by its occasional, ad hoc and opportunistic nature. In addition, save with respect to Europol, the external dimension of EU action has suffered from the absence of an overall policy framework in this sphere. This Brussels has recently started to address.

The primary catalyst for change in this regard was provided by the Hague Programme of November 2004,[117] which, in its introduction, emphasised the priority which had to be afforded to this matter in respect of crimes of particular concern such as terrorism, organised crime and the smuggling of human beings, which are inherently transnational in nature. In its words:

'Notably in the field of security, the coordination and coherence between the internal and external dimension has been growing in importance and needs to be vigorously pursued.' To that end, for example, the Commission and the Council were urged to take measures 'to ensure coherence between the EU and the international legal order and continue to engage in closer relations with international organisations . . .'.[118] The subsequent Action Plan set out seven specific measures, ranging from the examination of the case for agreements between the EU and third countries on extradition and mutual legal assistance to the conclusion of the UN Convention against Corruption on behalf of the EC.[119] To date, progress has been steady but partial.[120]

More importantly, however, the Hague Programme also called for a comprehensive strategy to be developed by the end of 2005 on the external dimensions of the Union policy on freedom, security and justice:

> All powers available to the Union, including external relations, should be used in an integrated and consistent way to establish the area of freedom, security and justice. The following guidelines should be taken into account: the existence of internal policies as the major parameter justifying external action; need for value added in relation to projects carried out by the Member States; contribution to the general political objectives of the foreign policies of the Union; possibility of achieving the goals during a period of reasonable time; the possibility of long-term action.[121]

It should similarly take appropriate account of the EU's special relations with specific third countries and regions.

Pursuant to this mandate, in December 2005 the Council adopted 'A Strategy for the External Dimension of JHA: Global Freedom, Security and Justice'.[122] This articulates a range of underlying principles, delivery mechanisms and tools as well as addressing the need to achieve maximum coordination in the execution of policy initiatives. Coreper (the Permanent Representatives Committee responsible for preparing the work of the Council) is entrusted 'with cross-pillar responsibility for ensuring coherence across Council work in this area'.[123] The Commission and the Council Secretariat are charged with monitoring progress on a systematic basis and reporting to the Council every 18 months. The first such report was submitted in late 2006.[124] This reflected on progress to date, established priorities for forward action, and set out options to improve cooperation with specific countries and regions. This important development not only holds out the prospect of ensuring a far greater and much needed degree of coherence between the internal and external dimensions to European criminal justice policy in the future, but also of maximising the practical impact, both formal and informal, that the EU can have in this increasingly important area of international concern.[125] Notwithstanding its limited formal powers, its potential international influence in this high-priority sphere is considerable.

NOTES

1. D. McGoldrick (1997), *International Relations Law of the European Union*, London: Longman.
2. J. Monar (2004), 'The EU as an international actor in the domain of justice and home affairs', *European Foreign Affairs Review*, **9**, 395–415, at p. 395.
3. See Chapter 1.
4. Note Article 37 EU, which reads: 'Within international organisations and at international conferences in which they take part, Member States shall defend the common positions adopted under the provisions of this title. Articles 18 and 19 shall apply as appropriate to matters falling under this title.'
5. See, generally, (1998) *Commentary on the United Nations Convention Against Illicit Traffic in Narcotic Drugs and Psychotropic Substances 1988: done at Vienna on 20 December 1988*, New York: United Nations.
6. See W. Gilmore 'Drug trafficking and the control of precursor and essential chemicals: the international dimension', in W. Gilmore and A. Brown (eds) (1996), *Drug Trafficking and the Chemical Industry*, Edinburgh: Edinburgh University Press, 1–24.
7. See W. Gilmore (2004), *Dirty Money: The evolution of international measures to counter money laundering and the financing of terrorism*, 3rd edn, Strasbourg Council of Europe Publishing, at pp. 89–91.
8. The only other full institutional member of the FATF is the Gulf Cooperation Council.
9. W. Gilmore, above at n. 7, at pp. 173–6.
10. Ibid., pp. 92–111.
11. Ibid., pp. 123–9.
12. Ibid., pp. 92–4.
13. See generally, M. Levi and B. Gilmore (2002), 'Terrorist finance, money laundering and the rise and rise of mutual evaluation: a new Paradigm for crime control?', *European Journal of Law Reform*, **4**(2), 337–64.
14. W. Gilmore, above at n. 7, at pp. 137–8 and 146–9.
15. Ibid., at pp. 138–9.
16. This in the context of the FATF's NCCT initiative launched in 2000. See, ibid., at pp. 146–9.
17. V. Mitsilegas (2007), 'The external dimension of EU action in criminal matters', *European Foreign Affairs Review*, **12**, 457–97, at pp. 492–3. See, also, V. Mitsilegas and B. Gilmore (2007), 'The EU legislative framework against money laundering and terrorist finance: a critical analysis in the light of evolving global standards', *International and Comparative Law Quarterly*, **56**, 119–41.
18. Council Directive 91/308/EEC of 10 June 1991 on prevention of the use of the financial system for the purpose of money laundering (OJ L 166, 28.6.1991, p. 77).
19. See P. Koutrakos (2006), *EU International Relations Law*, Oxford: Hart, at p. 8.
20. J. Monar, above n. 2, at pp. 404–5.
21. OJ L 26, 29.1.2004, p. 3.
22. OJ L 292, 21.10.2006, p. 1.
23. S. Peers (2007), *EU Justice and Home Affairs Law*, 2nd edn, Oxford: Oxford University Press, at p. 85.
24. Ibid., p. 84.
25. See, e.g., OJ L 37, 12.2.2000, p. 1.
26. S. Peers, above n. 23, p. 36.
27. Council of Europe Treaty Series/198.

28. An official Explanatory Report, following normal Council of Europe practice, was also drafted in respect of this Convention and is available on its official website: www.coe.int.

29. Council of Europe Treaty Series/141.

30. OJ L 331, 9.12.1998, p. 1.

31. OJ L 182, 5.7.2001, p. 1.

32. Explanatory Report, above n. 28, at pp. 3–4.

33. COM (2004) 444 final, 25.6.2004, Art. 2.

34. Art. 3.

35. As of the time of writing it had not yet entered into force. Of the EU Member States only Poland and Romania had ratified.

36. See, e.g., Arts 12 and 14.

37. See Art. 7. and Arts 17–19.

38. See Art. 2.

39. Explanatory Report, above n. 28, at para. 306.

40. Council document 9778/2/05, Brussels, 10 June 2005, at p. 24.

41. See Commission document SEC (2007) 896, Brussels, 3.7.2007.

42. See, also, H. Nilsson (2003), 'Organs and bodies of the third pillar as instruments of external relations of the Union', in G. de Kerchove and A. Weyembergh (eds), *Sécurité et Justice: enjeu de la politique extérieure de l'Union Européenne*, Brussels: Editions Université de Bruxelles, at p. 206.

43. OJ C 316, 27.11.1995, p. 1.

44. OJ C 26, 30.1.1999, p. 19.

45. H. Nilsson, above n. 42.

46. See, e.g., Council Act of 12 March 1999 governing the transmission of personal data by Europol to third States and third bodies (OJ C 88, 30.3.1999, p. 1).

47. OJ C 106, 13.4.2000, p. 1.

48. Ibid.

49. S. Peers, above n. 23, at p. 558.

50. Ibid., at p. 26.

51. OJ L 63, 6.3.2002.

52. Ibid., at Art. 1.

53. Ibid., at Art. 27.

54. See, e.g., V. Mitsilegas (2006), 'Judicial cooperation in criminal matters between the EU and Third States: international agreements', in M. Leaf (ed.), *Cross-Border Crime* (JUSTICE, 2006), pp. 79–92.

55. H. Nilsson, above n. 42.

56. See 2006 Annual Report, at pp. 52–5.

57. See, e.g., M. Anderson, M. den Boer, P. Cullen, W.G. Gilmore, C.D. Raab and N. Walker (eds) (1995), *Policing the European Union*, Oxford: Clarendon Press, pp. 53–6.

58. See, ibid., at p. 119.

59. See, generally, B. Gilmore (2003), *The Twin Towers and the Third Pillar: Some Security Agenda Developments*, Florence: European University Institute (Working Paper Law No. 2003/7).

60. 'Conclusion and Plan of Action of the Extraordinary European Council Meeting on 21 September 2001', Council of Europe document GMT (2001) Inf. 31, p. 1.

61. See, ibid.

62. Resolution of 4 October 2001 on the extraordinary European Council meeting in Brussels on 21 September 2001.

63. Reproduced as Council of Europe doc. GMT (2001) Inf. 33.

64. See House of Lords, Select Committee on the European Union, 'EU/US Agreements on Extradition and Mutual Legal Assistance', Session 2002–03, 38th Report, HL Paper 153, at p. 9.

65. 'Conclusions adopted by the Council (Justice and Home Affairs)', document 12156/01, 25/9/2001, p. 12.

66. B. Gilmore, above n. 59, at p. 10.

67. See, V. Mitsilegas (2003) 'The new EU–USA cooperation on extradition, mutual legal assistance and the exchange of police data', *European Foreign Affairs Review*, **8**, 515–36, at p. 515.
68. B. Gilmore, above n. 59, at p. 10.
69. V. Mitsilegas, above n. 67, at p. 526.
70. Council of Europe Treaty Series/190.
71. See Art. 10.
72. See Art. 49.
73. V. Mitsilegas, above n. 67, at p. 24.
74. See, ibid.
75. Background paper issued by the Danish Presidency at the informal JHA Ministerial meeting in Copenhagen, 13–14 September 2002. Copy of typescript on file with the authors.
76. House of Lords, above n. 64, at p. 9.
77. See Article 4, OJ L 181, 19.7.2003, p. 27.
78. Unpublished typescript on file with the authors, at p. 8.
79. House of Lords, above n. 64, at p. 40.
80. OJ L 181, 19.7.2003, p. 34.
81. OJ C 197, 12.7.2000, p. 1. For the explanatory report see, OJ C 397, 29.12.2000. See also, E. Denza (2003), 'The 2000 Convention on Mutual Assistance in Criminal Matters' *Common Market Law Review*, **40**, 1047–74.
82. OJ C 326, 21.11.2001, p. 1. For the explanatory report see, OJ C 257, 24.10.2002, p. 1.
83. Council of Europe Treaty Series/182.
84. Ibid., Art. 31.
85. V. Mitsilegas, above n. 67, at p. 533.
86. See, ibid., pp. 523–6.
87. V. Mitsilegas, above n. 17, at p. 476.
88. Ibid., pp. 476–7.
89. See Council document 5916/2/07, Brussels, 17.10.2007, p. 2.
90. Ibid.
91. V. Mitsilegas, above n. 17, p. 477.
92. For the Council Decision on the conclusion of the Agreement see, OJ L 183, 20.5.2004, p. 83. For the Commission Decision as adequate protection, see OJ L 235, 6.7.2004, p. 11.
93. Joined cases C-317/04 and C-318/04, *European Parliament* v *Council and Commission*, judgment of 30 May 2006.
94. V. Mitsilegas, above n. 17, p. 481.
95. OJ C 219, 12.9.2006, p. 1.
96. OJ L 298, 27.10.2006, p. 29.
97. See OJ L 204, 4.8.2007, at pp. 16 and 18.
98. B. Gilmore, above n. 59, at pp. 11–12.
99. See, ibid., at p. 13.
100. The text is to be found on the Europol website: www.europol.europa.eu.
101. See Arts 1 and 3.
102. Art. 1. These terms are defined in Art. 2.
103. See Art. 8.
104. The text is to be found on the Europol website: www.europol.europa.eu.
105. V. Mitsilegas, above n. 67, at p. 520.
106. See OJ C 2, 6.1.2004, p. 1.
107. V. Mitsilegas, above n. 67, at pp. 521–2.
108. See, ibid., at p. 522.
109. Letter from Lord Filkin, Parliamentary Under Secretary of State, Home Office to Lord Grenfell, Chairman of the House of Lords Select Committee on the European Union, 10 January 2003. Copy on file with the authors.
110. V. Mitsilegas, above n. 67, at pp. 517–18.
111. Agreement between Eurojust and the United States of America of 6.11.2006. Text available on the Eurojust website: http://eurojust.europa.eu.

112. Ibid., see Preamble.
113. Ibid., Art. 2.
114. Ibid., Art. 3(2).
115. Ibid., Art. 4.
116. See, e.g., Ibid., Arts 9–18.
117. The Hague Programme: strengthening freedom, security and justice in the European Union, 4–5 November 2004 (OJ C 53, 3.3.2005, pp. 1–14).
118. Ibid., para. 3.4.5.
119. See Council document 9778/2/05, Brussels, 10 June 2005, at p. 24.
120. See Commission document SEC (2007) 896, Brussels, 3.7.2007.
121. The Hague Programme, above n. 117 at '4. External Relations'.
122. See Council document 15446/05, Brussels, 6 December 2005.
123. See ibid., at para. 14. For more on the role of the Council in criminal matters, see Chapter 2.
124. See Council document 15001/06, Brussels, 20 November 2006.
125. See, e.g., V. Mitsilegas, above n. 17, at pp. 457–69.

6. Substantive criminal law

CONTEXT AND GENERAL OVERVIEW

Dealing with the issue of substantive EU criminal law, one is faced with a methodological problem. On the one hand, it is clearly there, and one could without too much difficulty provide an exhaustive list of the existing instruments harmonising the definitions of certain offences in the EU. On the other hand, substantive EU criminal law is frustrating in that it almost defies the legal urge to systematise and to categorise. While there are rational explanations for each individual EU instrument harmonising the definitions of a particular criminal offence, one is hard-pressed to identify the underlying rationale for the collection of criminal offences thus defined. In order to convey this characteristic of EU substantive criminal law, this chapter will begin by providing a short outline of what the EU has achieved in this field. While this list at least has pretentions to exhaustiveness, the matter is such that it cannot be excluded that one or other provision with an influence on substantive criminal law will 'slip through the net'. After this brief outline the chapter will proceed with a more detailed discussion of the main motivating factors behind EU harmonisation of criminal offences. In the context of this discussion, we will look into some of the individual instruments in more detail.

Overview of Criminal Offences defined by the EU

A chronological approach to the task of listing the criminal offences defined by the EU provides a clear illustration of the catalytic effect of the Treaty of Amsterdam and its introduction of the framework decision into the institutional armoury of the EU. Before the advent of the framework decision, very little was accomplished in the field of substantive criminal law. The Convention on the protection of the European Community's financial interests[1] defined the concept of fraud against the EC's financial interests and the Convention on the fight against corruption involving officials of the European Communities or officials of Member States of the European Union[2] defined active and passive corruption involving public officials. In a different category is the Joint Action concerning the information exchange, risk assessment and the control of new synthetic drugs.[3]

While it did not have a direct effect on the criminal legislation of Member States in relation to drugs, it did so indirectly by, in its Article 5, mandating the Council to enjoin Member States to include newly discovered and assessed substances in their criminal legislation in relation to drugs. This Joint Action was repealed by a later Council decision[4] which replaced the enforcement mechanism in relation to newly discovered and assessed substances. However, the latter left in place those Council decisions adopted under Article 5 of the old joint action and there are thus three decisions enjoining Member States to act on a total of seven synthetic drugs.[5]

Probably the most significant legislative achievement in the pre-Treaty of Amsterdam era in the field of substantive criminal law was the 1998 joint action on making it a criminal offence to participate in a criminal organisation in the Member States of the European Union.[6] This instrument enjoined Member States to criminalise both active and supportive participation in a criminal organisation. The definition of a 'criminal organisation' given by the 1998 joint action will be discussed in detail in the context of the discussion on the framework decision defining terrorism for which it is a definite precursor.

As was explained in previous chapters, the pre-Amsterdam institutional framework did not provide the EU with any truly effective tools to influence national approaches, let alone legislation, in the field of criminal law, and substantive criminal law was no exception. Joint actions were little more than aspirational and conventions required passage through standard national ratification procedures in order to be actionable before the courts. It is not improbable that the feeling that it was not very constructive to spend political capital and time on negotiating instruments unlikely to lead very far in practice is one of the explanations for the limited legislative output in the field of criminal justice in general and substantive criminal law in particular in the years between the creation of the third pillar with the Treaty of Maastricht and the institutional amendments brought in by the Treaty of Amsterdam.

Post-Amsterdam, the list of legislative achievements is both longer and simpler. The simplicity stems from the fact that the framework decision has become the absolutely dominant means by which to lay down common definitions of criminal offences. In chronological order of adoption, framework decisions now lay down common definitions of offences in the following fields: counterfeiting,[7] fraud and forgery in respect of non-cash means of payment,[8] money laundering,[9] terrorism,[10] trafficking in human beings,[11] illegal migration,[12] corruption in the private sector,[13] sexual exploitation of children and child pornography,[14] drugs offences,[15] and hacking.[16] The framework decision harmonising the offence of ship-source pollution[17] was recently annulled by the ECJ.[18]

As will be understood by the mention of the challenge to the framework decision on ship-source pollution, the issue of EU definitions of substantive offences is hardly uncontroversial, not even between different EU institutions. So, whereas a list such as the one provided above can give an indication of EU activity in this field, it does nothing to explain why certain offences are singled out for EU harmonisation, nor what the potential boundaries for EU action in the field of substantive criminal law are. In this respect, it has been said that 'examples testify that a good deal of the approximation has been finalized more as a knee-jerk reaction than as a result of a deep and substantive reflection on its need and contents'.[19] In any case, the motives behind the legislative choices made in this field need clarifying. These are the issues to which we now turn.

PROTECTING EU OBJECTIVES AND POLICIES

The great majority of the EU's objectives are of a kind which could be described as 'civil'. The traditional EC objectives – the four freedoms, free and undistorted competition, non-discrimination, etc. – are not part of what could be called the 'core' of the criminal law, by which it is meant, essentially, offences against the person and property offences. However, as is well known, the criminal law long ago extended beyond these traditional confines as it has been thought expedient to make use of criminal penalties to deal with infringements of various regulatory schemes such as taxation, production standards, migration, and also, lately, environmental regulations and competition policy. So it is easy to see that, while the EC Treaty did not confer any express criminal competence on the European institutions, by virtue of their subject-matter EC enactments would inevitably have an indirect effect on the application of national criminal law at the enforcement level. Hence the ECJ pointed out that, if national law provided for criminal prosecution in respect of violations of purely national regulations in a particular field, the principles of remedial effectiveness and equality dictated that the same sanctions be made available for violations of regulations of EC origin in the same field.[20] Likewise, it has been established that rights conferred by a directive can provide an absolute bar to national criminal proceedings.[21]

But these influences of traditional EC law on the criminal law were indirect and incidental. As previously stated, there is no express competence to legislate on criminal matters in the EC Treaty and some articles which deal with EC competences in areas which may in some Member States be regulated through the criminal law even expressly exclude direct EC influence on the application of criminal law. Examples of this can be found in

Articles 135 EC (customs cooperation) and 280(4) EC (fraud against the Community's financial interests). However, the EC Treaty cannot be said to be entirely consistent in this respect. As has been pointed out, notably by Steve Peers,[22] an article which by the same criteria could have been issued with the same reservation with respect to criminal law has not been. This is Article 63(3)(b) EC which enjoins the EC to adopt measures on 'illegal immigration and illegal residence'.

This distinction between the regulatory competence of the EC and the sovereign competence of the Member States to choose to discipline violators of these regulations by way of their national criminal laws was long thought unassailable. The upshot was that, if the EU as a whole considered that criminal measures were required in order to enforce rules and regulations established in pursuance of an EC competence, a parallel, third pillar measure had to be adopted as well: the so-called 'double-text mechanism'. A good example is Directive 2002/90/EC of 28 November 2002 defining the facilitation of unauthorised entry, transit and residence.[23] Adopted on the basis precisely of Article 63(3)(b) EC this directive defines the regulatory breach of intentionally assisting entry and residence in violation of the applicable laws on migration. It stops short of directly imposing on Member States the obligation to criminalise this behaviour. That imposition, however, is found in a framework decision of the same date on the strengthening of the penal framework to prevent the facilitation of unauthorised entry, transit and residence.[24] The framework decision refers to the definitions of the regulatory violations contained in the directive and enjoins Member States to criminalise them. It also provides a certain level of harmonisation in the applicable sanctions.

This almost schizophrenic approach to regulation in areas of established EC competence was based on the idea, already discussed in previous chapters, that to recognise EC competence on any aspect of criminal law, even in the 'quasi-criminal' or 'criminal-regulatory' fields, would constitute a serious intrusion into the jealously guarded sphere of national sovereignty.[25] The Commission, however, did not subscribe to this vision of there being a watertight division between the regulatory competence of the EC and the, if necessary, harmonised reinforcement of the sanction schemes by recourse to the criminal law which had to go through the third pillar.[26] The conflict came to a head when the Commission presented a proposal for a directive based on Article 175(1) EC to deal with environmental offences by way of criminal sanctions. The Council felt that 'the proposal went beyond the powers attributed to the Community by the Treaty establishing the European Community and that the objectives could be reached by adopting a framework decision on the basis of Title VI of the Treaty on European Union'. Consequently, the Council proceeded to adopt

Framework Decision 2003/80/JHA of 27 January 2003 on the protection of the environment through criminal law.[27] Having reserved itself against this solution, the Commission brought an action challenging the legality of the framework decision. Spontaneously, it might be thought an overreaction on behalf of the Commission; its objectives had been met and criminal legislation for environmental offences was now harmonised. It needs to be kept in mind, however, that the differences between the legislative procedures applicable in the first and third pillars are significant. If there were EC competences to impose criminal legislation, it would imply that national criminal law could be modified against the will of an individual Member State since, in most areas of the first pillar, legislation is adopted by a qualified majority vote in Council. Also, EC competence in criminal law would give the EP a say over criminal law in the EU. As we saw in Chapter 2, Article 39(1) EU limits the EP's role in the adoption of third pillar instruments to the right to be consulted by Council; the Council is then free to ignore what the EP had to say. By contrast, under Article 175 EC directives are adopted following the procedure laid down in Article 251 EC. Commonly referred to as 'co-decision', this procedure gives the EP an equal say in legislation with Council and can, *inter alia*, definitively reject a proposal. But the Commission's challenge was even more fundamental than that. The Commission claimed that, by using third pillar instruments to legislate in areas properly covered by the first pillar, the Council had infringed Article 47 EU. This article, it will be recalled, provides that 'nothing in this Treaty shall affect the Treaties establishing the European Communities or the subsequent Treaties and Acts modifying or supplementing them'. In short, if the EC is competent to regulate an area using criminal law, there is no third pillar competence to do the same. As applied to the area involved in the case at hand: if the EC was competent to criminalise certain environmental offences, the Council had violated Article 47 EU by adopting a framework decision criminalising such offences.

On 13 September 2005, the Grand Chamber of the ECJ ruled in favour of the Commission.[28] It stated that, further to Article 47 EU, it was the '*task of the Court to ensure that acts which, according to the Council, fall within the scope of Title VI of the Treaty on European Union do not encroach upon the powers conferred by the EC Treaty on the Community*'.[29] The Court felt that it was '*clear*' that the objective of the framework decision was '*the protection of the environment*'.[30] On the issue of criminal law, the Court held that while '*[a]s a general rule, neither criminal law nor the rules of criminal procedure fall within the Community's competence*',[31] this did

> *not prevent the Community legislature, when the application of effective, proportionate and dissuasive criminal penalties by the competent national authorities is*

an essential measure for combating serious environmental offences, from taking measures which relate to the criminal law of the Member States which it considers necessary in order to ensure that the rules which it lays down on environmental protection are fully effective.[32]

The Court concluded that, 'on account of both their aim and their content, Articles 1 to 7 of the framework decision have as their main purpose the protection of the environment and they could have been properly adopted on the basis of Article 175 EC'.[33] Consequently, it annulled the framework decision for infringement of Article 47 EU.

The whole question now is of course to what extent the reasoning of the ECJ in *Environmental crimes* can be applied to the other objectives and policy areas of the EU. The Commission quickly issued a communication on how it read the ECJ's ruling.[34] Unsurprisingly, it considers that the reasoning in *Environmental crimes* is applicable to all the areas where the EC is competent and where criminal sanctions are deemed essential to the effective enforcement of the rules and regulations laid down under the first pillar.[35] In a resolution, the European Parliament also supports this interpretation.[36] In an annex to the communication, the Commission lists a number of framework decisions which it considers have been adopted on an erroneous legal basis. This list includes pretty much all the framework decisions which can be said to provide criminal enforcement to recognised EC policies, i.e. the framework decisions on counterfeiting, fraud and forgery in respect of non-cash means of payment, money laundering, illegal migration, corruption in the private sector, hacking, and ship-source pollution. The Commission also puts the EP and Council on notice with respect to a pending proposal in respect of which it, presumably, had faced some hesitance in Council and which it feels the ruling in *Environmental crimes* ought to have dispelled: Proposal for a Directive of the European Parliament and of the Council on the criminal-law protection of the Community's financial interests (PIF).[37] Lastly, the Commission feels that one pending 'double-text' proposal should be reconsidered: Proposal for a European Parliament and Council Directive on criminal measures aimed at ensuring the enforcement of intellectual property rights and for a Council Framework Decision to strengthen the criminal law framework to combat intellectual property offences.[38,39] The Commission states that, although formally voidable, the majority of these instruments are safe for the moment because the time limits for introducing a direct action against them has expired. That, however, was not the case with the framework decision on ship-source pollution.[40] The Commission has attacked this latter framework decision seeking its annulment and, additionally, a confirmation that its extensive reading of the *Environmental crimes* ruling is correct.[41]

At issue is a 'double-text mechanism' comprising Directive 2005/35/EC on ship-source pollution[42] and the abovementioned framework decision. The directive lays down the regulatory definition of polluting discharges from sea-going vessels and states that such discharges are 'regarded as infringements if committed with intent, recklessly or by serious negligence. These infringements are regarded as criminal offences by, and in the circumstances provided for in, Framework Decision 2005/667/JHA supplementing this Directive'.[43] Article 2(1) of the framework decision then states that 'each Member State shall take the measures necessary to ensure that an infringement within the meaning of Articles 4 and 5 of Directive 2005/35/EC shall be regarded as a criminal offence'. The arguments are essentially the same as in *Environmental crimes* and it may even seem that the subject-matter is nigh on identical. That may very well be true, but what adds additional flavour is that Directive 2005/35/EC was adopted on the basis of Article 80(2) EC which mandates the Council, 'acting by a qualified majority', to decide 'whether, to what extent and by what procedure appropriate provisions may be laid down for sea and air transport'. This is a peculiar provision which essentially mandates a two-step approach to legislation in this area: first, Council has to decide that regulation is 'appropriate' and, second, to go about the actual legislating using the procedure laid down in Article 251 EC, i.e. co-decision. In practice, the first step has been deemed implicit in the final legislative act. Although it might be formally unorthodox, there seems little to object to in this approach. Given that the voting arrangements in Council are identical for the two decisions, it does indeed seem excessively formal to insist on a formal declaration of an intention to legislate prior to the actual legislation the adoption of which, surely, in and of itself attests to such an intention. Be that as it may, the minimum consequence of a ruling annulling the framework decision for infringement of Article 47 EU is that the EC is deemed competent to oblige Member States to adopt criminal legislation in the area of aerial and maritime transport. It would then be very difficult to argue that the EC's competence to impose criminal legislation in the areas of its substantive competence is limited by any other criteria than necessity and proportionality.

Attesting to the potential importance of the *Ship-source pollution* case, an unprecedented 19 Member States were granted leave to intervene, all in support of the Council. The European Parliament was granted leave to intervene in support of the Commission. A rather uncomfortable EU family reunion, in other words. The Council, supported by the intervening Member States, seeks to limit the ambit of the ECJ's ruling in *Environmental crimes*. It puts forward two main arguments: first, that the protection of the environment is an EU objective of exceptional

importance. So important, in fact, that the EC competence to oblige
Member States to impose criminal provisions is limited, or at least virtually
limited, to this singular EC objective. To this end, the Council draws upon
paragraphs 41 and 42 of *Environmental crimes* where the ECJ states that
'*protection of the environment constitutes one of the essential objectives of
the Community*' and justifies this with reference to mentions of this objective in the gateway Articles 2, 3 and 6 EC. Second, the decision of legislative intent implicit in the directive and formally required by Article 80(2)
EC should be read so as to have limited the ambit of any potential legislation in the area so that EC action, by decision of Council, did *not* include
criminalising ship-source pollution. The upshot of this argumentation is of
course that the Council must be seen to leave it an open question whether
a directive containing an obligation on Member States to criminalise ship-
source pollution is theoretically possible.

On 23 October 2007, the ECJ ruled that '*Framework Decision 2005/667,
in encroaching on the competence which Article 80(2) EC attributes to the
Community, infringes Article 47 EU and, being indivisible, must be annulled
in its entirety.*'[44] Although this does represent a victory for the Commission
in the instant case, the reasoning which led to this decision is far from conclusive on the principled point of the extent of the EC's competence to legislate in the field of substantive criminal law. The Court's reasoning very
much focuses on the specific circumstances of the case, i.e. Article 80(2) EC
and appears very purposefully free from any statements of principle. Right
at the outset, the ECJ quickly does away with the Council's contention that
Article 80(2) EC empowers it to define not only the extent to which it will
exercise its competences but also the extent itself of those competences:
'*[. . .] the existence of the legislative competence conferred by Article 80(2)
EC is not dependent on a decision by the legislature actually to exercise that
competence*'.[45] The issue is then purely that of whether the provisions of the
framework decision on ship-source pollution could have been adopted
under Article 80(2) EC. This is where the ECJ decides to stay very close to
shore. Instead of making a statement of principle on the extent of the EC's
competence to protect its regulatory schemes by way of the criminal law,
the Court focuses on the *de facto* material link between the issue in *Ship-
source pollution* and that in *Environmental crimes*, i.e. the protection of the
environment. It refers to the ruling in *Environmental crimes* and restates
that environmental protection is '*one of the essential objectives of the
Community*' and as such must, '*according to Article 6 EC, "be integrated into
the definition of . . . Community policies and activities."*' The upshot is that
environmental protection '*must be regarded as an objective which also forms
part of the common transport policy*' and that the EC '*may therefore, on the
basis of Article 80(2) EC and in the exercise of the powers conferred on it by*

that provision, decide to promote environmental protection'.[46] The principles laid down in *Environmental crimes* could then be applied *mutatis mutandis* to the present case:

> *Although it is true that, as a general rule, neither criminal law nor the rules of criminal procedure fall within the Community's competence [. . .] the fact remains that, when the application of effective, proportionate and dissuasive criminal penalties by the competent national authorities is an essential measure for combating serious environmental offences, the Community legislature may require the Member States to introduce such penalties in order to ensure that the rules which it lays down in that field are fully effective.*[47]

The ECJ can therefore proceed to annul Framework Decision 2005/667/JHA without formulating any wider principles than it had in *Environmental crimes* because its provisions '*relate to conduct which is likely to cause particularly serious environmental damage as a result, in this case, of the infringement of the Community rules on maritime safety*'.[48]

This very cautious approach by the ECJ needs to be contrasted with the approach adopted by Advocate General Mazák in his opinion of 28 June 2007. He interprets *Environmental crimes* as having been '*fundamentally motivated by and born out of the concern to ensure the full effectiveness of Community law*'.[49] For the Advocate General it therefore followed that '*the Community objective of environmental protection and its* effet utile *would, according to the* ratio *of th[at] judgment, be compromised if the Community did not have the power to adopt the criminal law measures necessary to ensure that the rules which it lays down on environmental protection are fully effective*'.[50] Crucially, then, AG Mazák agreed with the central argument of the Commission that '*there is indeed no sound basis for regarding the power to provide for criminal measures as being limited [to the protection of the environment]*'.[51]

It is this latter Commission argument which the ECJ very consciously omits to rule on. It could even be said that the Court goes some way to endorsing the Council's view that *Environmental crimes* was an exceptional ruling motivated by the exceptional nature of the subject matter, i.e. environmental protection. Whether one considers this to be the case will to a large extent depend on how one reads the judgment's pivotal paragraph:

> *since Articles 2, 3 and 5 of Framework Decision 2005/667 are designed to ensure the efficacy of the rules adopted in the field of maritime safety, non-compliance with which may have serious environmental consequences, by requiring Member States to apply criminal penalties to certain forms of conduct, those articles must be regarded as being essentially aimed at improving maritime safety, as well as environmental protection, and could have been validly adopted on the basis of Article 80(2) EC.*[52]

It is entirely possible to take from the above paragraph that the EC's competence to legislate in the field of substantive criminal law is indeed limited to the protection of the environment only that such protection is a transversal objective of EC action which can be a motivating factor in legislative activity in *all* fields of EC action. The consequence would be that the EC could potentially mandate the criminalisation of activities in all its competence areas as long as such action is motivated by concerns of the environmental impact of those activities. On the other hand, this passage can equally well be read as merely saying that, in the instant case, no further elaboration on the EC's competences in the field of substantive criminal law is necessary.

Finally, the Court predictably confirms its holding in *Environmental crimes* that the '*determination of the type and level of the criminal penalties to be applied does not fall within the Community's sphere of competence*'.[53]

The only little clarification provided by the ECJ in *Ship-source pollution* relates to the criterion of necessity of the harmonisation of criminal law laid down in *Environmental crimes*. Here it would seem that, as long as there is evidence to the effect that Council considered such action to be necessary, the Court will not second-guess it.[54] It is of course the case that this inference is much easier to make in relation to a third pillar framework decision in so far as the Council had to be unanimous in order to adopt it. If a first pillar directive was to be challenged on this basis by an outvoted Member State, we really do not know what criteria the Court would apply. Presumably, it would stick to the purely political criterion laid down in *Ship-source pollution*, since any departure from it would imply that it could overrule also a unanimous Council on the issue of the necessity of any given instrument of criminal approximation.

As will have been understood, *Ship-source pollution* did not provide the clarification sought on the extent of the EC's powers to approximate aspects of substantive criminal law. The result is continued uncertainty in this rather important area. Fortunately, it is far from unlikely that the ECJ will have further opportunities to clarify the situation. In addition to a proposed directive on environmental crimes, the Commission has submitted a proposal for a directive criminalising certain violations of EC regulations in the fields of intellectual property,[55] and more are likely to follow, in particular as the Commission goes to work on revising the framework decisions mentioned in the Annex to its communication on *Environmental crimes* which will certainly entail their redrafting as EC directives. If, for instance, a directive criminalising violations of intellectual property was to be challenged, the ECJ would not be able to continue to refer to environmental protection to justify EC action and the principles of EC competences in this area would have to be ironed out.

The likelihood is that, in future, EU criminal law will have to be subjected to the same division as national criminal laws generally are. One part will be the *core criminal law*, dealing with those rules which, for want of a better expression, are 'socially axiomatic'. By that it is meant those rules which are held to be ends in themselves and not means to achieve further, political objectives. This part of EU criminal law will continue to be governed by the third pillar. Then there will be the *regulatory criminal law* which will cover all criminal provisions aimed at achieving the political objectives of the EU: protection of the environment, the four freedoms, free and undistorted competition, etc. This part of EU criminal law is likely to be divided between the first and third pillars, the principle of incrimination and the specific definitions of the offences belonging to the first pillar and the more detailed provisions on penalties, if deemed necessary, belonging to the third. Further, as in national criminal law, it is likely that the regulatory criminal law will be quantitatively much more significant than the core criminal law. Finally, it needs to be remembered that the express exclusion of EC criminal legislation in the areas of customs cooperation and fraud against the Community's financial interests remains.[56] In view of the developments outlined above, one would be forgiven for thinking it an anomaly ripe for correction.

BOX 6.1

As was briefly touched upon in Chapter 2, the new TFEU formalises the above distinction between core and regulatory criminal law. Specific offences in specified areas of core criminal law may, under Article 69 B(1) TFEU, be approximated because they are considered 'particularly serious' and have a 'cross-border dimension'. In relation to regulatory criminal law, Article 69 B(2) TFEU establishes an EU competence to approximate the 'definition of criminal offences and sanctions' if such approximation proves 'essential to ensure the effective implementation of a Union policy in an area which has been subject to harmonisation measures'. In short, if the EU has adopted regulatory measures in any area and the effectiveness of those regulations is deemed to require the application of criminal sanctions, the EU shall be competent to approximate such offences and the sanctions to be applied. This is a neat solution to the rather complex situation which arose as a result of the judgment in *Environmental crimes* and which unfortunately remains after the ruling in *Ship-source pollution*.

Although likely to grow in importance, at the present time this regulatory EU criminal law is only in its infancy. Consequently, the majority of EU criminal law is found in instruments adopted under Title VI EU. The rest of this chapter will look at the motivations behind the provision of EU-wide definitions of certain offences falling within the category core EU criminal law.

THE FACILITATION OF CROSS-BORDER JUDICIAL COOPERATION

The definition of offences is but one of the factors which has traditionally rendered interjurisdictional cooperation in criminal justice difficult. In fact, in the large majority of cases, the facts making up an offence in one jurisdiction are very likely to be accepted as constituting an offence in another, albeit perhaps qualified differently. Nevertheless, looking at traditional extradition law it is apparent that the requirement that the actions for which an individual's extradition was sought constitute an offence in both jurisdictions (the dual criminality requirement) was considered extremely important.[57] Also, simple provision of judicial assistance to a foreign investigation may be conditioned on the substantive definition of the offence investigated. This is an expression of the fact that nation states want to be in total and complete control over the criminal law which is applied on their territories. The reasons for this are essentially twofold: the protection of the sovereignty of the nation state as a political unit *vis-à-vis* other nation states, and the protection of the terms of the relationship between the individual and the state.[58] In other words, the state can be said to have an interest in guaranteeing that it has the monopoly on violence on its territory undisturbed by the pretentions of other nation states.

The individual, on the other hand, can be said to have an interest in knowing precisely under which circumstances that violence will be exercised. If violence is exercised with reference to the laws of a nation state which the individual has had no opportunity to affect, it is arguable that there is a problem of democratic legitimacy.[59] This latter concern is perhaps better illustrated by another aspect of traditional extradition law, namely the 'nationality exception'. This principle will be found in many jurisdictions of the civil law tradition and essentially holds that no national can be extradited from her or his home country.[60] With increased integration in the EU, it was obvious that the old systems of cooperation in criminal matters would be put under increasing stress as the virtually effortless movement of suspects, witnesses and evidence demanded intensified cooperation between law enforcement bodies in the Member States.[61]

The EU Treaty established clear competences for the purpose of facilitating cross-border cooperation with a view to making the criminal justice system more effective in the struggle against cross-border criminality. In Article 29 EU, the third means mentioned in order to achieve the objective 'to provide citizens with a high level of safety within an area of freedom, security and justice' is precisely 'approximation, where necessary, of rules on criminal matters in the Member States, in accordance with the provisions of Article 31(e) [EU]'. This latter article then confers competence on the EU to take action by 'progressively adopting measures establishing minimum rules relating to the constituent elements of criminal acts and to penalties in the fields of organised crime, terrorism and illicit drug trafficking'.

Examples: Organised Crime, Terrorism and Trafficking

One of the first areas in which it was deemed important to agree to common minimum definitions was that of organised crime and, increasingly since 9-11, terrorism. There are essentially two reasons for this. First, it is clearly so that the popular perception of criminality with cross-border aspects is very much linked to the popular conception of organised criminal syndicates. Thus, the clear mandate in the EU Treaty for the EU to take action in the field of organised crime is supplemented by a strong public expectation that it do so.[62] Second, this was an area ripe for harmonisation for the very simple reason that there was no agreement on the legal definitions of the phenomena of organised crime and terrorism. All agreed that they were serious problems but cooperation was hampered by the single fact that legislative approaches differed greatly.[63] The first legislative result was the joint action defining a 'criminal organisation', discussed at the beginning of this chapter.[64] It is however doubtful that this instrument was of much practical use because, when terrorism leapt to the top of the agenda, it was clearly deemed insufficient merely to incorporate the definition of a criminal organisation given in the joint action in a more effective framework decision. Perhaps it was felt that the terrorism which faces us now is qualitatively very different from the organised crime the joint action targeted. Whatever the reasons, Framework Decision 2002/475/JHA[65] provides a separate and additional definition of a 'terrorist group'. For comparative purposes, the two definitions are here set side-by-side:

'*Criminal organisation*' as defined by Article 1 of Joint Action 98/733/JHA:	'*Terrorist group*' as defined by Article 2(1) of Framework Decision 2002/475/JHA:
a structured association, established over a period of time, of more than two persons, acting in concert with a view to committing offences which are punishable by deprivation of liberty or a detention order of a maximum of at least four years or a more serious penalty, whether such offences are an end in themselves or a means of obtaining material benefits and, where appropriate, of improperly influencing the operation of public authorities.	a structured group of more than two persons, established over a period of time and acting in concert to commit terrorist offences. 'Structured group' shall mean a group that is not randomly formed for the immediate commission of an offence and that does not need to have formally defined roles for its members, continuity of its membership or a developed structure.

There is no doubt that terrorist offences were contemplated when the 1998 joint action was drafted. That much is clear from the inclusion of the proviso that not only offences committed with a view to accumulating 'material benefits' were covered but also offences aimed at 'improperly influencing the operation of public authorities'. So even if terrorism *per se* might not have been criminalised in all Member States, terrorist actions in themselves were. Had the joint action definition of a criminal organisation been replicated in a framework decision, there would have been an implied obligation to criminalise membership of terrorist organisations. This solution would have been much more elegant. The definition of a criminal organisation had already been agreed and, despite some academic reticence,[66] it seems fit for purpose. A second alternative would have been to include a reference to the 1998 joint action in the framework definition defining terrorism, thus making it a separate offence to be a member of a criminal organisation set up for the commission of terrorist offences specifically. This option has been retained in a number of other framework decisions defining other offences, notably Framework Decision 2002/629/JHA on human trafficking, which we will discuss later on.

The conclusion must be that the reason for which the EU legislature opted for a separate definition of the 'terrorist group' is more a reflection of a will to agree to a common definition of the offence of terrorism itself and to set it apart from 'common' criminality than of a desire to provide any legal added value or to remedy a *lacuna* in the already existing definition of organised crime. And, unsurprisingly, it is the definition of the offence of terrorism which has attracted the most attention. Article 1(1) of Framework Decision 2002/475/JHA lays down that a series of substantive offences, if committed 'with the aim of . . . seriously intimidating a population, . . . unduly compelling a Government or an international organisation to perform or abstain from performing any act, or . . . seriously destabilising or destroying the fundamental political, constitutional, economic or social structures of a country or an international organisation', shall be deemed 'terrorist offences'. The substantive offences are the actual commission of, or the threat to commit, offences against the person, kidnapping or hostage taking, criminal damage, hijacking, weapons offences (including research into biological and chemical weapons), causing environmental damage endangering human life, and interference with the supply of basic commodities (water, power, etc.) likely to endanger human life.

This definition has been criticised for being too broad and for potentially covering activities deemed legal and even salutary in a democratic society, activities such as civil disobedience and demonstrations.[67] This criticism is difficult to understand. Given that the framework definition provides a cumulative definition under which a conviction of a terrorist offence requires the establishment of both a substantive offence *and* the defined 'terrorist motive', it is hard to conceive of any activity which would previously have been legal which would now be deemed terrorist activity. The criticism which can be levelled at the framework decision is precisely the weight placed on the motive of an offence. It is essential here to distinguish between the subjective element of an offence, the *mens rea*, and the motive. The former is merely the requirement that criminal responsibility requires the perpetrator of a criminal act to have been subjectively aware of what she or he was doing. The motive, on the other hand, refers to the subjective *explanation* for *why* the perpetrator committed an intentional offence. The requirement in the framework decision that a *prima facie* criminal act be defined with reference to the motives of the perpetrator is problematic. Normatively this is a major departure from the traditional view in criminal law that the eventual motive behind an offence is irrelevant as far as classifying it is concerned. With a few unhappy exceptions, be they mythical,[68] or real,[69] an intentional homicide is classified as murder whether the 'reason' for it was intense jealousy, family honour or political conviction. The rejection of motive as a relevant consideration in the classification of offences is a principled standpoint underlining the fact that society punishes acts and not ideological convictions. If we are to introduce motive as a consideration in the classification of terrorist offences, it is difficult to see why we should stop there. Is not motive always relevant? Is it not even more justified to distinguish the Jean Valjeans of this world who steal to feed their families from the Fagins motivated by mere monetary gain?

At any rate, the choice has been made and perpetrators of offences motivated by prescribed ambitions must now be sentenced to 'custodial sentences heavier than those imposable under national law for such offences in the absence of the special intent required pursuant to Article 1(1), save where the sentences imposable are already the maximum possible sentences under national law'.[70]

One other framework decision laying down a common minimum definition of an offence can be said to have been very much motivated by the need to facilitate cross-border cooperation in its enforcement. Framework Decision 2002/629/JHA[71] is perhaps the most obvious of all the substantive law measures adopted by the EU in that it defines trafficking in human beings – an offence which commonly includes the crossing of borders. Now 'the recruitment, transportation, transfer, harbouring, subsequent reception of a person, including exchange or transfer of control over that person' for the purposes of 'exploitation of that person's labour or services' or 'the exploitation of the prostitution of others or other forms of sexual exploitation', constitutes an EU-wide offence if use is made of 'coercion, force or threat', or of 'deceit or fraud', or if there has been 'an abuse of authority or of a position of vulnerability', or, finally, if 'payments or benefits are given or received to achieve the consent of a person having control over another person'.[72]

Harmonisation of Substantive Criminal Law and Mutual Recognition

As has been discussed in previous chapters, the methodological instrument chosen by the EU to work to achieve the AFSJ is mutual recognition. Mutual recognition has a significant impact on the substantive criminal law of the Member States since the object of mutual recognition is that legislative differences should no longer constitute obstacles to the EU-wide effectiveness of judicial decisions in criminal matters taken in the individual Member States. It is clear that some Member States were very positive towards the adoption of mutual recognition as the working principle of the AFSJ because they felt that this would at least dampen the momentum to proceed with legislative harmonisation which was seen as much less intrusive.[73] The greatest victory of this approach was undeniably the EAW and the list in Article 2(2) of categories of offences for which the requirement of dual criminality is inapplicable.

As has been mentioned earlier, traditional extradition law included a number of deeply rooted principles which were more or less universally applied, one of which was the principle of dual criminality. What this entailed in practice was that a request for extradition would only be granted if the facts which constituted the alleged offence for which extradition was requested also sufficed to make up that offence in national law. In the vast majority of cases, this requirement posed little difficulty but in a small minority of cases conflicts did arise. These were most noticeable either when the alleged offence did not exist in the law of the requested state (as was sometimes the case with terrorism) or where one element or other in the definition of the offence did not correspond. When the EU decided to facilitate extradition between its Member States, it could go down one of two routes. Either it could proceed to harmonise national definitions of offences one by one, something which would have been extremely difficult, given the jealousy with which Member States guard their own, traditional solutions (not to mention the legislative resources this option would have tied up) or it could opt for one or other variant of the scheme finally included in the EAW. There is little doubt which solution is the most elegant. In terms of the obstacle to cross-border cooperation constituted by differences in the definition of substantive offences, the EAW cuts the proverbial Gordian knot. Instead of having to verify that the facts making up the alleged offence in a request for extradition corresponded to the definition of that offence in national criminal law, now all the executing state needs to know is that the facts contained in the EAW correspond to one of the 32 categories in Article 2(2) *according to the law of the issuing state* and that the maximum penalty upon conviction is at least three years' imprisonment.

The EAW may be an elegant solution to a thorny problem but one will only feel able to appreciate that if one is fundamentally satisfied that the detailed provisions coming within the categories of offences in Article 2(2) EAW are treated well in every single Member State.[74] If, for instance, abortion was treated as a form of 'murder' in one Member State, many other Member States might feel very reluctant to assist that Member State in enforcing its anti-abortion laws. Likewise, a Member State which has legalised some form of euthanasia will be reluctant to assist another in the enforcement of its murder laws if the suspect or accused is a person who would have been covered by the executing Member State's euthanasia provisions. With reference to precisely these types of considerations, Weyembergh comes down a strong advocate for the position that mutual recognition requires quite extensive prior harmonisation in order to be justifiable.[75] As we have seen in Chapter 4, similar considerations lie behind many of the calls for harmonisation in the area of criminal procedure and, in particular, procedural rights and safeguards. In this respect, Weyembergh draws a parallel with two other sectors of EU action: the 'new approach' to the construction of the single market and judicial cooperation in civil and commercial matters. In the former, she points out that minimum harmonisation of safety standards was considered necessary before mutual recognition of detailed, national standards could be imposed. In the field of judicial cooperation in civil and commercial matters too, common minimum rules – notably on jurisdiction – preceded mutual recognition of national judgments. According to Weyembergh, if harmonisation was considered a precondition in these, arguably less contentious, areas, *a fortiori* it ought to be so considered in the area of criminal justice. Peers is also very critical of mutual recognition without prior harmonisation.[76] He makes the same comparison as Weyembergh with the operation of the principle in the construction of the single market but he also adds a second consideration:

> Since sovereign States are free to take different views as to what should be criminalized and to what extent, and these differences are rooted deeply in different cultures and national identities and represent different choices resulting from the democratic process in each State, why should States in principle be obliged to assist another State to apply its criminal law where the two States differ on whether the relevant act should be criminalized?[77]

It has also been pointed out that, even if the principle of recognising the definition of the offence of the issuing Member State is accepted, the practical application of the categories listed in Article 2(2) of the EAW is not at all straightforward, as it perhaps may seem at first glance. Flore has suggested that the executing Member State should make sure that the objective constituent elements of the offence category, as defined by the issuing Member State, correspond to the objective constituent elements of that category in the law of the executing Member State.[78] That solution is perhaps tempting in that it enables some measure of control to be retained by the executing Member State. But it is far from unproblematic. An example is the 28th category listed in Article 2(2): 'rape'. In England and Wales, rape is defined as having sexual intercourse with a non-consenting person while knowing of or being reckless as to that absence of consent.[79] In Sweden, in order for the same behaviour to be classified as rape, an additional factual element has to be proven, namely the application of actual or threatened violence, or that the non-consenting party was in a defenceless position.[80] There is thus the possibility that an EAW issued for rape by a UK court would fail if the Swedish judge applied the principles laid down by Flore. On the other hand, it seems unlikely that the EU legislator imagined that the executing judge would disregard completely the facts making up the alleged offence, if for no other reason than that the model EAW which figures in the annex to the framework decision contains a box where the circumstances of the alleged offence should be described. What seems likely is that national judges, when faced with a marginal situation, will apply a common sense test and treat the categories as generic descriptions of type-offences: a criminal version of the Platonic 'ideas'. Difficult to describe but, one would hope, fairly obvious in practice.

The EAW does address these issues by including a provision giving Member States the possibility to refuse execution of EAW if issued for acts which the executing Member State considers have been committed in whole or in part on its territory[81] or if issued for acts having been committed outside the territory of the issuing Member State and the executing state does not claim extrajudicial competence for the same offence.[82] The idea is that national objections to specific offences are less (or even not at all) justifiable when the offence itself has taken place outside the national territory. At the very least, no individual risks being charged with an offence which does not exist in her or his home country as long as she or he stays there; if she or he goes somewhere else, the familiar saying 'when in Rome . . .' applies. In this way the EAW does much to strengthen jurisdiction based on the principle of territoriality and discourages claims to extraterritorial jurisdiction.

However, theoretically possible, if not plausible, scenarios can be constructed where, for instance, a Belgian doctor having performed legal euthanasia on a French national in Belgium finds herself or himself the subject of an EAW issued by French prosecutors who claim jurisdiction based on the passive personality principle (i.e. the victim was a national of France),[83] while in Belgium the doctor will be safe, the 'offence' having been committed on Belgian soil. Should she or he ever leave Belgium, however, there is a risk that she or he will be apprehended in a Member State which, like France, claims extraterritorial jurisdiction over homicide cases based on the passive personality principle (jurisdiction based on the nationality of the victim). Then there is a risk that the Belgian doctor, having performed a perfectly legal procedure in Belgium, will find herself or himself turned over to the French authorities for prosecution. This and similar scenarios are far-fetched and very unlikely ever to occur, but the theoretical possibility might cause some to be sceptical of the scheme put in place by the EAW framework decision.

If EU law can be said in this way to cause difficulties, it should, in fairness, be stated that it also provides a possible solution. The 1990 Convention implementing the Schengen agreement[84] (CISA) contains a provision which serves to prevent an individual from being tried again in a second Member State on account of acts for which she or he has already stood trial in a first, commonly referred to as the principle of *ne bis in idem*.[85] The way the ECJ has interpreted this provision again constitutes a victory for the view that mutual recognition renders harmonisation less important. What this provision entails is that the outcome of a criminal trial in one Member State is conclusive throughout the EU with respect to the *facts* – and *not the offences* – tried.[86] The ECJ has explicitly stated that this is the effect irrespective of *'the possibility of divergent legal classifications of the same acts in two different [Member States]'*.[87] On the EU level, this means that the decision made in one Member State as to the legality of any given set of actions imposes itself on all the other Member States. For our imagined (and legally extremely well advised) Belgian doctor, if she or he fears the possibility of prosecution because her or his patient is, for instance, a French national, this case law provides a way out: she or he should could turn herself or himself over to the Belgian authorities and have them investigate the circumstances of the euthanasia procedure. If they close the case in such a way that it prevents further proceedings in Belgium, for instance because there was nothing illegal with the procedure, that decision will be final for the rest of the EU as well.[88] France will no longer have jurisdiction to try the doctor on those facts and the EAW would lapse.

The fact that EU law provides answers to most of the possible fears associated with the application of the principle of mutual recognition, and the effects this will have on the interrelation of various substantive criminal laws in the EU, does not necessarily end the debate. As will have become clear, opinions are far from agreed on how best to conceive of the relationship between mutual recognition and harmonisation, and the objection which is almost impossible to counter is the one that the criminalisation or, for that matter, the decriminalisation of a particular act is so wrong in principle that a refusal to assist in the application of such a law ought to be possible no matter the circumstances. However, once reduced to this, it is no longer so much an argument against mutual recognition in general and the EAW in particular, but an argument of moral philosophy.

The last main argument often put against the application of mutual recognition without prior harmonisation is of a more practical nature. It highlights the quite plausible fact that individual judges will be reluctant to give effect to judgments from different Member States in circumstances where she or he is uncomfortable with the law at the origin of that judgment. Asp is a good representative of this view:

> Recognition despite lack of harmonization of substantive criminal law is equal to recognition despite differences in substance and in areas closely connected to moral standards, such as criminal law, recognition of decisions displaying such differences will almost certainly be controversial. Thus it is fair to assume that there is some sort of correlation between the degree of harmonization and the degree of willingness to recognize each other's judgements.[89]

There are some empirical findings which seem to support this statement.[90] The question is how significant this really is. The degree of unwillingness exhibited by national judges faced with a judicial decision from another Member State is one thing, another for national legislators to provide them with the legal means to act upon it. In the context of the EAW, it is well known that national implementing legislation in many cases gives far more leeway for national judges to refuse surrender than is contemplated in the framework decision itself.[91] Many national laws transposing the EAW framework decision are thus, strictly speaking, unlawful and only 'get away with it' because there is no third pillar equivalent to the first pillar infringement proceedings under Article 226 EC.

BOX 6.2

As we saw in Chapter 2, the new TFEU does not link approximation of substantive criminal law to the principle of mutual recognition. Instead, it provides purely material and/or impact-related criteria for when EU approximation of specific areas of criminal activity are necessary. This decision is clearly controversial and is likely to lead to much criticism. To the extent that this criticism will be based on the familiar arguments described above, we would merely like to recall that the TFEU also gives the EU an express competence to settle conflicts of jurisdiction. Given that the application of a controversial criminal law ought only to be a threat to the harmonious coordination of the Member States' systems of criminal justice if allowed an extraterritorial application, it is our guess that the better exercised the competence to prevent and to settle conflicts of jurisdiction is, the less the need for approximation of laws will be felt under a system of mutual recognition.

The debate on whether it is correct to proceed with the mutual recognition programme in the absence of a greater degree of harmonisation, not least of substantive criminal law, is likely to go on. What is clear, though, and which will have transpired in this chapter, is that the EU, and in particular the Council, has clearly opted for mutual recognition so as to avoid all the difficulties associated with an extensive harmonisation programme. Putting to one side the objections to one or other piece of national criminal legislation which may be made from a political point of view, from a purely legal perspective, the mutual recognition programme is working without too many glitches. In a sense, the EU has come up with a way to defuse tension by providing a procedural solution to a substantive problem. The ultimate test of this proposition is to imagine there not being any EU legislation harmonising the offences described here, namely participation in organised crime, terrorism and trafficking. They all figure in the list in Article 2(2) of the EAW framework decision. In fact, they are numbers one, two and three on that list. This of course raises the question of the direction of the third pillar harmonisation programme. If most of the competences to harmonise 'regulatory criminal law' to protect the EU's political objectives are set to be exercised in the first pillar, and if the mutual recognition programme has made the harmonisation of substantive criminal law less of an issue, what will motivate the EU to exercise its competence to harmonise substantive criminal law?

MORAL EXEMPLARITY AND SUBSIDIARITY

Whether it is true or not, it is a common opinion that 'law cannot be considered simply as a system placing limits on individual freedom in order to enable the survival of the collective'.[92] Consequently, and similar to the way criminal law is being instrumentalised everywhere, it is a common opinion that one of the objectives of a European criminal law should be the influencing of human behaviour.[93] Probably the main reason why criminal law is such a sensitive subject is precisely because it enshrines the values of any given society: what it considers socially unacceptable and therefore punishes, but also, and probably more significantly, what it chooses to leave unpunished.[94] Slightly contentiously, a good argument can be made that, quantitatively speaking, criminal law is used as much to show outrage at what is considered morally unacceptable behaviour as it is used to prevent and to punish behaviour that is objectively harmful.[95] This is not the place to discuss the effects of the criminal law having become more of a *prima* than an *ultima ratio*,[96] suffice to say that it is a common and politically convenient response of legislators everywhere to throw criminal legislation at all types of perceived social ills. The EU is no different.

First of all it needs to be clarified that moral outrage need not be objectively unjustified. It seems fairly clear that the terrorism framework decision did not criminalise behaviour which had previously been tolerated or that, following the adoption of the EAW, there would have remained significant difficulties with intra-EU cooperation in combating it. However, no-one can deny that terrorism poses a grave threat to the physical integrity of individual citizens or that the acts committed by what is called 'terrorist groups' do not constitute serious criminal offences. When the EU legislates in the area of terrorism it should *also* be seen as a statement of fundamental values.

Likewise, the framework decision on human trafficking can be seen in this same light. It may very well be a genuinely useful coordinating instrument, but at the same time it is hard to imagine that the act of trafficking a human being in the conditions described in the framework decision was legal somewhere before its adoption or, again, that intra-EU cooperation and in particular extradition would have posed difficulties even following the advent of the EAW. But again, trafficking constituted and constitutes a serious problem and, at the time of the preparation and adoption of the framework decision, the world was starting to become aware of the horrors and prevalence of this 'industry'. The EU, quite legitimately, made another value statement through legislating on substantive criminal law.

The framework decisions on terrorism and trafficking can thus be seen from both the perspective of the objective to facilitate cooperation and coordination *and* that of using the substantive criminal law as a means to express the values of the EU. Where there is this dual justification, the fact that moral exemplarity is one facet of the reasoning is fairly uncontroversial. There are, however, initiatives which can only with great difficulty be said materially to facilitate cooperation and coordination and for which moral exemplarity seems the *only* justification. As always, such legislation constitutes more of a difficulty. The prime example of this is Council Framework Decision 2004/68/JHA of 22 December 2003 on combating the sexual exploitation of children and child pornography. With respect to the sexual exploitation of children, the framework decision enjoins Member States to ensure that their national legislations treat as punishable offences the 'coercing' or 'recruiting' of a child 'into prostitution or into participating in pornographic performances' or 'profiting from or otherwise exploiting a child for such purposes'. Equally, should be treated as a punishable offence the 'engaging in sexual activities with a child' when use has been made of 'coercion, force or threats', 'money or other forms of remuneration' or a 'recognised position of trust, authority or influence over the child'.[97] Legally-technically speaking, this is a good and comprehensive treatment of the problem addressed.

However, things get slightly more complicated when the framework decision moves on to deal with the issue of child pornography. Article 3(1) enjoins Member States to criminalise the 'production . . . distribution, dissemination or transmission . . . supplying or making available . . . [and] acquisition or possession of child pornography'. It also provides a harmonised definition of child pornography by which is now intended throughout the EU pornographic depictions of 'a real child', 'a real person appearing to be a child', or 'realistic images of a non-existent child'.[98] Trying for a moment to put to one side the distastefulness of the topic, this definition does raise an interesting problem. The difficulty the

EU legislator had to face in dealing with this matter was whether to limit its action to the criminalisation of the direct and indirect abuse of children, *or* whether to deal with the much thornier and more difficult issue of paedophilia as well. It opted for the second of these two options: the definition is clearly intended to cover 'real' as well as simulated, and computer-generated and otherwise animated depictions of children in pornographic situations. That is not entirely unproblematic. Paedophilia is a form of sexual deviance which most people find utterly horrifying. However, research suggests that the vast majority of people with paedophilic tendencies live their lives without ever acting on these tendencies in such a way as to pose an actual danger to real children. If we define paedophilia as the condition of being sexually attracted to minors there is nothing *inherently* harmful in it. On a comparative note, the United States Supreme Court held this to be enough to hold a similar provision of federal legislation unconstitutional on free speech grounds. In *Ashcroft v The Free Speech Coalition*,[99] Kennedy J, presenting the majority opinion, stated that such a provision '*prohibits speech that records no crime and creates no victims by its production. Virtual child pornography is not "intrinsically related" to the sexual abuse of children*'.[100] Finally, from a purely practical perspective, what we must ask ourselves is whether it is conducive to preventing as many paedophiles as possible from ever acting on their urges to criminalise those of their potential outlets which have been produced without any child ever being harmed. This last point is not merely detached academic musing: the *prevention* of crime appears in Article 2 EU as one of the EU's objectives and is reiterated in Article 29 EU where 'offences against children' is specifically mentioned. Further, in para. 41 of the Tampere declaration,

> [t]he European Council calls for the integration of crime prevention aspects into actions against crime as well as for the further development of national crime prevention programmes. Common priorities should be developed and identified in crime prevention in the external and internal policy of the Union and be taken into account when preparing new legislation.

It thus seems arguable that the Council made light of the crime prevention aspect when drafting the framework decision on combating the sexual exploitation of children and child pornography.

That is, however, not to say that the EU legislator was unaware of these issues but the compromise which has been incorporated into the framework decision is not entirely convincing. When it comes to depictions of adults 'appearing to be a child', Member States may opt to exclude such material from the ambit of its child pornography legislation.[101] Likewise, having defined a 'child' as 'any person below the age of 18',[102] but recognising that children under the age of eighteen but over the age of sexual consent are legally sexually active, the framework decision allows Member States to exempt from punishment the production and possession of 'images of children having reached the age of sexual consent [if] produced and possessed with their consent and solely for their own private use'.[103] However, and rather oddly, when it comes to computer-generated or animated images, the framework decision only allows Member States to exempt material 'produced and possessed by the producer solely for his or her own private use'.[104] One can see the logic in so far as it might be a laudable objective to prevent the spreading of such disturbing material. Nevertheless, one can also question the wisdom in conclusively settling the questions relating to the correct balance between repression and prevention in relation to paedophilia at the EU level, thus preventing the debate within as well as between Member States on what is the most constructive solution.

The EU legislation on child abuse and child pornography deals with serious problems which, all can agree, need to be fought one way or another. But, in the EU context, it is necessary always to bear in mind that the objectives of the EU 'shall be achieved . . . while respecting the principle of subsidiarity as defined in Article 5 [EC]'.[105] From this perspective, it is doubtful whether the perceived need to make a value statement, no matter how noble the value, is enough to justify EU action. In this respect, the background of the framework decision on child abuse and child pornography highlights the difficulties associated with the institutional set-up in the third pillar and, in particular, the combination of a right of initiative of Member States, unanimity in Council and weak judicial oversight:

Back in 1996, a scandal which has come to be known as the 'Dutroux affair' caused massive political and judicial upheavals in Belgium. At the heart of the affair was a very disturbed man who abducted, abused and murdered a number of children. He was arrested, escaped and, finally, was rearrested. As a consequence of their perceived mishandling of this case, a number of questions were asked as to the competence and integrity of Belgian law enforcement authorities. The Belgian government needed to act and one of the ways in which they did this was to submit a proposal for an EU joint action on child abuse and child pornography.[106] The result was Council Joint Action 97/154/JHA of 24 February 1997 concerning action to combat trafficking in human beings and sexual exploitation of children.[107] This instrument was a bit of a catch-all in that it enjoined Member States to ensure that sexual abuse of children, child pornography, trafficking in children and trafficking in adults were sufficiently dealt with in their national criminal legislations. It also enjoined Member States to 'grant each other the widest possible judicial cooperation in the investigations and judicial processes relating to the[se] offences'.[108] This instrument put both the issue of sexual exploitation of children and the issue of trafficking on the EU agenda. For the actors involved, it was a win–win situation. The Belgian government was able to put what was a purely domestic problem on the European agenda and the EU was given the opportunity to be seen to be doing something in an area where popular feeling runs very high. And, of course, which other Member State would want to be seen opposing legislation against child abuse? In any case, the issue was now an established EU concern which the Commission was quick to develop. Consequently, a couple of years later, there followed Council Decision 2000/375/JHA of 29 May 2000 to combat child pornography on the Internet[109] and, most recently, the two framework decisions on trafficking and on child abuse and child pornography, the latter of which formally repealed Joint Action 97/154/JHA.

This phenomenon, the 'europeanization'[110] of domestic issues, is problematic from a number of perspectives. Commenting on this, de Hert draws a parallel with the principle of non-interference in public international law: 'states may not interfere in another state's internal affairs by putting domestic issues on supranational agendas. There must be a meaningful relationship between these issues and the goals pursued by the supranational institution. Illegitimate "jumping of scale" should be prevented.'[111] The tendency of Member States sometimes to 'jump scales' by placing issues which cause them or, more correctly, their governments, difficulties domestically on the EU agenda, highlights the very particular tensions in the institutional set-up of the third pillar. De Hert's starting point is national sovereignty. Stretching or even ignoring the competence constraints of the EU to suit a particular national agenda may cause legislation to be brought in at the EU level the legality of which is at the very least doubtful. The consequence is that the residual area of national competence and legislative sovereignty is constrained in ways not contemplated in the founding treaties.

From the opposite perspective, the EU's sovereignty in *its* competence sphere is also threatened by this practice. The whole logic of the EU law system is dependent upon the principles of conferred powers to the EU and, consequently, residual powers to the Member States. The primacy of EC law is only conceivable within the confines of a system where the area within which EC law can operate is clearly delimited and where legislation is subject to strict competence review instigated by the interested parties. The EC – first pillar – system fulfils these 'requirements'. The third pillar system does not. As we described in an earlier chapter, the only parties able directly to challenge a legislative instrument adopted under Article 34 EU are the Member States, the Council and the Commission. The first two are unlikely ever to do so, given that unanimity is required from the Member States at the time of adoption by Council. The Commission, on the other hand, has twice challenged framework decisions for infringement of the EU Treaty,[112] but it has yet to do so in a situation which would in fact *limit the EU's competence to the benefit of the competence of Member States*. In an ideal world, the Commission would transfer its first pillar office of 'guardian of the Treaties' to the third pillar and exercise it also to *restrict* its ambit. However, it is perhaps too much to ask that an institution seeking to construct the EU's identity in a relatively new competence area should also work to limit its own competence. Currently, then, the only realistic counterweight to the legislative supremacy of the Council is the possibility that preliminary references challenge the legality of doubtful instruments. When it happens, as it inevitably did for the EAW,[113] it is certainly extremely salutary for the legitimacy of the instrument itself, but also for EU action in the field of criminal justice in general. But, as was explained in a previous chapter, the preliminary reference system in the third pillar, with its double variable geometry, is far from guaranteed to provide a sufficient counterweight to the varied forces imposing their agendas on the EU's legislative efforts, unconcerned by formal competence constraints.

The conclusion one must draw is that, at present, there are very weak checks in place to make sure that third pillar legislation complies with the principle of attributed powers. At the same time, it is becoming increasingly clear that the ECJ views the strength of third pillar legislation much the same as it does EC legislation. The decisions in *Maria Pupino*[114] and the cases on Article 54 CISA attest to this. Just like EC legislation, the effectiveness of third pillar legislation requires primacy. But if the primacy of third pillar legislation is to be arguable, let alone strong enough to withstand the likely challenges from superior courts in the Member States, a more developed system of safeguarding the principle of conferred powers has to be put in place. The short-term gain for the Commission in jumping at every possibility to extend the substantive scope for EU legislative action, such as the framework decision on child abuse and child pornography, is easily understandable. What the Commission ought to bear in mind, though, is that in the medium-to-long-term, such a course of action might undermine the larger, and surely more important, issue of ensuring the primacy and effectiveness of third pillar legislation generally.[115] Ironically, and probably contrary to popular belief, a change from unanimity to qualified majority in Council could have a limiting effect on the legislative output in the third pillar since Member States which then are outvoted in Council are likely to be motivated to challenge legislation before the ECJ which, in its turn, would be beneficial to the principle of legality which, in its turn, would strengthen the claim for primacy of third pillar legislation.

BOX 6.3

New Article 3a EU would make it clear that 'competences not conferred upon the Union in the Treaties remain with the Member
States'. New Article 3b EU then clarifies the exact interplay of the
principles governing the exercise of legislative power in Europe. It
is again laid down that EU action is limited to the exercise of 'competences conferred upon it by the Member States in the Treaties
to attain the objectives set out therein' (new Article 3b(2) EU).
Further, the principle of subsidiarity is expressly limited to the
areas of EU action 'which do not fall within its exclusive competence' (new Article 3b(3) EU). Finally, it is established that the 'principle of proportionality' shall guide all action by EU institutions in
the sense that 'the content and form of Union action shall not
exceed what is necessary to achieve the objectives of the Treaties'
(new Article 3b(4) EU).

What new Article 3b EU would provide is greater clarity, in that
it is very pedagogical. In comparison with the present Article 5 *EC*,
which it would replace, legally speaking it is very doubtful whether
new Article 3b EU really adds anything new. The principles of conferral, subsidiarity and proportionality are all there already. On the
other hand, the force with which the principle of conferral is
emphasised might lead to a change in emphasis away from simple
discussions of legal basis and onto the principled ground of division of powers. The wording of the new EU principle of conferral is
very similar to the federal idea of residual powers as found, *inter
alia*, in Article 30 of the German constitution. As is well known, in
German constitutional litigation, the respect for the substantively
separate sovereignties of the constituent parts of the *Bund* has an
inherent, principled importance which the present legal basis litigation of the EU could be said to lack.

It also seems likely that an increased involvement of the European
Parliament (EP) in third pillar legislation could help prevent the worst cases
of legislative overreach. However, where the lack of input of the EP in EU
legislation on substantive criminal law is most felt at present is in the drafting process itself. Although technically a legislative body, the EU Council
is nevertheless composed of national executives. Beyond the obvious
problem in terms of state theory and the separation of powers, there is
justifiable concern for the consequences in terms of a deterioration of leg-

islative quality. When executive interests become the prevailing legislative perspective, there is an unfortunate loss in terms of the range of institutional interests given a voice.[116] An open and contentious debate appears necessary if not vital in any system which proposes to define criminal offences and thereby the circumstances under which individuals are to be convicted and, probably, sent to prison. If such a debate does not take place, there is a very real risk that legislation will be adopted without proper thought having been given to all aspects of any given problem. Already, examples of EU legislation in the field of substantive criminal law which can be said to have suffered from this lack of institutional perspectives are not hard to come by. The problematic definition of terrorism and the issue of animated and computer-generated child pornography, both discussed in this chapter, are but two examples where a full parliamentary debate is likely to have highlighted the problems contained in the proposed definitions and to have contributed to more thought-through solutions.

A final, very recent, example of 'legislative posturing' is the proposed framework decision on combating racism and xenophobia which awaits final adoption by Council.[117] The background to this piece of legislation is the perceived need to update Joint Action 96/443/JHA concerning action to combat racism and xenophobia.[118] This joint action enjoins Member States to make sure either that, essentially, public expressions of racism and Holocaust denial are criminalised, or remove the requirement of dual criminality with respect to such offences committed abroad. The incorporation of this option in the text is of course due to the fact that there are a wide variety of opinions among the different Member States on how to approach criminal legislation in this field and even whether such legislation is compatible with freedom of speech, and so whether 'hate speech' should be the subject of criminal sanction at all. After the publication of the Commission's proposed framework decision, the EAW was adopted and 'racism and xenophobia' figures as a category under Article 2(2) which means that, as long as such offences are punishable in the issuing state by a maximum sentence of at least three years' imprisonment, lack of dual criminality can no longer be invoked to refuse surrender. With that, one might think, the main problem of inter-state cooperation in the enforcement of local hate speech laws ought to have disappeared and the need for further substantive harmonisation forestalled. Nevertheless, consecutive presidencies have considered this to be an issue of such symbolic importance that discussions are still ongoing in Council six or so years after the presentation of the original proposal. During the first half of 2007, Germany held the EU presidency and in April claimed success in finalising the negotiations on this framework decision.[119] It remains unadopted.

From a motivational perspective it seems fairly clear that 'moral posturing' was the sole impulsion in relation to the framework decision dealing with abuse of children and child pornography, and the proposed framework decision on combating racism and xenophobia. However, proponents of these measures can and do argue that, even if this was the case, that is irrelevant since the EU Treaty provides a specific mandate for action in these two fields. In fact, the first paragraph of Article 29 EU treats 'preventing and combating racism and xenophobia' as an element of the creation of the AFSJ. The second paragraph of the same article states that crime should be prevented and combated and 'in particular . . . trafficking in persons and offences against children . . .'. Given that these two fields of action are expressly mentioned in the portal article of Title VI, how can it be suggested that instruments adopted to give effect to these mentions are of dubious legality? The question is far from settled but the argument will have to centre on how to read the general applicability of the subsidiarity principle to all EU legislative action, established in Article 2 EU, in combination with the specified areas of competence mentioned in the substantive articles. Put differently, does the fact that a subject area is made an EU concern entail that the principle of subsidiarity ceases to operate with respect to EU action within that subject area? If the answer to that question is 'yes' there can be no objection to the two framework decisions discussed. However, the problem with such a reading has already been outlined: subsidiarity is an aspect of the principle of attributed powers and, if this principle is not respected, it will be difficult to insist on the primacy of EU legislation. This consideration seems to us serious enough to reject the suggestion that the sole fact that a subject area is mentioned as an area of EU competence should obviate the need for a separate subsidiarity check. The consequence is that, in order for the EU to be able to legislate in the field of substantive criminal law, not only should there be an adequate legal basis in the EU Treaty but there should *also* be an established *material* need for EU action.[120] In this regard, the mere absence of a common approach is not enough to justify EU harmonisation as there is most likely good reason for this state of affairs.

If that is the case, what then remains of an EU competence if the principle of subsidiarity erects a *prima facie* obstacle to EU harmonisation of the substantive offences concerned? As we have already mentioned earlier in this chapter, by virtue of the success of the mutual recognition programme and the possibility of providing procedural solutions to substantive problems which it entails, the need for harmonisation in the field of substantive criminal law has been substantially diminished. This, however, does not exhaust the usefulness of EU competence in the field of substantive criminal law. One aspect of substantive criminal law which can be said to have received merely perfunctory treatment might in future prove to be more central to the good functioning of the AFSJ than the detailed definition of substantive offences. This is the field of sanctions and its corollary, ordinal justice.

In all this discussion of the need to harmonise substantive criminal laws it can easily be forgotten that, when it comes to the recognition of the criminality of certain actions and the definition of offences, there is large agreement between the Member States of the EU.[121] What is more, indications are that the various systems of criminal justice tend to converge rather than diverge.[122] This is perhaps not surprising given that it has become good legislative practice to conduct comparative studies before proceeding with legislative reform and that, if a country's legislation is decidedly different from what appears to be the international consensus on any given issue, that in itself tends to be a strong argument in favour of reform.[123] To drive home the point, if individuals in all the Member States of the EU were asked to list the actions they would expect to be universally criminalised, chances are that not only would those lists look very similar but they would also pretty much conform to existing legislation throughout the EU. The starkest differences are likely to be found in the area of regulatory criminal law but, as we have seen earlier in this chapter, this area is likely to become a first pillar concern.

However, where there cannot be said to exist a general consensus among the Member States of the EU is in the field of sanctions. When it comes to EU criminal law and its effects on sanctions, there are two aspects which need to be kept separate. First, the great diversity in the levels of sanctions imposed for any given offence in different Member States is a source of distrust and suspicion between the criminal justice systems in these Member States. And even if, as Nuotio suggests, this diversity 'is a natural outcome of the diffuse forces and traditions behind the development of legal systems',[124] it can nevertheless be perceived as problematic that a person who can travel freely, even (unfortunately) for the commission of offences, should incur drastically different sentences for the same type of offence for the entirely contingent reason of where she or he happens to be at any given time.[125] The second aspect of sanctions and EU criminal law is the question of *ordinal justice*, or, put differently, the view a given community takes on the comparative seriousness of different offences, which translates into how severe a sentence one offence should incur relative to another. A simple example is that murder tends to be viewed as more serious than theft and that murder therefore incurs the more severe penalty. The provisions on sanctions contained in the existing EU instruments providing common definitions of various offences are only harmonising in a very loose sense. Generally limiting themselves to specifying a minimum maximum sentence, they allow for Member State discretion on two levels. First, Member State legislatures are very free as to how they choose to transpose these provisions in national law; not only can the maximum sentence be raised but there could also be inserted mandatory minimums or, on the contrary, very 'lenient' alternative sentences. There is indeed nothing preventing a national jurisdiction from providing for any number of alternative forms of punishment; fines, community work, compulsory treatment are only a few of the possibilities available reflecting the wide variety of opinions on the purpose of the criminal sentence. Second, individual courts still have to apply the provisions enacted by the legislature and they will do this in accordance with the prevailing, local practice and very much inspired by local principles of ordinal justice. One criticism which has been directed at this system is that it represents a 'repressive orientation'[126] and that it risks exacerbating an already existing tendency to 'overpenalise'.[127] Given the considerable discretion left to the national legislators in transposing these provisions in national law, it is difficult to see how the chosen system of minimum maximum sentences would necessarily have these consequences.

What must be conceded though is that the general imposition of a mandatory minimum maximum sentence risks 'upsetting the balance in national penal codes'.[128] In order to explain this a distinction needs to be made between sentencing practice and potential sentences and what that means in terms of ordinal justice. We have seen that the imposition of minimum maximum sentences does not *necessarily* have to affect the existing diversity in sentencing practices between EU Member States. However, it does not seem entirely far-fetched to imagine that it will. And this is because, in terms of ordinal justice, the measure of how serious a community considers a particular offence to be, relative to others, is the maximum sentence imposable for that offence. National systems differ in the degree of discretion generally left to individual courts by the legislature; the only legislative guide can be a maximum sentence,[129] or the legislature can be more detailed providing both maximum as well as minimum sentences.[130] Whatever the system in operation, the maximum sentence will constitute the reference by which offences are compared with each other and will be a very important consideration for the individual court when exercising its sentencing discretion. The introduction of a relatively high maximum sentence by way of EU legislation is therefore likely to pull national sentencing practices for that offence in the direction of greater severity.

Be that as it may, what we are concerned with at present is that such an introduction may cause national sentencing provisions, and therefore the national system of ordinal justice, to look bizarre indeed. When in Article 1(3) of Framework Decision 2002/946/JHA the EU mandates Member States to punish organised people smuggling with a minimum maximum of eight years' imprisonment, that may seem reasonable. But if we imagine that a Member State's criminal law punishes manslaughter or rape with a lower maximum sentence we are forced to concede that the effect in terms of ordinal justice of Framework Decision 2002/946/JHA in that Member State is that organised people smuggling is considered a more serious offence than both manslaughter and rape. We are not saying that that is necessarily wrong. What we are pointing to is that EU legislation, although it does not necessarily cause any great convergence in actual sentencing practices, it necessarily does affect the systems of ordinal justice of the Member States.

Whether it is necessary to proceed with a more dedicated effort to harmonise sentencing practices between the Member States is a political issue which, ultimately, is for each and every one to decide. What seems to impose itself, though, is that the effects of EU legislative instruments on national systems of ordinal justice need to be taken into account to a greater extent than is currently the case.[131] One approach would be for the EU merely to impose sentences with reference to procedural effects, i.e. whether the offence should come within the ambit of the EAW and similar instruments or, even, if the requirement of dual criminality, to the extent that it could apply, should be set aside. This approach would have minimum impact on national systems of ordinal justice while ensuring maximum EU cooperation. In fact, up to, and including, the framework decision on combating corruption in the private sector, framework decisions all include a general opening paragraph enjoining Member States to ensure that the offences criminalised are subject to '*effective, proportionate and dissuasive criminal penalties, which may entail* [or "*can give rise to*"] *extradition*'.[132] Since then, however, with one exception,[133] framework decisions have specified the sanctions Member States are to apply. A more robust approach would be for the EU, in conjunction with its Member States, to start drawing up guidelines on ordinal justice and then to make sure that its harmonising legislation conforms to those guidelines. Those guidelines should be as comprehensive as possible and also take into account offences on which the EU is unlikely to be competent to legislate. This to ensure that the criminal law is treated as a coherent whole, but also in recognition of the fact that the individual citizen in any given moment is subject to a singular criminal law irrespective of whether the source of its substantive provisions and sanctions is a national or the EU legislature.

NOTES

1. Council Act of 26 July 1995 drawing up the Convention on the protection of the European Communities' financial interests (OJ C 316, 27.11.1995, p. 49).
2. OJ C 195, 25.6.1997, p. 2.

3. OJ L 167, 25.6.1997, p. 1.
4. Council Decision on the information exchange, risk-assessment and control of new psychoactive substances (OJ L 127, 20.5.2005, p. 32).
5. Council Decision defining 4-MTA as a new synthetic drug which is to be made subject to control measures and criminal penalties (OJ L 244, 16.9.1999, p. 1); Council Decision concerning control measures and criminal sanctions in respect of the new synthetic drug PMMA (OJ L 63, 6.3.2002, p. 14); Council Decision 2003/847/JHA concerning control measures and criminal sanctions in respect of the new synthetic drugs 2C-I, 2C-T-2, 2C-T-7 and TMA-2 (OJ L 321, 6.12.2003, pp. 64–5); Council Decision 2008/206/JHA of 3 March 2008 on defining 1-benzylpiperazine (BZP) as a new psychoactive substance which is to be made subject to control measures and criminal provisions (OJ L 63, 7.3.2008, p. 45).
6. OJ L 351, 29.12.1998, p. 1.
7. Council Framework Decision 2000/383/JHA of 29 May 2000 on increasing protection by criminal penalties and other sanctions against counterfeiting in connection with the introduction of the euro (OJ L 140, 14.6.2000, p. 1), amended by Council Framework Decision 2001/888/JHA of 6 December 2001 amending Framework Decision 2000/383/JHA on increasing protection by criminal penalties and other sanctions against counterfeiting in connection with the introduction of the euro (OJ L 329, 14.12.2001, p. 3).
8. Council Framework Decision 2001/413/JHA of 28 May 2001 combating fraud and counterfeiting of non-cash means of payment (OJ L 149, 2.6.2001, p. 1).
9. Council Framework Decision 2001/500/JHA of 26 June 2001 on money laundering, the identification, tracing, freezing, seizing and confiscation of instrumentalities and the proceeds of crime (OJ L 182, 5.7.2001, p. 1).
10. Council Framework Decision 2002/475/JHA of 13 June 2002 on combating terrorism (OJ L 164, 22.6.2002, p. 3).
11. Council Framework Decision 2002/629/JHA of 19 July 2002 on combating trafficking in human beings (OJ L 203, 1.8.2002, p. 1).
12. Council Framework Decision 2002/946/JHA of 28 November 2002 on the strengthening of the penal framework to prevent the facilitation of unauthorised entry, transit and residence (OJ L 328, 5.12.2002, p. 1).
13. Council Framework Decision 2003/568/JHA of 22 July 2003 on combating corruption in the private sector (OJ L 192, 31.7.2003, p. 54).
14. Council Framework Decision 2004/68/JHA of 22 December 2003 on combating the sexual exploitation of children and child pornography (OJ L 13, 20.1.2004, p. 44).
15. Council Framework Decision 2004/757/JHA of 25 October 2004 laying down minimum provisions on the constituent elements of criminal acts and penalties in the field of illicit drug trafficking (OJ L 335, 11.11.2004, p. 8).
16. Council Framework Decision 2005/222/JHA of 24 February 2005 on attacks against information systems (OJ L 69, 16.3.2005, p. 67).
17. Council Framework Decision 2005/667/JHA of 12 July 2005 to strengthen the criminal-law framework for the enforcement of the law against ship-source pollution (OJ L 255, 30.9.2005, p. 164).
18. C-440/05 *Commission* v *Council* ('*Ship-source pollution*'), judgment of 23 October 2007.
19. A. Weyembergh (2005), 'Approximation of criminal laws, the Constitutional Treaty and the Hague Programme', *Common Market Law Review*, **42**(6), 1567–97, at p. 1586.
20. See 68/88 *Commission* v *Greece* ('*Greek Maize*'), judgment of 21 September 1989.
21. See, e.g., 80/86 *Kolpinghuis Nijmegen*, judgment of 8 October 1987.
22. S. Peers (2006), *EU Justice and Home Affairs Law*, (2nd edn), Oxford: Oxford University Press.
23. OJ L 328, 5.12.2002, p. 17.
24. See above n. 12.
25. See, e.g., Donysios Spinellis (2003), 'Opportunité et légitimité de l'harmonisation – Issues for discussion', in M. Delmas-Marty, G. Giudicelli-Delage et al. (eds), *L'harmonisation des sanctions pénales en Europe*, Paris: Société de législation comparée.

26. On this, see Daniel Flore (2003), 'Introduction – Un droit pénal européen: hasard ou nécessité', in D. Flore, S. Bosly et al. (eds), *Actualités de droit pénal européen*, Bruxelles: La Charte; and M. Wasmeier and N. Thwaites (2004), 'The "Battle of the Pillars": does the European Community have the power to approximate national criminal laws?', *European Law Review*, **29**(5), 613–35.

27. OJ L 29, 5.2.2003, p. 55.

28. C-176/03 *Commission* v *Council* ('*Environmental crimes*'), E.C.R. [2005] I-7879.

29. Ibid., at para. 39.

30. Ibid., at para. 46.

31. Ibid., at para. 47.

32. Ibid., at para. 48.

33. Ibid., at para. 51.

34. Communication from the Commission to the European Parliament and the Council on the implications of the Court's judgment of 13 September 2005 (Case C-176/03 *Commission* v *Council*), COM(2005) 583 final.

35. On this, see S. White (2006), 'Harmonisation of Criminal Law under the First Pillar', *European Law Review*, **31**(1), 81–92; and also the measured House of Lords report: 'The Criminal Law Competence of the European Community', Session 2005–2006, HL Paper 227, 28.7.2006.

36. Resolution on the consequences of the judgment of the Court of 13 September 2005 (C-176/03 *Commission* v *Council*) (2006/2007(INI)).

37. OJ C 240E, 28.8.2001, p. 125.

38. COM(2005) 276 final.

39. For the record, the Commission makes clear that it considers the pending proposal for a framework decision on combating racism and xenophobia (COM(2001) 664 final) to be correctly framed but that, if criminal provisions to fight discrimination were contemplated, they would have to be framed under Article 13 EC.

40. See above n. 17.

41. C-440/05 *Commission* v *Council* ('*Ship-source pollution*').

42. Directive 2005/35/EC of the European Parliament and of the Council of 7 September 2005 on ship-source pollution and on the introduction of penalties for infringements (OJ L 255, 30.9.2005, p. 11).

43. Ibid., Article 4.

44. C-440/05, para. 74.

45. Ibid., para. 59.

46. Ibid., para. 60.

47. Ibid., para. 66.

48. Ibid., para. 67.

49. Opinion, para. 89.

50. Ibid., para. 90.

51. Ibid., para. 92.

52. Judgment, para. 69.

53. Ibid., para. 70.

54. Ibid., para. 68.

55. Amended proposal of 26 April 2006 for a Directive of the European Parliament and of the Council on criminal measures aimed at ensuring the enforcement of intellectual property rights (COM(2006) 168 final).

56. See above, n. 22.

57. See, e.g., J. Dugard and C. Van den Wyngaert (1998), 'Reconciling extradition with human rights', *American Journal of International Law*, **92**, 187–212.

58. See A. Weyembergh (2004), *L'harmonisation des législations: condition de l'espace pénal européen et révélateur de ses tensions*, Bruxelles: Editions de l'Université de Bruxelles, especially at p. 143.

59. Paul de Hert (2004), 'Division of competencies between national and European levels with regard to justice and home affairs', in J. Apap (ed.), *Justice and Home Affairs in the EU: Liberty and Security Issues after Enlargement*, Cheltenham, UK and

Northampton, MA, USA: Edward Elgar; see also E. Guild (2004), 'Crime and the EU's constitutional future in an area of freedom, security, and justice', *European Law Journal*, **10**(2), 218–34.

60. See, e.g., Z. Deen-Racsmány and R. Blekxtoon (2005), 'The decline of the nationality exception in European extradition?', *European Journal of Crime, Criminal Law and Criminal Justice*, **13**(3), 317–63.
61. See, e.g., Henri Labayle (1995), 'L'application du titre VI sur L'Union Européenne', in M. Delmas-Marty (ed.), *Vers un droit pénal communautaire?*, Paris: Dalloz.
62. See E. Denza (2002), *The Intergovernmental Pillars of the European Union*, Oxford: Oxford University Press.
63. See L. Ferola (2002), 'The fight against organized crime in Europe – building an area of freedom, security and justice in the EU', *International Journal of Legal Information*, **30**(1), 53–91.
64. See above, n. 6.
65. See above, n. 10.
66. V. Mitsilegas (2001), 'Defining organised crime in the European Union: the limits of European criminal law in an Area of "Freedom, Security and Justice"', *European Law Review*, **26**(6), 565–81.
67. See, e.g., S. Douglas-Scott (2004), 'The rule of law in the European Union – putting the security into the Area of Freedom, Security and Justice', *European Law Review*, **29**(2), 219–42.
68. E.g. *crimes de passion*.
69. E.g. 'honour killings'.
70. Article 5(2) of Framework Decision 2002/475/JHA.
71. See above, n. 11.
72. Ibid., Article 1(1).
73. See, e.g., H. Brady and M. Roma (2006), 'Let justice be done: punishing crime in the EU', London: Centre for European Reform (policy brief).
74. See, e.g., S. Douglas-Scott (2004), above n. 67; and S. Alegre and M. Leaf (2004), 'Mutual recognition in European judicial cooperation: a step too far too soon? Case Study – the European arrest warrant', *European Law Journal*, **10**(2), 200–217.
75. See A. Weyembergh (2004), above, n. 58.
76. S. Peers (2004), 'Mutual recognition and criminal law in the European Union: has the Council got it wrong?', *Common Market Law Review*, **41**, 5–36.
77. Ibid., at pp. 24–5.
78. D. Flore (2002), 'Le Mandat d'Arrêt Européen: Première mise en Oeuvre d'un Nouveau Paradigme de la Justice Pénale Européenne', *Journal des tribuneaux* (6050), 273–281.
79. Section 1 of the Sexual Offences Act 2003.
80. *Brottsbalken*, chapter 6, para. 1.
81. Article 4(7)(a).
82. Article 4(7)(b).
83. We are indebted to Rob Blekxtoon for this example.
84. OJ L 239, 22.09.2000, pp. 19–62.
85. Article 54.
86. See C-436/04 *Van Esbroek*, judgment of 9 March 2006; C-150/05 *van Straaten*, judgment of 28 September 2006; C-288/05 *Kretzinger*, judgment of 18 July 2007; and C-367/05 *Kraaijenbrink*, judgment of 18 July 2007.
87. *Van Esbroek*, at para. 31.
88. This follows from the rulings in *van Straaten*, and C-467/04 *Gasparini*, judgment of 28 September 2006.
89. Petter Asp (2005), 'Mutual recognition and the development of criminal law cooperation within the EU', in E.J. Husabø and A. Strandbakken (eds), *Harmonization of Criminal Law in Europe*, Antwerpen – Oxford: Intersentia, at p. 32.
90. J. Sievers (2007), 'The European arrest warrant: the potential and prerequisites of mutual recognition as a mode of governance', *3rd Challenge Training School: Police and*

Judicial Cooperation in Criminal Matters in the EU: Which Future for EU's Third Pillar?, Brussels: CEPS.
91. The UK Extradition Act 2003 is a good example.
92. S.P. Fragòla and P. Atzori (1990), *Prospettive per un diritto penale europeo*, Padova: CEDAM – Casa Editrice Dott. Antonio Milani., at p. 127.
93. Ibid.
94. E.g. M. Hildebrandt (2007), 'European criminal law and European identity', *Criminal Law and Philosophy*, (**1**), 57–78.
95. For a good discussion of this in the context of drugs legislation, see S. Harris (2005), *The End of Faith*, New York: W.W. Norton & Company.
96. On this, see discussion in B. Schünemann (2007), 'Alternative-project for a European criminal law and procedure', *Criminal Law Forum*, **18**(2), 227–51.
97. Article 2.
98. Article 1(b).
99. 535 U.S. 234 (2002).
100. At para. 111.
101. Article 3(2)(a).
102. Article 1(a).
103. Article 3(2)(b).
104. Article 3(2)(c).
105. Article 2 EU.
106. See J. Monar (2001), 'The Dynamics of Justice and Home Affairs: Laboratories, Driving Factors and Costs', *Journal of Common Market Studies*, **39**(4), 747–64.
107. OJ L 63, 4.3.1997, p. 2.
108. Title III, para. A.
109. OJ L 138, 9.6.2000, p. 1.
110. Monica den Boer (2004), 'The European Convention and its Implications for Justice and Home Affairs Cooperation', in Apap, J. (ed), *Justice and Home Affairs in the EU: Liberty and Security Issues after Enlargement*, Cheltenham, UK and Northhampton, MA, USA: Edward Elgar.
111. Paul de Hert (2004), see above n. 59.
112. *Environmental crimes* and *Ship-source pollution*.
113. C-303/05 *Advocaten voor de Wereld*, judgment of 3 May 2007.
114. C-105/03 *Maria Pupino*, judgment of 16 June 2005.
115. See discussion on pre-legislative scrutiny and post-adoption monitoring mechanisms in Chapter 4.
116. This is one aspect of the so-called 'inter-institutional balance' deemed to form an integral and crucial part of the justification for the 'Community method' of decision making.
117. COM(2001) 664 final (original proposal).
118. OJ L 85, 24.7.1996, pp. 5–7.
119. 'EU agrees breakthrough hate-crime law', EUobserver.com, 20 April 2007.
120. See also discussion on the proposed framework decision on procedural rights in Chapter 4.
121. See Fragòla, S.P. and P. Atzori (1990), above n. 92.
122. See Cadoppi, A. (1996), 'Towards a European Criminal Code?', *European Journal of Crime, Criminal Law and Criminal Justice*, **4**(1), 2–17.
123. See, e.g., Delmas-Marty, M. and J.R. Spencer (2002), *European Criminal Procedures*, Cambridge: Cambridge University Press.
124. Kimmo Nuotio (2003), 'Reasons for maintaining the diversity', in Delmas-Marty, M., G. Giudicelli-Delage, et al. (eds), *L'harmonisation des sanctions pénales en Europe*, Paris: Société de législation comparée, at p. 465.
125. On this, see e.g. Alessandro Bernardi (2003), 'Opportunité de l'harmonisation', in Delmas-Marty, M., G. Giudicelli-Delage, et al. (eds), *L'harmonisation des sanctions pénales en Europe*, Paris: Société de législation comparée.
126. Weyembergh, A. (2005), see above n. 19, at p. 1588.

127. Simon Claisse et Jean-Sébastien Jamart (2003), 'L'harmonisation des sanctions', in Flore, D., S. Bosly, et al. (eds), *Actualités de droit pénal européen*, Bruxelles: La Charte, at p. 71.
128. Ibid. at p. 61.
129. E.g. England and Wales.
130. E.g. Sweden.
131. In fairness, it should be mentioned that, exceptionally, Article 1(4) of Framework Decision 2002/946/JHA on the strengthening of the penal framework to prevent the facilitation of unauthorised entry, transit and residence allows Member States to apply a lower maximum sentence (six years) if the normal one (eight years) would disturb '*the coherence of the national penalty system*'.
132. Article 4(1) of 2003/568/JHA on combating corruption in the private sector does not require the possibility of extradition.
133. Article 6(1) of 2005/222/JHA on attacks against information systems.

Conclusion

What we hope to have shown in this book is that a fundamentally positive approach to the broad aims and ideals of EU criminal law and justice can be combined with rigorous criticism of many of its aspects. The ever-increasing social, economic and political integration in Europe, largely as a result of EU/EC initiatives, is a welcome development. However, we fundamentally believe that this development in our continent requires a profound rethinking of how the good of criminal justice – however defined – is to be delivered to those living there. As we hope has become apparent in the preceding chapters, this fundamental position is echoed by the institutions charged with developing the EU's AFSJ. At the same time, and as was stated in the introduction, the actual framing of the AFSJ suffers from a failure properly to consider the theoretical implications of providing the good of criminal justice at the EU level. In legislative action, judicial pronouncements, official reports, etc., ground-breaking novelties with far-reaching theoretical implications fail to deal with the fundamental theoretical issues involved.

Looking at EU criminal law and justice today, one is faced with a significant body of law potentially affecting most aspects of criminal justice. For us, the starting point for any inquiry into the nature of EU criminal law and justice must be this existing legal framework. Even though the decision makers have failed to consider the potential theoretical and conceptual implications of their actions, this does not rule out the possibility that these actions have in fact resulted in a reconceptualisation of criminal justice. Therefore, the first question which needs to be asked is whether we are *now*, as a result of the significant *acquis* of the AFSJ, faced with a de facto reconceptualised pan-EU system of criminal justice. This *legal* question must precede the arguably more *political* one of whether such a reconstitution is desirable. The importance of this theoretical exercise is of course that the concept we have of any system of criminal justice guides and determines the interpretation and development of its various instruments. To say that the legal determination of whether there has already been a fundamental shift in the conception of criminal justice in the EU should precede the political one of whether such a shift is desirable may be considered as putting the cart before the horse. To that we would say that no law can be interpreted and applied acontextually. If the legislator fails to provide the theoretical context, such a context needs to be deduced from the legislation itself.

It is our view that EU criminal law and justice currently uncomfortably straddles two not entirely compatible logics. On the one hand, the Member States and the EU institutions alike realise that the changed environment in today's EU requires common solutions to the side-effects of the ease of movement but also that the EU represents an opportunity to increase the effectiveness of law enforcement. They therefore fully subscribe to the view that the EU can provide practical benefits in the provision of the good of criminal justice. On the other hand, these same actors seem to be of the opinion that ground-breaking advances in cooperative practices as a result of common EU legislation can be introduced without changing the classical theoretical conception of criminal justice as the sharp end of national sovereignty. But, as we saw, for example in relation to legislative advances such as the EAW and the ECJ's interpretation of the principle of *ne bis in idem* enshrined in Article 54 CISA, it is becoming increasingly difficult to reconcile the advanced integration required of the EU's legislative instruments with the maintaining of complete national sovereignty over criminal justice.

In our opinion, it would be most helpful if those involved in the construction of the AFSJ took a moment's pause to reflect upon what exactly it is they are constructing. What is it that drives the development of EU criminal law and justice? Is it merely a multilateral project to review the traditional institutions of international cooperation in criminal justice? Is it a flanking measure to counter the unwanted side-effects of the internal market? Or is it the creation of a true, pan-EU criminal justice space? Are these mutually exclusive or different points on the same sliding scale? Will it mutate over time?

From a methodological perspective, the EU legislator makes use of a wide array of devices. In the realm of judicial cooperation, we saw that the two main methodologies are mutual recognition and approximation. However, we also saw that the rationales for when one is to be preferred over the other are not very clear. There are indications that mutual recognition was seen as a way for Member States to promote cooperation without having to approximate or, more likely, harmonise their national legislations. At the same time, it is clear to all that cooperation on some aspects of criminal law require approximating legislation. There is general agreement that both these methodologies are needed in EU criminal law, but there is great disagreement as to when it is appropriate to use one as opposed to the other. For example, it is often said with some force that mutual recognition without approximation can lead to great injustices.[1] As could be seen, particularly in Chapters 2 and 3, parallel to the EU's efforts to increase and facilitate judicial cooperation, initiatives are being taken to render cross-border police cooperation more effective. Here, the EU's methodology of choice has been to emphasise *practical* cooperation between national law enforcement agencies. This has been operationalised through, in particular, the setting up and strengthening of coordinating agencies such as Europol and the establishment of common databases to secure a more effective flow of information between domestic police and security authorities based upon a principle of 'availability'.

To some extent, all these methodological devices seek to forestall and minimise tensions due to the sociological fact that national institutions tend to be inherently suspicious of the way things are done abroad. Mutual recognition has a lot of support from Member States where there is great reluctance to introduce 'foreign-influenced' elements into the national legislation. Approximation, on the other hand, is favoured by those who do not trust the others to 'get it right' without commonly agreed rules. It all seems to come down to 'trust'. What the discussion in Chapter 4 showed was that the issue of mutual trust is very live in discussions on, and the application of, potential and actual instruments, respectively, in the AFSJ. We even have judicial pronouncements to the effect that 'mutual trust' exists.[2] Despite this, very little effort is made to explain what is meant by 'mutual trust' or who exactly it is that is meant to have it, and in what. It takes a lot of imagination and good will to accept the common image of 'Member States' having trust in each other. At the other end of the spectrum, it is unlikely that many judges, for instance, would claim that they *do not* trust individual colleagues in other Member States. However, what we are given almost daily expressions of is the definite lack of trust of lay individuals in the systems of criminal justice of other Member States and, maybe, a certain scepticism of professionals regarding certain aspects, real or imagined, of those systems.

The problem is that the 'mutual trust' we so aim to speak of needs to be located somewhere between the very general and the very particular, between the rather esoteric notion of one whole country trusting another, to the prejudices of 'the man in the street'. When the relevant *locus* of mutual trust has been identified, a further question has to be asked. Put somewhat crudely, that is, 'So what?' If we begin by taking the trust the man in the street may or may not have in the criminal justice systems of a Member State other than his own, we can draw a parallel with national polling on confidence levels in various public institutions. From such polling it is well known that public confidence in various national public institutions varies greatly along all kinds of variables: age, socioeconomic group, rural v. urban, etc. Although low levels of confidence in the judiciary may be seen as problematic, that tends not to be an argument for the judiciary to stop doing its job. We will hazard a guess and state that, in any given Member State, and with very few exceptions, confidence levels in the judiciary of any other Member State will be lower than for the national judiciary. Without any objective parameters justifying popular confidence levels in judiciaries in general, and in foreign judiciaries in particular, why should such confidence levels be any more relevant to the development of legislation organising the judiciary on the EU level than it is to legislation organising the judiciary nationally?

If we then take the more or less informed scepticism of professionals towards certain aspects of the systems of criminal justice of other Member States, the normative relevance of mutual trust is even more doubtful. Judicial actors may or may not personally approve of specific pieces of legislation they are mandated to apply. However, in their judicial function, they are obliged to uphold the law as it stands. If that law mandates that under certain circumstances they give effect to the legislation of other Member States, that is something they will have to do whether they personally like it or not. This is not to say that lack of mutual trust of professionals does not constitute a *practical* problem and research suggests that it is.[3] There is, however, a world of difference between upholding 'mutual trust' as a practical problem which can be helped by, say, educational measures, and saying that it is a *normative* problem which should preclude further legislative developments.

While all these questions remain unanswered, the Member States and the EU institutions continue to build on the *acquis* of the third pillar. The EU is already engaged in the provision of the good of criminal justice in a very real way and is poised to become even more so. As we have seen, among other things EU instruments now define criminal offences, the conditions under which a convicted criminal's possessions can be seized, and also essentially determine where a defendant is to stand trial and thereby also what procedure she or he will be subjected to. These developments would have benefited greatly from more substantial discussions on the rationale of the system under construction.

In this context, the role of the European Parliament (or, rather, lack thereof) takes centre-stage. While we would not go so far as to say that the lack of direct parliamentary decision-making powers causes EU criminal law to fall foul of the principle of legality,[4] we do think that the European Parliament would be the logical forum for the discussions called for above. We also think that parliamentary control has the potential to check some of the excesses of EU legislative practice in the field of criminal justice. As we stated in Chapter 1, the institutional set-up of the third pillar is very reminiscent of what Agamben would call a 'state of emergency'.[5] Admittedly, the institutional particularities of the third pillar, notably the unanimity requirement, tend to prevent swift action. However, as we saw clearly in the period immediately following the criminal attacks of 11 September 2001, the ability of these institutional particularities to prevent swift or even rash action is very relative. Given the right circumstances they can in fact serve as a catalyst to such action. It seems that the third pillar provides a permanent framework for dealing with states of emergency.

This all adds up to something which should be obvious: the most important effect of giving the European Parliament a decisive role in EU legislation in matters of criminal justice is that it would serve to balance the preponderance of executive power. Currently, the executives of the Member States can initiate and adopt legislation without having to take the views or concerns of other 'branches of Government' into account. The circumscribed competence of the ECJ to annul legislative acts provides too unsecure and temporally distant a possibility to provide the necessary *a priori* check needed. This is particularly evident in relation to the almost universal drift to use the criminal law to discipline ever wider areas of human activity. As we saw in Chapter 6, in particular, the administrative regulations governing economic activity are being reinforced or even replaced by criminal legislation. We also saw that the urge to use the criminal law morally to condemn behaviours which are not unequivocally harmful also leads to the expansion of the remit of criminal law. These developments serve to undermine the logic of the criminal law as the *ultima ratio* of society. The answer to the question, 'Should it be criminal?' does not necessarily follow from the answer to the question, 'Is it undesirable or even repugnant?' These kinds of considerations are currently not given much room in EU criminal law and justice and the hope is that a strengthening of the role of the European Parliament will change that.

It has been stated several times in the above chapters that the system of judicial supervision in the AFSJ is too weak. In particular, the variable geometry of the preliminary reference procedure and the absence of an equivalent to the Article 226 EC enforcement procedure appear as real obstacles to the harmonised and effective implementation of the AFSJ *acquis*. Here in the conclusion, we will limit ourselves to reiterating that changes to this state of affairs would be most welcome and that, until this happens, formal political monitoring and reporting mechanisms will remain crucial.

From an institutional point of view, the AFSJ is a very interesting subject-area. Many of the discussions and debates which coloured the early days of the EC can be observed in the new context of the third pillar. An obvious example is the issue of supremacy and whether it is at all transferable to the third pillar and, if so, with what, if any, limitations. The ruling of the ECJ in *Pupino*,[6] even though 'supremacy' was not expressly mentioned, can be seen as the first instalment of a no doubt long judicial debate on the applicability of this institution in EU criminal law and justice. *Obiter dicta* by the German *Bundesverfassungsgericht* in their judgment annulling the first German law implementing the EAW seem to indicate that certain national constitutional courts seem very willing, if not eager, to help shape the future of EU criminal law and justice.[7]

Further, the fact that Council legislates unanimously has given rise to interesting – and sometimes very confused – discussions on issues of competence and legal basis. On this point, it must first be clarified that legal basis and competence are not necessarily the same thing. That is because, even if the EU has a formal legal basis to legislate within a given sphere, its *competence* to do so will be constrained by a number of other factors, such as subsidiarity, proportionality and, sometimes, the empirical evidence available. The above is true of EU/EC law in general, but in the third pillar the fact that Council legislates unanimously has led to some conflation of issues of legal basis and competence and issues of political will and expediency. This was seen most clearly in the discussion on the now defunct FDPR in Chapter 4. A number of authors and institutions essentially claimed that the issue of competence was directly linked to the unanimity requirement. Essentially, they argued, if the Council is unanimous, the EU is competent. We know this is blatantly false, if for no other reason than that the ECJ accepts challenges to legislation adopted unanimously. But the larger issue lurking behind all this relates to the legal nature of the EU's third pillar. Is it an integral part of the EU, or is it a formalised division of public international law?

Those who are willing to equate unanimity with competence implicitly equate the third pillar with standard public international law cooperation. We believe that this is a very dangerous position and wish strongly to insist on the specificity of the EU *vis-à-vis* public international law. While Member States are still free to meet outside of the institutional framework of the EU and conclude agreements under public international law, if they choose to operate within the confines of the EU framework, the institutional requirements of that framework have to be respected. This debate is implicit in the *Environmental crimes* and *Ship-source pollution* cases and fortunately the ECJ has taken a strong principled stance on this particular issue. This can be deduced from the use the ECJ makes of Article 47 EU which, it will be remembered, states that nothing in the EU Treaty shall limit the EU's competence under the EC Treaty. Had the ECJ accepted the argument that the third pillar is essentially a forum under public international law, it could not have annulled the challenged framework decisions on the basis that they ought to have been adopted under legal bases in the

EC Treaty. The fact that the ECJ did implies that the EU has to be seen as a legal whole, with an internal distribution of competences which has to be respected irrespective of the unanimous will of the Member States. Put differently, once Member States decide to act within the confines of the EU structure, they have to act according to the procedures assigned to that particular area by that structure. Just because the 27 Member States of the EU could have concluded an international convention under public international law criminalising ship-source pollution this does not give them the right to adopt a third pillar framework decision for that purpose if the Treaties are deemed to specify that the correct instrument for such action is a first pillar directive. To us it follows that the pillars are not to be seen as separate legal orders, but as mere parts in a general scheme where the procedural rules applicable to legislative activity in the EU are allocated according to the subject-matter concerned.

This legal specificity of the *EU as a whole* is an important element in the debate on the institutional effects of measures adopted under any of its different procedures. The strict conception of the EU's competence implied by this is, in our view, an argument in favour of the transferability of first pillar concepts such as supremacy to the third pillar.

Another testimony to the distinctive nature of the EU and public international legal orders, as well as an illustration of an undisputable consequence of the unanimity requirement in third pillar matters, is that certain developments of the AFSJ agenda badly wanted by some Member States but resisted by others have been adopted outside of the EU framework. The 1985 Schengen agreement and the associated 1990 CISA are early examples of this and, in Chapter 3, the more recent example that is the Prüm treaty was discussed. These texts all started out politically closely linked to the EU, but legally completely unrelated to it. As we know, Schengen has been incorporated into EU law and Prüm is well on the way to being so. This use of extra-EU initiatives expressly aimed at affecting the EU agenda has been severely criticised in some quarters.[8] We feel no need to argue about this, given that there is no legal argument against proceeding in this way. The EU cannot have a vocation completely to substitute the operation of public international law as between its Member States and by the same token it cannot legally object to some of its Member States going further in their integration than the unanimous agreement of all Member States would allow for. We also wish to point to the fact that both Schengen and Prüm constitute significant advances in European integration.

From a purely political perspective, it might be thought to be somewhat unfortunate that developments which are aimed at being included into the EU *acquis* are forced outside of the EU framework because a sufficient minority of Member States – indeed just one in the context of the third pillar – are opposed to them. Already, in the Treaty of Maastricht, the possibility of what is today known as 'enhanced cooperation' was introduced into the EU framework to attempt to strike a balance between the wish of some Member States to move more quickly on some issues, the reluctance of others, and the need to prevent too great a fragmentation of EU law. Given that the Treaty of Prüm was concluded outside of the EU framework, we can conclude that the enhanced cooperation mechanism in its present form has failed to strike the correct balance.

On this, and on many other issues, the Reform Treaty constitutes a significant advance, particularly in that it specifies the circumstances in which enhanced cooperation can be resorted to. As we saw in Chapter 1, enhanced cooperation is an option in the field of criminal law if a measure approximating legislation has the requisite majority but one or several Member States are of the opinion that the measure in question would 'affect fundamental aspects of its criminal justice system'. It should be restated that enhanced cooperation is *not* available for measures implementing the principle of mutual recognition; i.e., if there is a sufficient majority, the minority cannot block and force the majority to have recourse to enhanced cooperation. Also here it is worth emphasising the distinction (in our view correct) between measures implementing the principle of mutual recognition which do not require changes to the substantive or procedural criminal legislation of Member States and approximating measures which do. Considering, as the drafters of the Treaties do, that enhanced cooperation is a way to render the transition from unanimity to qualified majority more palatable to Member States fearing for the integrity of their national systems of criminal justice, limiting enhanced cooperation to approximating measures makes sense. The internal integrity of a national system of criminal justice is never threatened by the enhanced coordination *between* systems of criminal justice.

While the Reform Treaty should logically decrease the likelihood that recourse will be had to extra-EU cooperation, it cannot, nor should it, completely exclude it. A significant majority of Member States which still falls short of a qualified majority as defined may wish to press ahead with approximating measures or even improve on the principle of mutual recognition between them. Be that as it may, the clarity of the procedure established by the Reform Treaty is to be welcomed, in particular as it will make the proceedings more transparent, something which should promote accountability.

Further to the discussion in Chapter 6 on the principles of conferral of powers and subsidiarity, it is worth again emphasising the clarity with which these principles are explained in new Articles 4 and 5 EU. It remains to be seen whether, under the new provisions, there will follow a shift in emphasis away from legal basis and onto the more principled ground of division of powers – something which the provisions appear to be open to. It will also be interesting to see whether the principle of subsidiarity will – finally! – be justiciable. As was stated in Chapter 6, there are some existing measures, in particular in the domain of the approximation of substantive criminal law, which seem very difficult to justify with respect to the principle of subsidiarity. A link should also be made to what was said above about the growing tendencies to subject an ever larger area of human activity to the criminal law and the dilution of the idea that the criminal law is the *ultima ratio* of society. These considerations, in our view, amount to a strong argument in favour of the justiciability of the principle of subsidiarity as a complement to the principle of conferral of powers. A failure to respect the principle of subsidiarity in fact constitutes a failure to respect the principle of conferral of powers. The two are linked and, if one is justiciable, so should the other be.

Finally, we wish to reiterate the main contention of this book: that profound reflection is needed on the theoretical underpinnings of EU criminal law and justice so that a coherent conceptual framework for the application of existing and future provisions in the area can develop. At the heart of this inquiry there must be the question of whether there is a common idea of criminal justice that unites the different systems of criminal justice which currently make up the EU's AFSJ. In view of the substantial EU *acquis* in the area of criminal law and justice, as well as the important extra-EU *acquis* made up of the ECHR and the case law of the ECtHR, we believe that there is. Moreover, we believe that this common idea is sufficiently strong to bear the completion of the already initiated intra-EU detachment from the von clausewitzean conception of international cooperation as an aspect of international relations.[9] However, this conclusion merely states that the old conceptual framework is insufficient in order to make sense of EU criminal law and justice. The challenge over the coming years is to elaborate the conceptual framework which will help build EU criminal law and justice into a system capable of delivering the good of criminal justice in the context of our ever-closer and yet ever-more diverse Union.

NOTES

1. See, e.g., A. Weyembergh (2004), *L'harmonisation des législations: condition de l'espace pénal européen et révélateur de ses tensions*, Bruxelles: Editions de l'Université de Bruxelles.
2. See Joined Cases C-187/01 and C-385/01 *Gözütok and Brügge* and the discussion in Chapter 4 above.

3. See J. Sievers (2007), 'The European Arrest Warrant: the potential and prerequisites of mutual recognition as a mode of governance', 3rd Challenge Training School: Police and Judicial Cooperation in Criminal Matters in the EU: Which Future for EU's Third Pillar?
4. For a contrary opinion, see B. Schünemann (2007), 'Alternative-project for a European criminal law and procedure', *Criminal Law Forum*, **18**(2), 227–51.
5. G. Agamben (2003), *Stato di eccezione*, Torino: Bollati Boringhieri.
6. C-105/03, see discussions in Chapters 1 and 4, above.
7. See above, Chapter 4.
8. See, e.g., E. Guild and F. Geyer (2006), 'Getting local: Schengen, Prüm and the dancing procession of Echternach', Centre for European Policy Studies.
9. See Introduction, above.

Annex

THE EFFECTS OF EU CRIMINAL JUSTICE ON THE UK AND IRELAND UNDER THE REFORM TREATY

Designated as one of the UK government's 'red lines', EU criminal justice as described in this book will be subject to a derogatory scheme in relation to the UK and Ireland. The basis is the Protocol on the position of the United Kingdom and Ireland annexed to the Treaty of Amsterdam[1] which 'compensated' the UK and Ireland for the loss of their vetoes in respect of the 'communitarisation' of asylum and immigration. The Treaty of Lisbon amends the old protocol and makes it applicable to the whole of the Title IV TFEU. For ease of discussion, we have made a consolidated version of the protocol as it will look using the text of the Reform Treaty. However, *this is not an official consolidated version and should not be cited!*

The basic principles of the scheme are as follows:

Article 2 establishes the principle that no legal instrument adopted in pursuance of the EU's AFSJ, or any judgment of the ECJ interpreting such instruments are applicable to the UK and Ireland. Article 3 gives the UK and Ireland the opportunity to declare that they wish to participate in any proposed legal instrument in this area. However, Article 3(2) makes it clear that, if either the UK or Ireland, after such a declaration, nevertheless makes life so difficult for the other Member States, they will be excluded according to the principle of Article 2. The UK and Ireland will thus not be able to opt in only to sabotage a proposed instrument. Article 4 makes it possible for the UK and Ireland to accept an instrument after it has been adopted.

In Article 4a which is a completely new addition, the position in relation to instruments amending existing instruments which the UK and Ireland participate in is regulated. The principle of non-participation applies even for these amending instruments, *but* the UK and Ireland will potentially pay a high price for non-participation. According to Article 4a(2), if they decide not to opt in, and the other Member States formally decide that that particular instrument will be 'inoperable' without their participation, the *original* measure will cease to apply to them. This means that an existing instrument such as the EAW, if an important amendment is proposed and, say, the UK decides not to participate in this amendment, can cease to apply to the UK. It is hoped that all sides will show political restraint in the use of these provisions to prevent a too significant fragmentation of EU criminal justice.

Protocol on the position of the United Kingdom and Ireland in respect of the area of freedom, security and justice

THE HIGH CONTRACTING PARTIES,

DESIRING to settle certain questions relating to the United Kingdom and Ireland,

HAVING REGARD to the Protocol on the application of certain aspects of Articles 22a and 22b of the Treaty on the Functioning of the European Union to the United Kingdom and to Ireland,

HAVE AGREED UPON the following provisions which shall be annexed to the Treaty establishing the European Community and to the Treaty on European Union,

Article 1
Subject to Article 3, the United Kingdom and Ireland shall not take part in the adoption by the Council of proposed measures pursuant to Title IV of Part Three of the Treaty on the Functioning of the European Union. For the purposes of this Article, a qualified majority shall be defined in accordance with Article 205(3) of the Treaty on the Functioning of the European Union. The unanimity of the members of the Council, with the exception of the representatives of the governments of the United Kingdom and Ireland, shall be necessary for decisions of the Council which must be adopted unanimously.

Article 2
In consequence of Article 1 and subject to Articles 3, 4 and 6, none of the provisions of Title IV of Part Three of the Treaty on the Functioning of the European Union, no measure adopted pursuant to that Title, no provision of any international agreement concluded by the Community pursuant to that Title, and no decision of the Court of Justice interpreting any such provision or measure shall be binding upon or applicable in the United Kingdom or Ireland; and no such provision, measure or decision shall in any way affect the competences, rights and obligations of those States; and no such provision, measure or decision shall in any way affect the

Community or Union *acquis* nor form part of Community law as they apply to the United Kingdom or Ireland.

Article 3

1. The United Kingdom or Ireland may notify the President of the Council in writing, within three months after a proposal or initiative has been presented to the Council pursuant to Title IV of Part Three of the Treaty on the Functioning of the European Union, that it wishes to take part in the adoption and application of any such proposed measure, whereupon that State shall be entitled to do so.

    The unanimity of the members of the Council, with the exception of a member which has not made such a notification, shall be necessary for decisions of the Council which must be adopted unanimously. A measure adopted under this paragraph shall be binding upon all Member States which took part in its adoption.
2. If after a reasonable period of time a measure referred to in paragraph 1 cannot be adopted with the United Kingdom or Ireland taking part, the Council may adopt such measure in accordance with Article 1 without the participation of the United Kingdom or Ireland. In that case Article 2 applies.
3. Measures adopted pursuant to Article 61 C of the Treaty on the Functioning of the European Union shall lay down the conditions for the participation of the United Kingdom and Ireland in the evaluations concerning the areas covered by Title IV of Part Three of that Treaty.

For the purposes of this Article, a qualified majority shall be defined in accordance with Article 205(3) of the Treaty on the Functioning of the European Union.

Article 4

The United Kingdom or Ireland may at any time after the adoption of a measure by the Council pursuant to Title IV of Part Three of the Treaty on the Functioning of the European Union notify its intention to the Council and to the Commission that it wishes to accept that measure. In that case, the procedure provided for in Article 280 F(1) of the Treaty on the Functioning of the European Union shall apply mutatis mutandis.

Article 4a

1. The provisions of this Protocol apply for the United Kingdom and Ireland also to measures proposed or adopted pursuant to Title IV of

Part III of the Treaty on the Functioning of the European Union amending an existing measure by which they are bound.

2. However, in cases where the Council, acting on a proposal from the Commission, determines that the non-participation of the United Kingdom or Ireland in the amended version of an existing measure makes the application of that measure inoperable for other Member States or the Union, it may urge them to make a notification under Article 3 or 4. For the purposes of Article 3 a further period of two months starts to run as from the date of such determination by the Council.

    If at the expiry of that period of two months from the Council's determination the United Kingdom or Ireland has not made a notification under Article 3 or Article 4, the existing measure shall no longer be binding upon or applicable to it, unless the Member State concerned has made a notification under Article 4 before the entry into force of the amending measure. This shall take effect from the date of entry into force of the amending measure or of expiry of the period of two months, whichever is the later.

    For the purpose of this paragraph, the Council shall, after a full discussion of the matter, act by a qualified majority of its members representing the Member States participating or having participated in the adoption of the amending measure. A qualified majority of the Council shall be defined in accordance with Article 205(3)(a) of the Treaty on the Functioning of the European Union.

3. The Council, acting by a qualified majority on a proposal from the Commission, may determine that the United Kingdom or Ireland shall bear the direct financial consequences, if any, necessarily and unavoidably incurred as a result of the cessation of its participation in the existing measure.

4. This Article shall be without prejudice to Article 4.

Article 5

A Member State which is not bound by a measure adopted pursuant to Title IV of Part Three of the Treaty on the Functioning of the European Union shall bear no financial consequences of that measure other than administrative costs entailed for the institutions, unless all members of the Council, acting unanimously after consulting the European Parliament, decide otherwise.

Article 6

Where, in cases referred to in this Protocol, the United Kingdom or Ireland is bound by a measure adopted by the Council pursuant to Title IV of Part

Three of the Treaty on the Functioning of the European Union, the relevant provisions of the Treaties shall apply to that State in relation to that measure.

Article 6a
The United Kingdom and Ireland shall not be bound by the rules laid down on the basis of Article 15a of the Treaty on the Functioning of the European Union which relate to the processing of personal data by the Member States when carrying out activities which fall within the scope of Chapter 4 or Chapter 5 of Title IV of Part Three of that Treaty where the United Kingdom and Ireland are not bound by the rules governing the forms of judicial cooperation in criminal matters or police cooperation which require compliance with the provisions laid down on the basis of Article 16b.

Article 7
Articles 3, 4 and 4a shall be without prejudice to the Protocol on the Schengen *acquis* integrated into the framework of the European Union.

Article 8
Ireland may notify the Council in writing that it no longer wishes to be covered by the terms of this Protocol. In that case, the normal Treaty provisions will apply to Ireland.

This specific protocol is, however, not the end of the matter. With respect to the *UK only*, Article 10, paragraphs (4) and (5) of the Protocol on Transitional Provisions creates yet another special solution prompted by the UK government's intransigent line at the negotiations of the RT. As was outlined in Chapter 1, the TFEU's general scheme of judicial enforcement will only apply to measures adopted under Title VI EU five years after the entry into force of the TFEU, unless they have been amended after the entry into force of the TFEU. Article 10(4) specifies that up to six months prior to the expiry of this transitional period, the UK may notify to the Council that it does not accept the extension of the ECJ's powers. If it does make such a notification, as from the date of expiry of the transitional period *all such measures shall cease to apply to the UK.*

Article 10(5) specifies that at any time following the eventual disapplication to the UK of the pre-TFEU measures, the UK may notify the Council 'of its wish to participate in acts which have ceased to apply to it'. In such case, Article 4 of the Protocol on the position of the United Kingdom and Ireland in respect of the area of freedom, security and justice shall apply. This must be read as meaning that, from this position, the UK can pick and choose which measures it wishes to participate in.

It is submitted that Article 10, paragraphs (4) and (5) of the Protocol on Transitional Provisions present a much greater danger to the coherence of the AFSJ than does the Protocol on the position of the United Kingdom and Ireland in respect of the area of freedom, security and justice. It is true that the UK's eventual wish to avoid the extension of the ECJ's powers will be tempered by the drastic consequence of the disapplication to it of the *entire* AFSJ *acquis*. That effect however is significantly lessened by the fact that Article 10(5) then grants the UK the possibility to 'cherry-pick' from the 'outside'. This may prove to be a perverse incentive for a UK government dissatisfied with some of the measures adopted under Title VI EU. Article 10, paragraphs (4) and (5) would then provide the UK government with the option first to cause the whole of the AFSJ *acquis* to be disapplied to the UK after which it could attempt to 're-accept' only those measures it thinks are palatable. It should be emphasised that the feasibility of the above described procedure depends on the political will of the other Member States to play along.

NOTE

1. OJ C 340, 10.11.1997, p. 99.

Index